**Lake Tahoe Community College
Learning Resources Center
So. Lake Tahoe, CA   95702**

THE AMERICAN ROOTS
OF EZRA POUND

Ezra Pound in 1909
(Courtesy of the American Literature Collection,
the Beinecke Rare Book and Manuscript Library,
Yale University)

THE AMERICAN ROOTS
OF EZRA POUND

J. J. Wilhelm

Garland Publishing, Inc.
New York & London
1985

Library of Congress Cataloging in Publication Data
Wilhelm, James J.
The American roots of Ezra Pound.
Bibliography: p.
Includes index.
1. Pound, Ezra, 1885–1972. 2. Poets, American—
20th century—Biography. I. Title.
PS3531.082Z887 1985   811'.52 [B]   84-26007
ISBN 0-8240-7500-5 (alk. paper)

Printed on acid-free, 250-year-life paper
Manufactured in the United States of America

ACKNOWLEDGMENTS AND THANKS

Since this book depends almost wholly on primary sources (census rolls, city directories, birth ledgers, newspapers, letters, and government documents), standard footnoting is out of the question. I have created a section called Documentation at the end of the book which tells where the sources I have used are located. In almost every case, a date or a number is the primary way to locate this information, and these facts are given in the text itself. I was fortunate in that *Paideuma: A Journal Devoted to Pound Studies* allowed me to publish four of the more significant chapters in a very different form, and there the reader may find an exact explanation of the research procedures employed here. I have also created a special repository of documents uncovered in my researches at the Alexander Library of Rutgers University, which is open to public inspection. As for secondary sources, these are detailed either in the Documentation section or in Works Cited In the Text at the end of the book.

So many people have assisted me in writing this book that it would be exhausting to mention them all. Let me simply cite a few of the most important: John Swan and the staff of the Lilly Library at Wabash College; Frank Lorenz and the staff of the Burke Library at Hamilton; Daniel Traister and the staff of the Van Pelt Library at the University of Pennsylvania; Mary de Rachewiltz and the staff of the Beinecke Library at Yale; John Kirkpatrick and the staff of the Humanities Research Center at the University of Texas, Austin; the New York Public Library, the New York City Archives, the State Historical Societies of Wisconsin and Minnesota; the Hopkinton, Crawfordsville, and Chippewa Falls Public

Libraries; the *Wood River Journal* of Hailey, the National Archives, the Hampton Veterans' Home and National Cemetery; the Nyack, Peekskill, Utica, and Plainfield Public Libraries; the Presbyterian Historical Society of Philadelphia; the Society of Friends Genealogical Service of New York under the direction of Elizabeth Mooger; the Arch St. Presbyterian Church along with Dr. G. H. Todd; the Loomis Institute; and the Public Relations staff of St. Elizabeths Hospital.

Others who kindly assisted me are: Rujie Wang, with the letter of Robert Winter; Omar Pound, with advice on the early Pound ancestry; Mary de Rachewiltz, with a variety of hints and clues; Janice S. Robinson with information about Hilda Doolittle; Malcolm Rosholt on Wisconsin lumbering; R. C. Brown on Wisconsin railroads; James Rader, whose researches were indispensable for the writing of Chapter 11; Carl Gatter, whose researches furnish the foundation for Chapter 4; the recently deceased Ben Kimpel, who knew Pound's correspondence inside and out, and directed me with unerring aim to the right place for the right quotation; and, for their encouragement, Hugh Kenner, George Kearns, and Wendy Stallard Flory, whose own work ignited an interest in Pound's biography.

I hereby gratefully acknowledge my thanks to New Directions, Inc., for permission to quote from the following copyrighted material:

Grateful acknowledgment is made to New Directions Publishing Corp. for permission to quote from the following works of Ezra Pound: *A Lume Spento.* Copyright © 1967 by Ezra Pound; *The Cantos of Ezra Pound.* Copyright © 1934, 1937, 1940, 1948, 1956, 1959, 1962, 1963, 1966, 1968, and 1972 by The Estate of Ezra Pound; *Collected Early Poems of Ezra Pound.* Copyright © 1976 by The Trustees of the Ezra Pound Literary Property Trust. All rights reserved; *Pavannes and Divagations.* Copyright © 1958 by Ezra Pound; *Personae.* Copyright 1926 by Ezra Pound; *Selected Letters.* Copyright 1950 by Ezra Pound; *Selected Poems.* Copyright 1926 by Ezra Pound.

Acknowledgment is also made to New Directions for permission to quote from the following works: H. D., *End to Torment.* Copyright © 1979 by New Directions Publishing Corp.; H. D.,

Other acknowledgments for quotations are made in the Documentation section at the back of the book, while courtesy lines for pictures appear with the captions.

LIST OF ILLUSTRATIONS

CONTENTS

Introduction

A headline on page one of the *New York Times* of July 27, 1943, proclaimed: "8 FROM U.S. INDICTED AS AIDING AXIS." The article went on to name seven people who were believed to be broadcasting in a treasonable way for Hitler and the Nazis: Robert Henry Best, the son of a Methodist preacher from South Carolina, who had worked as a freelance agent in Germany for New York newspapers; Douglas Chandler, a Baltimore journalist who had been "wiped out" in the stock-market crash of 1929 and was working as a lecturer in Europe; Edward L. Delaney, a former actor who was subsisting as an overseas film agent; Constance Drexel, a German-born journalist who passed herself off as one of the Philadelphia Drexels; Max O. "Okay" Koischwitz, who had taught German at Columbia University and Hunter College before returning to his native Germany in 1935; Jane Anderson, a stylish art and music critic who had divorced the critic Deems Taylor and had married the Fascistic Count de Cienfuegos of Spain; and Frederick Wilhelm Kaltenbach, a graduate of Grinnell College, Iowa, who was called "the American Lord Haw-Haw" because of his caustic humor. Only one of the eight was alleged to be working for Benito Mussolini and the Italian Fascists: Ezra Pound, one of the greatest American poets of the twentieth century.

After the indictments had been handed down, Pound immediately stopped his broadcasts from Rome. He was clearly moved by the government's action, even though he always maintained that his broadcasts were anything but treasonable. He claimed later that he had merely exercised his constitutional right as an American citizen to air his views, and "free speech without free radio speech is as zero" (Canto 74, p. 426). Still, from his speech on February 10, 1942, he seems to have anticipated trouble, since the following words were read as a prologue to that talk and to others: "Rome Radio, acting in accordance with the Fascist policy of intellectual freedom and free expression of opinion by those who are qualified to hold it, has offered Dr. Ezra Pound the use of the microphone twice a week. It is understood that he will not be asked to say anything whatsoever that goes against his conscience, or anything incompatible with his duties as a citizen of the United States of America."

These words were clearly trying to provide a legal shelter for Pound, who had found himself for a variety of reasons (including the aged and sickly condition of his father) behind enemy lines during World War II. However "Dr." Pound—who only came close to gaining that prestigious degree from the University of Pennsylvania—seemed in the eyes of many to be guilty of treason because the law stipulates that one may be called a traitor simply by lending moral support to an enemy in time of warfare: "Whoever, owing allegiance to the United States, levies war against them, or adheres to their enemies, *giving them aid and comfort* within the United States or elsewhere, is guilty of treason."

On leafing through Pound's manuscripts, which have been edited by Leonard W. Doob, one can find numerous places where certain hearers might insist that Pound was both aiding and comforting the enemy:

> *February 3, 1942:* "The prospect of a 30 years war is not one to arouse mirth and hilarity even in a flighty, chicken-headed and irresponsible people such as the United States of Americans."
>
> *June 28, 1942:* "You are NOT going to win this war. None of your best minds EVER thought you could win it. . . . You have never had a chance in this war."

Even if he was not openly inciting the troops to mutiny or rebellion, Pound could scarcely be considered to be acting as an American patriot according to the legal definition of treason, with those difficult-to-define words "giving aid and comfort."

Some people, however, wondered if Pound was an American at all, since he had spent most of his life abroad, after leaving America in 1908 when he lost his teaching job at Wabash College in Crawfordsville, Indiana, because of a presumed affair with a stranded vaudeville actress. People associated Pound with London, where he had first gone to live, founding the school of Imagism and making translations, especially from Chinese, that profoundly changed the course of twentieth-century literature. Then he had moved to Paris in 1921, where his friends were Ernest Hemingway, James Joyce, and Jean Cocteau.

Finally, from 1924 to the time of the broadcasts, he had lived in Italy, largely in the lovely resort of Rapallo, where he stayed in a downtown hotel with his wife Dorothy, while his longtime lover, the violinist Olga Rudge, lived just above on a hill overlooking the Mediterranean Sea. Couldn't Pound really be considered an Italian? No. Pound had retained his American citizenship and insisted on the fact that he was American to the core. As he said in his speech of March 26, 1942, he was "Ezra Pound speakin' from Europe for the American heritage," and the Yankee accent and motifs ran throughout his impassioned addresses, where he frankly attacked President Roosevelt and his Cabinet for undermining the American Constitution and the traditions of John Adams and Thomas Jefferson. There was also the repeated mention of an ancestor, as on May 4, 1942: "This is my war, all right; I have been in it for 20 years. My Granddad was in it before me." During the following broadcast on May 9, Pound offered a portrait of this grandfather who haunted him, a former Congressman named Thaddeus Coleman Pound, whom he revered as an archetype of American enterprise, honesty, imagination, and courage.

The Italian government, despite some early successes, proceeded to lose the war. In fact, on the day before Pound was publicly proclaimed a traitor, *The New York Times* said: "MUSSOLINI OUSTED WITH FASCIST CABINET/BADOGLIO, HIS FOE, MADE PREMIER BY KING," and from there, it was downhill for Pound's adopted home. In May of 1945 Pound was apprehended by Communist partisans in the hilltop eyrie shared during wartime with Dorothy and Olga, and was sent to an American "detention camp"—a euphemism for a hellish wartime prison—within sight of the towers of Pisa. After a horrendous six months spent in part in what was called a "gorilla cage," Pound was whisked by plane to Washington to stand trial for treason.

Fortunately for the old and exhausted man, the trial never took place, because the wartime hysteria was still very much alive: for example, in 1946 Lord Haw-Haw (William Joyce) was executed. Pound was judged physically and mentally unfit to stand trial, and was remanded to St. Elizabeths Hospital in southwestern Washington, where he would languish until April of 1958. However unjust the treatment may have been in the long run—after all, Pound was denied a chance to refute the charge of treason (and there were technical reasons why the indictment might have been difficult to prove)—the shortrun solution may well have saved the poet's life.

This book is not concerned with the question of whether Pound was or was not a traitor. It is, instead, an inquiry into the way in which a man with very deep and profound American roots could finally turn his back (but not his mind) away from his native country. The poet always claimed that the story of his family background could be viewed as a miniature version of the social history of the United States. Up to now, these words have either been flatly rejected or rather indifferently accepted, sometimes with a touch of skepticism.

In the following pages, the first thorough examination of the poet's roots, we shall see that Pound's boast about his ancestry was anything but reckless or ill-taken. Not many in the United States have a history that reaches as far back in time and as broadly over the face of the whole nation as does that of Ezra Pound. These roots, in fact, are what make the charge of treason sound so incongruous and poignant. However, what follows is not simply concerned with verifying a man's genealogical claims. It is concerned with the problem of how any brilliant person—any "difficult individual" as Christian Herter, the Under Secretary of State, called Pound in 1958—succeeds or fails in his relations with the country of his birth. Pound's "treason" may ultimately have been more aesthetic than political.

There is no doubt that Pound always considered himself an

American. His compelling love for his native land drove him into making those dangerous speeches, into rushing back to the United States in 1939 when America was on the brink of war in order to try to talk to Roosevelt and certain Congressmen (as if he were Thaddeus Coleman Pound the politician), and frequently interspersing some rather embarrassing "MURRKANISMS" in his writings, especially his prose. In St. Elizabeths, in view of the dome of the United States Capitol, it was particularly touching to hear him insist on how American he truly was, especially when he adopted the persona of "Uncle Ez," a cracker-barrel philosopher who united at least two of his ancestors from the past, including his namesake, Ezra Brown Weston, formerly of New York City.

In the hospital, as the aged Pound lay back with his drawn face on the pillow, he could see himself and his family in a sweep of time extending back to the 1630s and in a geographical panorama that stretched from the wilds of Idaho to New Jersey and Massachusetts. In the reflecting mirror of America's social structure, he could number among his relatives a United States Congressman, a President of Harvard, a famous but currently out of vogue poet, a broken-down peddler of toothache pellets, a vivacious lady hotelkeeper, the man who saved the Connecticut Charter, several millionaire stockbrokers, a variety of lawyers and bankers, and the owner of The Wayside Inn, one of America's best-loved hostelries.

Of course, under the pressure of hostile charges, his mind tended at times to exhibit some of the delusions of grandeur that the psychiatrists accused him of having. Thaddeus Coleman Pound seemed to verge at times not only on the legendary but the mythic. But the white-haired guru of St. Elizabeths firmly refused to act like the European Father of Imagism; he insisted on being "the Idaho kid," as Hemingway had always called him, or "Montana," as Charles Olson liked to refer to him.

As we retrace Ezra Pound's steps through time, we shall find that most of Pound's statements about himself and his family's past were true. In his family's story, we can see the unfolding history of America. One of Pound's greatest virtues, even though it often hurt him, was his honesty. In this respect also, he was all too American. . . .

◆ ONE

THE WILDS OF IDAHO AND THE LEGEND OF THADDEUS COLEMAN POUND

He was born in a place that could only have existed in nineteenth-century America: the rough-and-tumble mining town of Hailey in the Territory of Idaho, in the shadow of the Sawtooth Mountains. The place had an air of myth about it. The little town nestled in the foothills that rise out of the green and fertile Snake River Valley and tower northward into the Bitterroot, Rocky, and Lost River Mountains. Due south was Shoshone, where the Wood River Branch of the Oregon Short Line connected with the main artery of the Union Pacific Railroad at a mighty cascade of waters. To the southeast were the desolate Craters of the Moon, while due north were sites that would later be developed as Sun Valley and Ketchum, where Pound's old boxing partner from Paris, Ernie Hemingway, would shoot himself to death.

The place was volatile and wild, full of characters with names like Blue Dick and Curley and Poison, and one Horace Morgan, a gambler who wore a black velvet frockcoat that reached down to his knees. There was one hotel, the Merchant's, but about fifty bars with colorful names, including the Kentucky Hardware, whose owner was too sheepish to admit to his relatives back in the Blue Grass State that he ran a saloon. There was an unpaved Main Street lined by plank sidewalks, and off it, in neat geometric rectangles, were other unpaved lanes with the names of numbers or minerals or trees. Ezra Pound was born at the corner of Second and Pine in a white frame house that was still standing there a

7

century later—the first house with plastered walls in the Idaho Territory, built proudly by Homer Loomis Pound for his newly wed wife Isabel.

The Pounds had come to this improbable place because Homer, the son of Congressman Thaddeus C. Pound of Wisconsin, was very much in need of work, and although Thaddeus was firmly opposed to nepotism, he had nevertheless wangled a job for his son in the recently opened Federal Land Office. President Chester Alan Arthur made the appointment in 1883, two years before baby Ezra was born on October 30, 1885. Aside from wanting some employment for his son, Thaddeus had another reason for shipping Homer off into the mountains: this restless politician, whose ownings during his life ran from a lumbering company to railroads to a spring-water bottling company, had purchased some silver mines while he was in Washington. It was dangerous to own such potential treasures and not keep watch over them. In fact, in May of the year of Ezra's birth, Thaddeus visited his son and daughter-in-law, and the *Hailey Times* reported that the ex-Congressman was outraged because two of his claims, the Alturas and the Acme, had been "jumped" by other prospectors on the grounds that he was not working them regularly. The move was illegal, but it took years of litigation before Thaddeus got his mines back, and by then it was too late to exploit them, for he was a tired old man.

Homer's job as register was to try to keep some kind of order in this lawless milieu. He would register the claims of the prospectors as they were filed and then would more or less stand guard over them—even though he did not personally carry a gun, the way most other men did in that environment. It was also his job to test or assay the silver or lead being mined to determine its purity. The experience that he gained on the Idaho frontier would serve Homer well later in life, since he would go on to work with minerals as an assayer for the United States Mint at Philadelphia.

Although Homer never got rich at his job, many of his neighbors did. Homer was fond of relating these get-rich-quick stories later in life: "One day a man would come and beg you for some work; you would hire him to saw some wood for you, and when you saw him the next week and asked him if he wanted to come

Home at Hailey Idaho. 1884.

The house in Hailey at Second and Pine Streets, where Pound was born. Taken from the Homer Pound Scrapbook, with Homer's handwriting above. (Courtesy of the American Literature Collection, the Beinecke Rare Book and Manuscript Library, Yale University)

A Fourth of July parade in the 1880s on the main street of Hailey. (*Courtesy of the Wood River Journal*)

back and work some more, he'd be flabbergasted and say: 'Saw wood! I got ten thousand in the bank!" A maid that Isabel Pound hired left the job to become the wife of an overnight millionaire, and when Isabel herself had to go to the hotel to live because she couldn't find anyone to help her, her former servant had to defend her when the other guests thought that she was a servant. Frontier society was indeed fluid.

From the start, Hailey was hardly the place to take a lady like Isabel Weston Pound to. She was a Wadsworth on one side of her family, with connections to the poet Henry Wadsworth Longfellow and the great Connecticut patriot Captain Joseph Wadsworth. When Isabel's mother, Mary Parker Weston, came to Hailey to visit the couple after the birth of the baby, she was so horrified by the place that she told Homer in no uncertain terms that he should not have brought her daughter there. In crossing the continent, Mary had had one misadventure after another. Forced to change trains in Cheyenne, Wyoming, she had decided to spend the night in a hotel, but she could not sleep because in the depths of the night some cowboys rode up and down the main street shooting up the place just for the fun of it. And the worst part was—there was no lock on her door! To a woman who could trace her American ancestry back to 1636—if not to the Battle of Crécy —this kind of conduct was intolerable. In Pound's masked autobiography *Indiscretions*, from which most of this material is gleaned (with the correct names for people and places substituted), Homer, who is described as "the naïvest man who ever possessed sound sense" (p. 8), told his son that if you had had a lock on your door, your neighbors would have "suspicioned" you.

Grandmother Weston was not the only person who could not fathom the mysterious workings of the Old West. Before the Pounds arrived in Hailey after an extended honeymoon, they had sent ahead a stylish black maid named Mary Beaton (at least this is the name that Pound gives her in *Indiscretions*). Mary was one of a group of black servants whom Pound's Uncle Ezra Weston (actually *great* uncle) had assembled over the years during his business dealings in the South, and especially after the Civil War. Mary had worked in Ezra's boardinghouse in Manhattan, where Isabel had grown up, since Harding Weston, Isabel's father, had more or less divorced himself unofficially from the family. Compared to the world of Manhattan, Hailey seemed a barbaric outpost to the maid, who found nothing to do (since the only other black within miles was a lowly, ignorant barber). She put on her Sunday finery and sashayed up and down the sidewalk plankings, trying to elude the ogles and catcalls of the love-starved miners. Finally she became so disgusted with the place that she left one night around midnight, not even bothering to take her elegant dresses along with her. It took several years before she reingratiated herself into the world of the Westons, who felt that she had let Isabel down.

Another servant was a Chinese gentleman who had probably arrived in Hailey to help build the railroads. He worked as a cook, a job which he did excellently, and as a general factotum. But one night while some of Homer's *nouveau-riche* prospecting friends were dining in the house, he mistakenly used a brush that was meant to clean fireplaces to scrape off crumbs from the table, and when his guests broke into laughter, he sullenly served the last courses and then disappeared forever into the pines. His departure left Isabel servantless and helpless, and so she moved into the hotel. She complained constantly about the altitude, but it was more the low life on Main Street that annoyed her than the rarefied air. And so, when Baby Ezra was not yet one-and-a-half years old, his parents decided to sell the plastered house and head back east.

It was not an easy thing for Homer to abandon this job, which seemed to have a future. After all, he had managed to sip his lemonade in the saloons with his friends, to appear to be "one of the boys," and to enforce some stern laws on claim-jumpers without getting shot. He was now almost thirty, and this was the only important job he had ever held. True, he had worked as a butcher in his native Chippewa Falls when times were tough, and he had had some business training in the Union Lumbering Company, owned by his father Thaddeus and his Uncle Albert, but his education was limited. Being one of the first white children born in the "primeval forests" of northern Wisconsin, he had been reared in childhood by an Indian nurse. When it came time for high school, Thaddeus had packed him off to a military academy in Shattuck, Minnesota, and so when college time rolled around, it seemed almost natural (since his father was embroiled in Wisconsin politics) that Homer would continue his schooling at West Point. The family even put him on a train bound for the military academy, but the usually docile Homer for at least once in his life rebelled and, halfway toward the Bear Mountain bend of the Hudson, he simply got off the train and went home. That was the end of that.

When Thaddeus Pound was elected to Congress in 1876, Homer continued to work for the family business, but at last the lure of the national capital was too strong. Homer soon after ventured eastward, joining his father in the exciting city of Washington, staying at the Ebbit House Hotel at 14th St. N.W. and F Street, which Thaddeus usually made his home away from home. In the capital, Homer plunged into the social life as far as a rather innocent young man from Wisconsin was able to do. When he was not listening to his father in the Capitol Building, he was off at the many parties being held around town. During the inaugural ball of the ill-fated President Garfield or some other event, Homer bumped into a vivacious lady from New York City whose name was Frances Amelia Wessells Freer [first husband?] Weston (with another name to be added later). To Ezra Pound, this was his beloved "Aunt Frank."

Frances Weston lived with her husband Ezra at his boardinghouse at 24 East 47th Street, and it was to the boardinghouse that she invited Homer to come for a visit—perhaps rather tentatively. But Homer, who had nothing else to do, took the invitation, whether meant seriously or not, at its face value and appeared there in Frances' wake. This did not in the least perturb either Frances or Ezra, who seemed to welcome anyone except the most serious felons into their world, and soon Homer felt that he had found something of a home. It was here that he met the woman he would marry—the stiffbacked but otherwise gracious Isabel Weston.

Isabel's life up to this point had not been the happiest. Her mother, the proud Mary Parker, had married Harding Weston, who "had ideas." As Pound put it in *Indiscretions* (but with false names that have here been corrected): "'He always had plenty of ideas.' He did not, for example, continue to support Mary; he had put [Isabel] in a convent school for a few months, and refrained from paying the bills; he had, as definite manifestation of kinetic potentialities, 'punched [Ezra's] head,' when the stubbier and more industrious brother had . . . declined finally and conclusively to lend [Harding] any more money" (pp. 20–21). Finally Mary had her fill of him. She was a winning Wadsworth through her mother, and was not about to tolerate a losing Weston. And so the two parted ways.

Mary Parker Weston did not approve of most people. She found the lively Frances Weston, whom many loved, too material-minded, too fond of baubles and jewels, and not very well-connected socially. (Aunt Frank hailed from a Dutch family of New York that had moved to Illinois and then back to New York; she was not related to any of the Brahmins of New England.) Nor did Mary quite approve of the simple, homespun Homer, with his "dangeds" and "darns" and coats that seemed to be made out of burlap or something else that no Fifth Avenue swain ever wore. Having been burned herself in marriage, Mary was hoping for far better things for her daughter.

However, there was no crowd of suitors storming the doors on 47th Street for Isabel's hand, and Homer was, after all, the son of a Congressman, who did have some lucrative lumbering and railway connections. So on November 26, 1884, with Clement French presiding as the pastor, Homer and Isabel were married—in the big parlor of the boardinghouse, surrounded by Uncle Ezra's little world of clients and admirers and black servants, such as Mary Beaton, who was sent on ahead to set things up in Idaho.

Homer and Isabel took a long honeymoon before arriving in Hailey. They traveled by train up the Hudson, across the Mohawk Valley to Rochester, where the Pounds and the Westons and the Loomises all had lived at one point, and to Niagara Falls, the classic place for a honeymoon in the 1880s. Then they traveled west to Milwaukee, and north to Chippewa Falls, the home of Thaddeus Coleman Pound, who was just leaving Congress and returning to his business career.

The Pound family, as Ezra proudly proclaims in *Indiscretions* (p. 11), stemmed originally from one John Pound, who arrived in the United States, probably in Connecticut, in the middle of the seventeenth century. He died in 1690 in New Jersey, in the Woodbridge-Piscataway area near the Atlantic Ocean. John is believed to have been a whaler originally, and may well have sailed from New Brunswick and the Raritan River, a center for that business in those days. His English origins are obscure. The name "Pound," of course, can mean anything from a blow to a unit of weight to a British form of money, but the poet sometimes chose to relate it to animal pounds, believing that his English ancestors were men who in some way had "the power over wild beasts" (Cantos 47, 49).

Because John Pound was a Quaker, it is easy to document his and his ancestors' progress, since that sect takes excellent care of its members' records. His son, John II, fathered an Elijah Pound, who himself fathered two more Elijahs. Elijah Pound III, who was born in 1802 and died in 1891, married Judith Coleman of Nantucket (again of fisherman stock) in 1826. They produced a son named Albert Pound in 1831 and Thaddeus in 1832 (often incorrectly given as 1833). The two boys were inseparable friends, dying at ripe old ages, just a year apart: Albert in 1913 and Thaddeus in 1914, when Ezra had already established himself as a poet in London.

In 1809, finding farming in the New Jersey area unprofitable, Elijah Pound III went with eight of his children and his ever-faithful brother Joel to Farmington, New York, just southeast of Rochester, to establish a Quaker community. When the land again proved intractable, he moved once more—this time to Warren County, Pennsylvania, in the northwest corner of the state on the New York border. There in the hamlet of Elk on December 6, 1832, Thaddeus was born.

The *United States Biographical Dictionary* (1877) recounts Thaddeus' early life in the colorful language of the day:

> His ancestors on both sides were Quakers, deeply imbued with the sterling principles taught by the wise and sagacious Penn; and they sought to ingraft upon their children these cherished sentiments of love, honesty and goodwill toward man, preëminent among the sect. His parents, Elijah and Judith Pound, could only give to their family a home of the most primitive style, scarcely

13

containing the necessaries of life. In 1838 the family removed to Monroe county, New York, where, in the following year, the mother died, leaving to her sons all that she had to give, the sacred memory of a mother's prayers . . .

Four or five years later we find the family in Rochester, the father and sons working in a woolen factory, Thaddeus at first receiving one shilling a day, his business being the assorting of wool, the initiatory step to "sorting" on a larger scale in other branches of business.

In the spring of 1847 the family immigrated to Wisconsin, and shortly afterward located in Rock county, renting a farm on Catfish Prairie; and here, even amidst the drudgery of farm and household duties, the boy felt the glowing inspiration of Western life, and improved the fragments of time snatched from labor, having an eager love of learning, until at the age of fifteen he was installed as teacher in the home district. This experience, so often a stepping-stone to American fame and fortune, brought the subject of our sketch to Milton Academy, in Rock county, where, between working in harvest-fields and teaching during vacation, he continued several terms. For the purpose of securing better opportunities in his pursuit of a liberal education, he taught, for a time, a high school at Caledonia, Livingston county, New York, and availed himself of the superior facilities for instruction to be had at the Rushford Academy in Alleghany county, of the same State. In the spring of 1856 he removed to Chippewa Falls, Wisconsin.

Before returning to Wisconsin, Thaddeus married Susan Angevine Loomis, the daughter of Nathan S. Loomis of Oneida County in Rochester on October 29, 1855. At the same ceremony, his brother Albert married her sister, Sarah Elizabeth. The two couples then headed west to find their fortunes.

Thaddeus' career has to be considered in a threefold way: as a lumberman, a railroad-builder, and a politician, since all three pursuits were intertwined. John Gregory, the grandfather of the poet Horace Gregory, described Thaddeus this way in his *Industrial Resources of Wisconsin*, which was published in 1870: "He is a pleasant speaker, and as a conversationalist has a sort of magnetic power little less than fascinating. All who come in contact with him, whether in business, the social circle, or in politics, acknowledge his kindly and genial nature" (p. 213). Earlier, in the

Hillier County & West name view

"Bird's eye view of Hailey from the top of Carbonate hill about one mile distant } {and office location} }residence. 1883.=

A panoramic view of Hailey taken from the Homer Pound Scrapbook. (Courtesy of the American Literature Collection, the Beinecke Rare Book and Manuscript Library, Yale University)

'CHIPPEWA FALLS UNION LUMBERI

The steamer *Buckeye* pushing a raft of lumber downstream on the thirteen-day voyage to St. Louis. This photograph was used for publicity purposes by the Union Lumbering Co.
(*Courtesy of Malcolm Rosholt*, Lumbermen on the Chippewa)

1850s, Thaddeus and his brother had demonstrated their ability to move crowds by touring the country towns of Wisconsin and putting on exhibitions of "animal magnetism" in order to debunk this pseudo-science. In 1856 Thaddeus had his first job in business: as a bookkeeper for a struggling lumber company; in 1859 he won his first political position: he was "chairman" of the village of Anson and was selected as a delegate to the Republican State Convention.

By 1862, Thaddeus was enjoying great prosperity. With his brother Albert, who delighted people by saying such outrageous things as that he preferred to believe in the Church of England because "it interfered neither with a man's politics nor his religion" (*Indiscretions*, p. 43), "Thad," as he was popularly known, reshaped the company in which they were working into a new firm called Pound, Halbert and Co. During the next seven years as the company was thriving, Thaddeus was elected to the Wisconsin State Assembly in 1864, 1866, 1867, and 1869, and was the Assembly Speaker in the last year. There seemed to be no end to his good fortune.

Pound always tended to romanticize this phase of Thaddeus' career. He saw his tireless grandfather out in the woods hewing the giant evergreens alongside the tall, blond, Scandinavian men who tended to work the forests. Thaddeus and friends would hack down the timber, then drag it to the many rivers, where they would secure the logs together, frequently in a gigantic raft, and float them downstream to the mighty Mississippi, where they would be sent outward into the world. Lumberjacks, wearing their colorful woolen shirts, would dance across the logs like nimble acrobats, directing their southward course, often with the help of steamers. Thaddeus and Albert went along with the men, arm-wrestling at night after a hard day's labor, while Grandmother Susan would cook up a huge supper back in the camp. This picture, or something like it, seems to have lain in the back of the young poet's mind: Grandfather Pound, the fearless pioneer and friend of the people.

In 1869, Thaddeus and Albert decided to press their luck further by expanding their lumber operation into a much larger firm called The Union Lumbering Company, including Mr. Halbert and other backers. Thaddeus and Albert each controlled $100,000 in shares of stock—an enormous amount of money in that day—while Thaddeus' salary as President of the company was $3,500 in 1870—also a considerable amount. A year later, Thaddeus was elected Lieutenant Governor of the state, and he performed his duties so admirably over the next two years that there was soon talk about his having a job in Washington. This materialized in 1876, when he defeated the Democrat George Cate and became the Republican Congressman from his northwestern district of Wisconsin.

Although his political career continued to flourish, Thaddeus' lumber concern did not. All during the 1870s, the water was very low in the Chippewa River, making log-driving and sawmilling difficult. It was partially for this reason that Thaddeus and others turned toward railroads as the solution to the problem of transporting their products. Then, too, there was a bank panic in 1873, followed by a general depression, which spelled trouble for a business that had taken in considerable new investments, was costly to operate, and had not established itself against older competitors. But there was yet another explanation: since Thaddeus had to spend about half of the year in the state capital at Madison—then later in Washington—he was simply unable to devote much time to the business, and apparently neither Albert nor Mr. Halbert had the proper expertise.

By 1870, Thaddeus was deeply engrossed in trying to improve rail traffic in Wisconsin, particularly to and from Chippewa Falls. During his terms in the State Assembly, he served on the railroad committee and constantly promoted bills to expand service. Perhaps his greatest achievement was his almost singlehanded building of the Chippewa Falls Northern and Eastern Railway Company, without any help from banks or other investors. When no one would advance him money for rails, Thaddeus returned to New York State to find them. Pound recalls this feat, which is documented elsewhere, in Canto 28:

> And they thought they had him flummox'd,
> Nobody'd sell any rails;
> Till he went up to the north of New York state
> And found some there on the ground

And he had 'em pried loose and shipped 'em
And had 'em laid here through the forest.

(p. 138)

In the same passage, Pound describes another adventure of T. C. P.
in the building of his line:

And one day he drove down to the whorehouse
Cause all the farmers had consented
            and granted the right of way,
But the pornoboskos wdn't. have it at any price
And said he'd shoot the surveyors,
But he didn't shoot ole pop in the buckboard,
He giv him the right of way.

Through courage and perseverance, he established service from
Chippewa Falls to Eau Claire on what became known as the
Chippewa Falls and Western Co. (now part of the Chicago North-
western Line).

During this period, Thaddeus Coleman Pound encountered
his nemesis, Frederick Weyerhauser, the robber-baron *extraordi-
naire.* Pound mentions this encounter prominently at the start of
Canto 22, where he disguises the adversary's name for legal reasons:

An' that man sweat blood
to put through that railway,
And what he ever got out of it? . . .
And there was the other type, Warenhauser,
That beat him, and broke up his business,
Tale of the American Curia that gave him,
Warenhauser permission to build the Northwestern railway
And to take the timber he cut in the process;
So he cut a road through the forest,
Two miles wide, an' perfectly legal.
Who wuz agoin' to stop him!

(p.101)

It is sad to note that the monopolist won, and Thaddeus' prosperous little line became absorbed in 1881 in Weyerhauser's Northern Pacific Railroad.

17

In addition, Thaddeus was a promoter for the construction of the St. Paul Eastern Grand Trunk Railway Co.—whose grandiose name matched the grandiose idea of linking the Great Lakes to the Mississippi at St. Paul—from Green Bay via Abbotsford and Chippewa Falls. This important railroad was also built, but it soon passed out of Thaddeus' hands too, becoming a part of the Wisconsin Central and then the Soo Line. In spite of these losses, Thaddeus promoted railroads constantly while he was in Congress, and was even accused by Representative Eden from Illinois of helping "to donate thirty-five millions of acres of land to a railroad corporation." Peculiarly enough, Thaddeus was backing House Bill No. 232 "extending the time for the construction of the Northern Pacific Railroad" (Weyerhauser's outfit!) into Oregon and Washington. On page 4870 of the *Congressional Record* for the Forty-Fifth Congress, Second Session, Thaddeus demanded that Eden's implication "that I was here in the employ of railroads" be stricken from the record. It was not. One wonders if Ezra ever got around to reading these musty records in attempting to document the career of his hero.

There is no doubt that Weyerhauser helped to destroy many of Thaddeus' dreams, just as he did to numerous other men. Malcolm Rosholt, one of the recognized authorities on lumbering in Wisconsin, chronicles the following sad ending to Thaddeus' lumber business in his *Lumbermen on the Chippewa*:

> The Union Lumbering Company survived the financial panic of 1873, but two years later went into bankruptcy. The mill was released by the court to A.E. Pound and T.W. Halbert, who struggled with it for two years and also failed. The court-appointed receiver, L.C. Stanley . . . kept the mill going until 1878, and, facing more debts than profits, he was forced to shut down. . . . [A] new corporation operated the mill until the entire organization was sold on March 1, 1881, to the Weyerhauser Mississippi River Logging Company which turned it back to Chippewa Lumber & Boom. . . .
>
> It is difficult at this point to understand why a mill, employing several hundred people, could not have made a profit for so many years. No doubt, the most important decision Weyerhauser made after he bought it was to appoint William Irvine as his production chief and general manager. Here was a man who had risen

from the ranks in the lumber industry, even to studying the machinery in the sawmill. He visited the logging camps frequently and took a personal interest in the drives every spring. Although he mixed freely with the mill hands and men in the woods, he always maintained a rather stiff personal decorum, even to wearing the high starched collar and tie when visiting camp.

(p. 112)

In short, the starched-collar Irvine was everything that Thaddeus was not—and to him and Weyerhauser went the entire concern, along with acres and acres of valuable timber land.

One of the things that most interested the mature Pound about his enterprising grandfather was the old man's manipulation of locally controlled money—or, as he called it, interest-free scrip: "by '78, T.C.P. said 'non-interest-bearing'" (Canto 97, p. 677). This laconic line conveys a wealth of meaning for the poet, who said the following in his essay "A Visiting Card":

> No one, perhaps, has ever built a larger tract of railway, with nothing but his own credit and 5,000 dollars cash, than that laid down by my grandfather. The credit came from the lumbermen (and in face of opposition from the big U.S. and foreign steel monopolists) by printing with his brother the paper money of the Union Lumbering Co. of Chippewa Falls, bearing the promise to "pay the bearer on demand . . . in merchandise or lumber." It was only when my father brought some old newspaper clippings to Rapallo in 1928 that I discovered that T.C.P. had already in 1878 been writing about, or urging among his fellow Congressmen, the same essentials of monetary and statal economics that I am writing about today [1942] (*Impact*, pp. 64–65).

Pound was always concerned in his mature life with the need for economic reform, especially with ways of preventing the vast international banking systems from gaining an octopus-like control of small communities. He always contended (along with William Carlos Williams and Charles Olson, as well as others) that the Federal Reserve System in America—or the Bank of England or France—were pernicious impostors, because they were not directly representative of the people, but were controlled by small cliques of bankers who had usurped the god-given right of every government to coin and control its money. The United States government, for example, cannot issue dollars on its own power; it has to issue them through the Federal Reserve System and its member banks, and there is a charge attached to this procedure. When the banks (the Federal Reserve not yet in existence) would not loan T. C. P. any money, he simply defied their tyrannical power and issued his own, some of which can be seen at the Humanities Research Center in Austin, Texas.

Pound applauded this slamming of the door on usurious Wall Street, precisely as the "little" people of the West did during the Populist uprisings of the 1890s. Thaddeus Coleman Pound was not a proto-Populist any more than he was a Greenback Democrat, even though he did advocate the use of greenbacks (money that had been issued by the United States Government during the Civil War) at one point to ease the shortage of money. But, as all the biographies of Thaddeus make clear, he was an old-line Republican during most of his career, and he soundly defeated a Greenback candidate, August R. Barrows, during the Congressional election of 1878.

This issuing of private currency by a company was a fairly common thing in Wisconsin during this period, as several historians make clear. However, its effects could also be pernicious: many a West Virginia coal company, to cite but one example, has enslaved its employees by doing the same, locking them deeply into the company's feudal embrace, where their pay can only be translated into goods within the company store. While I am not suggesting that Thaddeus was guilty of such avaricious endeavors, I feel that Pound's attempt to label his forebear as a pioneering economic reformer shows a zealousness on his part that is not quite in keeping with the historical facts. One does not want to dispel the legend here, merely modify it. After all, Ezra saw his grandfather only once—at the age of three—and all that he could remember was the old man's beard.

As far as Thaddeus' Congressional career is concerned, there is much to praise, although most of it is more workmanlike than dramatic. Pound notes at the opening of Canto 22 that his grandfather constantly tried to help the poor Indians whom he and his fellows were rather mercilessly displacing on the frontier:

And he said one thing: As it costs,
As in any indian war it costs the government
20,000 dollars per head
To kill off the red warriors, it might be more humane
And even cheaper, to educate.

A glance at the *Congressional Record* will quickly assure the reader that Thaddeus did originate many bills to aid the Indians, as well as women, another disadvantaged group to whom he felt partial:

1878	HOUSE BILL 5101: "to authorize the State of Wisconsin to select indemnity lands for . . . Indian reservations"
	HOUSE BILL 4549: Indian appropriations . . . female suffrage
1879	PAGE 227: for anti-polygamy laws
	HOUSE BILL 1138: for the Winnebago Indians . . . to promote their civilization
	HOUSE BILL 1140: relief for the Menomonee Indians
1881	HOUSE BILL 1858: for building Indian schools
	HOUSE BILL 1857: for relief of the Lac de Flambeau tribes. of Indians

Similarly, Thaddeus was a solid conservationist who was much interested in controlling the flow of water in rivers. Of course, skeptics may say that he had a selfish interest in these activities, since logging companies required free passage to transport their logs. Still, an impartial historian, Robert F. Fries, had this to say about Thaddeus in his *Empire in Pine*: "His plan called for the creation of artificial reservoirs at the headwaters of the Mississippi and its tributaries so that the water level could be kept fairly constant the year round. Although the project was enacted into law, the difficulties involved in securing lumbermen to support the plan because they feared it would aid their natural enemies, the steamboat interests, delayed the construction of the reservoirs, but by 1885 some progress had been made. The project was finally abandoned when the reservoirs failed to work as had been expected" (p. 57). Even if that scheme did not work, Thaddeus created other bills to improve navigation on the Chippewa River (House Bill No. 1456 in 1877), to build a railway bridge across the St. Croix River (House Bill No. 5497 in 1880), and to develop irrigation in Idaho (House Bill No. 5002 in 1881). He also promoted a bill to create jobs in land offices, which led to Homer's appointment in Hailey.

If Thaddeus had a weak spot beyond his inability to make his business schemes pay off, it had to be women. His love life began quietly enough with his marriage in 1856 to Susan Angevine Loomis of Durhamville, New York—whose roots will be discussed in connection with Hamilton College, where Ezra studied. She bore him a boy in 1858 who was named for a Greek poet rather than a Hebrew patriarch (like so many other members of the family) because Thaddeus' Uncle Jacob adored *The Iliad* and *The Odyssey*. When Ezra Pound christened his son Omar, he continued this tradition, blending the family name with the Persian poet Khayyam. Susan also gave Thaddeus a girl, christened Florence, who went on to marry a man named Foote. Florence lived as a music teacher on Estaugh Street in Philadelphia after the turn of the century, where she took care of her mother for about two decades. Susan Angevine also lived periodically with the Pounds in nearby Wyncote.

Pound says very little about Grandmother Susan in *Indiscretions,* and in his correspondence with Isabel, he often confuses her with her sister. He does say in his autobiography that Susan was very careful with her words, seldom saying anything more than "Harve was *like* that" (p. 11). She appears to have resembled the wooden woman whom the poet describes rather tongue-in-cheek in Canto 28:

> She sat there in the waiting room, solid Kansas,
> Stiff as a cigar-store indian from the Bowery
> Such as one saw in "the nineties,"
> First sod of bleeding Kansas
> That had produced this ligneous solidness . . .

(p. 135)

In any case, Susan was not a suitable spouse for the dramatic Thaddeus, and they soon went their separate ways. Pound said in 1920 when he was writing *Indiscretions:* "At the age of 160 she and *her* mother, who must have been by that time 180 (exactitude is no matter when one reaches these legendary numbers), lived in

Montana, not together, but each alone in her cabin with a good two miles of veldt between them. From her presumably I derive my respect for the human being as an individual, my dislike of herding, and of the encroachment of one personality upon another in the sty of the family" (p. 11). Although this passage is clearly humorous, it shows a further inclination toward the legendary, and a yearning for connections with the pioneering West. Many of the Footes and Pounds wound up in Montana, especially in Big Timber, and in the late eighties, Thaddeus even envisioned running for governor of the new state.

In the 1860s, when Thaddeus was serving in the Wisconsin Assembly, he seems to have taken up with another woman, who is described this way in *Indiscretions*: "She is reported to have been amiable and to have been 'good to' my father during some period of stress, presumably financial" (p. 14). When Thaddeus went to Washington, he took this woman with him, despite the possibility of scandal. We can see here a model for Pound's own amatory adventures, particularly his long love affair with Olga Rudge at the same time that he continued to live with Dorothy Shakespear Pound. But being a politician rather than a poet, Thaddeus was far more subject to public pressure. President Garfield promised to give Thaddeus a place in his Cabinet if he won the election: "But Garfield had made numerous promises, one notably to J.G. Blaine, who, in the event, declined 'to sit in the same cabinet with a man who was not living with his wife.' Mr. Blaine was the 'bigger man' and the domestic proprieties of high official circles were preserved for the time being" (p. 14).

Still, Thaddeus was vindicated. Garfield was suddenly assassinated and was followed by Arthur, who was not the least bit disturbed by adultery and was extremely friendly to the Congressman from Wisconsin, as Homer's job in Idaho proved. Later, in 1884, Mr. Blaine ran for the Presidency on the Republican ticket against Grover Cleveland, a Democrat. At his own expense, Thaddeus published a broadside in Milwaukee that turned the entire state against Blaine and led to his crushing defeat. His rhetoric is worth quoting, since it shows the kind of fearless promotion of public morality (without attention to private lives) that Pound always insisted upon as essential to a civilized society. After stating that any candidate for President should show common honesty, a decent recognition of fidelity, and wisdom, Thaddeus said:

> Mr. Blaine is not such a man, but, in my opinion, embodies most in American politics that is menacing to public morals and integrity in government. With a long public career, mainly distinguished for a sort of declamatory and pugilistic statecraft, he is not the inspiration of a single valuable policy or the author of an important statute, but, on the contrary, has often suggested and supported unwise and bad, and opposed good legislation. With a record clouded by suspicion and accusation of jobbery and corruption undefended, he brings to us personal antagonisms which have torn and weakened our party in the past, invading the Administration of the lamented Garfield with demands of personal vengeance so virulent as to inflame the spirit of assassination. . . .

These were powerful words, and they had their effect—both on the voters of Wisconsin and an adoring grandson.

There is one rather serious question to be raised about the affair of Thaddeus' adulterous lover: according to the *Milwaukee Sentinel* of November 7, 1872, Thaddeus took a second wife named Emily M. Fenn. She is strangely never mentioned by Pound or by any writer of Thaddeus' life, including those of obituaries. Did Pound know about this second marriage and choose to ignore it, possibly because he preferred to think of Thaddeus braving society's bluenosed puritans and carrying on his love affair unimpeded? In any case, young Ezra was aware of the fact that his idolized Grandpa was a man who insisted on living his life as he pleased.

It is interesting to note that when Thaddeus was in Washington in 1878, almost by chance Ezra B. Weston and his wife Frances were also living there, at 203 East Capitol Street. They had come there after the collapse of their hotel in Nyack, so it is possible that Homer met Isabel at that time, even before he went to visit the Westons in New York. In any case, both Aunt Frank and Isabel loved Washington with its unending social life. Pound recalled in the *Pisan Cantos* the ladies of this Victorian period sitting primly and properly in the gallery of the Senate listening to the politicians orate:

The Governor's Mansion in Chippewa Falls, Wisconsin. Taken from the Homer Pound Scrapbook, with Homer's description below. (*Courtesy of the American Literature Collection, the Beinecke Rare Book and Manuscript Library, Yale University*)

Family portrait of four generations of Pounds taken in 1888: on the left, Thaddeus C. holding Baby Ezra; Homer standing; and great-grandfather Elijah. (*Courtesy of the American Literature Collection, the Beinecke Rare Book and Manuscript Library, Yale University*)

and in my mother's time it was respectable,
it was social, apparently,
            to sit in the Senate gallery
or even in that of the House
      to hear the fire-works of the senators
(and possibly representatives) . . .

                                      (Canto 83, pp. 535–36)

Seen from the vantage point of the 1940s, the 1880s did indeed appear to be a kind of Paradise Lost.

Thaddeus Coleman Pound's final years are, however, unhappy. He died penniless in Chicago's Henrotin Hospital on November 21, 1914, having gone there to cure his failing eyesight. In the summer before his death he returned momentarily to Chippewa Falls, and voiced reminiscences that were recorded in a volume called *Chippewa County*, which also contains a Longfellow-like poem by Ezra Pound (doubtlessly written earlier) entitled the "Legend of the Chippewa Spring and Minnehaha, the Indian Maiden." One of the few bright spots in Thaddeus' later life was his discovery of a sparkling water-spring that is still used today. Thaddeus bottled the water, which soon proved to be very popular, and he intended to turn this into another fortune, but the high cost of transporting the bottles ruined his dreams of financial success.

On leaving Washington, Thaddeus spent most of his time in a large house in Chippewa Falls that he had built in his days of glory. Called The Governor's Mansion, it had a mansard slate roof with a cast-iron railing that ran around the top. After Thaddeus' death and burial in nearby Eau Claire, the house eventually became a headquarters for the Boy Scouts. When Baby Ezra and his parents visited the Mansion in 1888, Thaddeus was still in high spirits. He was eccentrically cutting off the horns of his cattle to test a new theory that said that this act would produce better milk. Instead, he almost lost his whole herd. Thaddeus' only salaried job at this time was that of a railroad inspector in 1887, but he remained active. When he was not helping to incorporate the first Edison Electric Light Co. in the northwestern part of the state, he contented himself with experiments on his farm: breed-

25

ing trout and growing new kinds of potatoes (like the Jefferson of Canto 31).

When he died, Thaddeus Coleman Pound was eulogized at length on the floor of the Wisconsin State Capitol. People praised him as an initiator of ideas rather than as an achiever. He was especially lauded for promoting "Pound's rule" in Congress, just before leaving in 1883, which prohibits the Speaker of the House from inhibiting debate. In the years before his death, Thaddeus seems to have become thoroughly disillusioned with both the Democratic and Republican Parties, just as his grandson would feel. He was interested in founding a new party along Progressive lines, but his death cut that dream short with all the others.

It is hard to assess the man behind the legend. Thaddeus Pound represented to the mature Ezra the American West in all of its untrammeled vigor and energy. He stood for what the country might have become, had it followed the basic precepts of Jefferson and Adams and not fallen prey to the selfish tactics of usurious bankers and greedy monopolists. Although we have to remember that Ezra saw Thaddeus only once in his life, the old man nevertheless remained an untouchable authority, a patriarch par excellence, who, even if he never did build the ideal city or create the ideal state, spent most of his life trying. Thaddeus stood up against monopoly—whether the Weyerhauser Lumber Co. or the Northern Pacific Railway—and he was an economic experimenter who would try to beat the system by issuing his own currency. Pound saw his grandfather as the archetypal pioneer, fighting meddling politicians (like the socialists, communists, and New Dealers of the future), as well as the Wall Street bankers, the Federal Reservists, and the robber barons running rampant in the last half of the nineteenth century, those men who were turning the Jeffersonian dream of the land belonging to everyone into the possession of a few. When he died, Thaddeus was called "a Republican of the radical type." To Ezra, this meant a freedom to assert one's individual rights. When he wrote *Jefferson and/or Mussolini*, Pound saw his grandfather firmly attached to Jefferson's side. The only viable alternative, he believed, was a totalitarian government—in the form advocated by Confucius or Mussolini—which allowed others to assume responsibility for social action. To

Pound, the danger lay on the left, where both socialism and communism were stifling the expression of the individual and dragging everyone down to the lowest common denominator. Either the rugged individualism of T. C. P. or the benign despotism of a Chinese Emperor seemed preferable to the rule of Big Brother.

No biographer could ever make the "real" Thaddeus Pound match the ideal in his grandson's mind. To Ezra, Thaddeus was as legendary as the town of his birth. In 1969, when he was safely back in Italy, Pound was seized by a powerful urge to visit the village where he had first seen light. He had heard many strange and exciting things about it, and he now wanted to see it for himself. He and Olga Rudge tried to plot a journey to this exotic place: they would first fly to New York . . . then to Salt Lake City . . . and then to the Hailey-Sun Valley Airport, and—it was all too complex, especially for a man well into his eighties. They decided to limit their visit to the Eastern Seaboard. The "real" can be both tiring and annoying, and we are often thrown for our true contentment upon our myths.

TWO

THE WARM LITTLE WORLD OF UNCLE EZRA WESTON

The trek back across the American continent was long and arduous, especially since the Union Pacific sleeper that the Pounds took ran straight into the teeth of the horrendous blizzard of '87. Baby Ezra contracted a whooping cold, and his all-night coughing, as they journeyed through the mountains, did little to enable the other travelers to sleep. But the inventor of a rotary snow plow that was being tried out on the train's locomotive came to the rescue. Over the fears of Isabel, he insisted that she pour some kerosene over a lump of sugar and feed it to the discomforted infant. The concoction worked, and the baby's croup was checked. Riding behind the first rotary snow plow was noted in the family annals as another Poundian first, even as Uncle Joel, the brother of Elijah III, had ridden the very first railroad train that had operated in America. The Pounds were proud of being first in achievements, and this tendency toward discovery would continue in little Ezra.

Back in the civilized world of Uncle Ezra Weston's boardinghouse, the Pounds introduced the baby, however tenuously, to the metropolis. Although he would officially grow up in the suburbs of Philadelphia, Ezra Pound was unofficially a New Yorker because of the Weston connection. Pound seems to have always wished that New York had the culture of London or the life of Paris or the beauty of Venice, but what it did have—raw, vital, sometimes violent energy—already made some sort of impact on the growing child.

Pound's first recollections of the city concern the five-storied boardinghouse (with cellar) at 24 East 47th Street, between elegant Fifth Avenue and Madison. This brownstone building had a steep set of stairs that led up to a small porch, then into an entrance hall and sizable parlor, with a communal dining room, kitchen, and private study in the rear. Upstairs were numerous small single rooms with folding beds that Pound remembered later as being both functional and comfortable. The Westons lived on the second floor, and their black servants, gathered largely from Uncle Ezra's business trips to the South before the Civil War, lived in the basement, above the well-stocked cellar. Number 24 was one of a series of identical brownstones on the south side of 47th Street. As the years passed, Ezra's wife, Frances or "Frank," acquired the adjoining properties stretching to No. 28 at the corner of Madison. She grandly called this operation "The Weston" in 1905, when she got a telephone. The entire parcel of lots extending from 22 to 28 was torn down after 1906, when Robert Goelet, an entrepreneur from Newport, Rhode Island, who was leasing the boardinghouse to Ezra, finally decided to erect a luxury hotel, the Ritz-Carlton, which would serve as a center for New York society into the 1950s.

In an early memory, Pound recalled lying in a baby carriage in the garden in back of the house, staring up at a window in the rear parlor, where Uncle Ezra "bulged from a small stubby comfortable red plush easy-chair; and he tied the end of his wife's 20 sewing cotton to the stem of a large crimson strawberry and lowered it" (*Indiscretions*, p. 42). The baby saw the fruit and reached up for it. He was then fed the berry, and the cotton was hauled up for a repeat performance. In this way, Uncle Ezra tried to enhance the child's perception, with Pavlovian tests and rewards.

Down at the Fifth Avenue end of the street were two places of note: the fashionable Hotel Windsor and the mansion of Helen Gould, the Jewish millionairess. The Hotel Windsor burned to the ground on St. Patrick's Day of 1899 in a catastrophic fire, whose aftermath is described in Canto 80 (p. 508):

East 47th Street looking eastward toward the Third Avenue
Elevated, with the mansion of Helen Gould on the left and on
the right an arcade built over the ruins of the Hotel Windsor.
Ezra B. Weston's boardinghouse, No. 24, once stood down the
street on the right, but has been torn down to create space for
the Ritz-Carlton Hotel, which looms empty in the distance.
*(Photo by Percy L. Sperr; courtesy of the U.S. History, Local History
and Genealogy Division of the New York Public Library)*

The elegant Hotel Windsor, later destroyed by a fire that began in
the first bay window on the right. (*Photo by Percy L. Sperr; courtesy
of the U.S. History, Local History and Genealogy Division of the
New York Public Library*)

"Funny looking wood, James," said Aunt F.
"it looks as if it had already been burnt"

[Windsor fire]

  "Part o deh roof ma'am."
  does any museum
contain one of the folding beds of that era?

The thirteen-year-old Ezra was probably away at Cheltenham
Military Academy when this disaster occurred, but the horror of
the event lingered on, especially since many parts of the hotel's
exterior and furnishings went up in a great vortex of smoke and
flames that caused the hotel to crumble into a heap of rubble in a
matter of hours. Well-dressed guests clung from their window
ledges or plunged to their deaths while the last vestiges of the
once festive parade straggled by. The event jarred the otherwise
pleasant days of the Gay Nineties in much the way that the
sinking of the Titanic would do a few decades later.

    The rest of the 47th Street neighborhood was largely residen-
tial. The sprawling Grand Central Station, whose open tracks had
to be crossed by bridges over Park (then Fourth) Avenue if the
Pounds wanted to go to Grandmother Weston's place at Lexington
and 52nd Street, had not yet attracted business uptown from 14th
and 23rd Streets. Columbia University was just up Madison
Avenue at 49th Street, and the professors in the School of Mines
overlooking the railroad gulch had to shout when the New York
Central trains chugged by on their way northward. St. Patrick's
Cathedral was just a block beyond at 50th Street, and across from
it was the site of what later was to become Rockefeller Center,
which in those days was a large rose garden and arboretum that
Columbia would later lease at an enormous profit to the Rockefeller family.

    The Westons were Presbyterians, and they attended either the
fashionable St. Bartholomews (the church of millionaires) at 44th
and Madison or the Palladian structure known as "Dr. Parkhurst's
church" on Madison Square. Another important nearby site was
the office of Dr. John Dowling at 41 West 40th Street, where baby
Ezra said some of his first words at the age of one year and ten
months. In answer to the doctor's question about what was wrong

with him, the baby gave, according to *Indiscretions* (p. 42), a precise answer that shocked everyone, and with no infantile silliness attached. Dr. Dowling attended all of the family's sicknesses, and was there when Uncle Ezra died on December 10, 1894.

The world of Ezra Brown Weston was, one gathers from *Indiscretions* and elsewhere, a very warm place in which to live. Uncle Ezra ran his boardinghouse in a truly genteel and hospitable manner. There is what might be called a "hotel syndrome" that is observable on this side of the family, especially with the Hows, with whom the Westons intermarried. Pound describes Uncle Ezra as follows in his autobiography: "He, after all, had always been comfortable; the first How (no terminal *e*) had hung his scutcheon in Duxbury [actually, Sudbury] and told his man to cook for his master and all and sundry; how else could a person accustomed to leisure be expected to maintain his wonted standard of victualling?" (p. 28). Pound also associates Ezra with a "plantation" in Massachusetts, and although he may have used the word to mean simply a large farm, he was well aware that the Westons also had relatives in the South, especially in Virginia. In fact, Uncle Ezra was trapped in the South behind the enemy lines during the outbreak of the Civil War. It was because of this, as well as other business dealings, that he acquired an entourage of black servants that included Mary Beaton, mentioned in the preceding chapter, and his man, "black Jim". The boardinghouse world, through its inhabitants and the personality of "Uncle Ezry" or "Ez," exuded Southern hospitality—with a New England accent.

During his first seven years of life, Pound would go over to see Grandmother Mary on Lexington Avenue for some private schooling in her Wadsworth ancestry, and on 47th Street he got his education in Westoniana. Uncle Ezra, like many Westons, believed that his family traced its roots back to one Thomas Weston, a wealthy London merchant who helped to transport Puritan refugees to America when neither the Dutch nor the British would do so. Thomas Weston thus stood in Pound's young mind as another pioneer of the New World—one who was willing to risk his life to help other people, however little Pound himself thought of the Puritans and however much profit Thomas made out of it. Most people believe that the town of Weston, Massachusetts, was named for Thomas, and it enters the lives of many of Pound's other ancestors. Edmund Weston, who is clearly the originator of Pound's branch of Westons in America, could possibly have been related to Thomas, but the connection, however hard Ezra the elder or junior tried to establish it, is uncertain. Still, when he was writing his Adams Cantos in the thirties in Fascist Italy, Pound tried to insist on the link, thereby connecting his family, at least geographically and spiritually, with the Adamses, whom he strongly admired:

> for the planting
> and ruling and ordering of New England
> from latitude 40° to 48°
> TO THE GOVERNOR AND THE COMPANIE
> whereon Thomas Adams
> 19th March 1628 . . .
> Merry Mount become Braintree, a plantation near Weston's
> (Canto 62, p. 341)

Edmund Weston arrived in America on the *Elizabeth and Ann* in 1635. He was a simple man, only a thresher of grain in the first appearance he made on the public rolls in Duxbury. But by 1639 Edmund had a partnership in farming with John Carver of Duxbury. The Weston lineage can be traced through the following men: Edmund Weston II; Zachariah, who moved to Middleboro, Massachusetts; James, who moved to New Braintree; and Abner, who moved to Barre, a pivotal town in the evolution of Pound's genealogical history. John Wheeler Weston (baptized July 2, 1797) lived in this city at the same time as David Wadsworth III (1767–1835). From John's marriage to Asenath How came Harding Weston, Pound's ne'er-do-well grandfather, as well as Uncle Ezra and several other siblings, most of whom died young. From David came Mary Wadsworth, who married Hiram Parker of Hopkinton and gave birth to Mary Parker, who through marriage with Harding became Grandmother Weston of Lexington Avenue. It was a small world. The three moves from a Massachusetts port to the inland town of Barre to New York State seem to have been made with marvelous synchronization in the time from the 1630s to the 1890s. This world was Anglo-Saxon, white, and privileged; it was almost hermetically sealed off from people like Helen Gould or the thousands of other "different" people who were flooding the metropolis in steady waves. Somehow the blacks were more acceptable to this society, because they were menials, trained to keep their place.

John Wheeler Weston's marriage to Asenath How creates the connection to the owners of the famous Wayside Inn of Sudbury, Massachusetts. Asenath was the daughter of Hannah How, who was married to Eliphalet How, the grandson of the man who had founded the famous hostelry, David How. Known first as the Red Horse, the inn later changed its name and was then immortalized by Henry Wadsworth Longfellow as the place where seven storytellers each tell three tales to while away the time. Grandmother Weston read these *Tales of a Wayside Inn* to Ezra, because Longfellow was related to the Wadsworths:

> One Autumn night, in Sudbury town,
> Across the meadows bare and brown,
> The windows of the wayside inn
> Gleamed red with fire-light through the leaves
> Of woodbine, hanging from the eaves
> Their crimson curtains rent and thin.
> As ancient is this hostelry
> As any in the land may be,
> Built in the old Colonial day,
> When men lived in a grander way,
> With ampler hospitality;
> A kind of old Hobgoblin Hall,
> Now somewhat fallen to decay,
> With weather-stains upon the wall,
> And stairways worn, and crazy doors,
> And creaking and uneven floors,
> And chimneys huge, and tiled and tall.

Longfellow goes on to mention "Squire" Lyman Howe (with the *e* added), who was a landlord in the latter part of the 1800s, up to 1897 when he sold it outside the family. The lovely inn was purchased by Henry Ford in the twentieth century and restored to its former grace and beauty, although Ford disposed of his control after a very bad fire in the 1950s.

Wayside Inn, Sudbury, Massachusetts

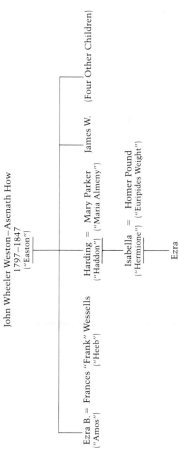

The Weston family genealogy from 1797 to Ezra Pound.

Just as the Pounds made a break from country life and agriculture to city life and business in the first half of the nineteenth century, so too the Westons decided to leave their farming at Barre behind and travel westward. Curiously enough, they went precisely to the same city that the Pounds had tried, Rochester. King's Directory of Rochester for 1844 lists John W. Weston running a "Bonnet Wareroom" at 11 State Street and owning a residence at 10 Allen. An advertisement for his store in this period shows a variety of hatware, ranging from bonnets to stovepipe hats and tams. By 1845–46, the establishment was being run by the oldest son, George, but two years later James Wheeler Weston was the proprietor. Father John died in 1847 at the age of fifty, while George would linger on in illness until 1853.

By 1850, the family was bored with the limited opportunities in Rochester and decided to try their luck in New York City, precisely as the Wadsworths were doing at about this time. Taking the profits from their haberdashery, they rented a house at 19 Wooster Street in southern Greenwich Village, and then at 164 Prince Street, where the 1851 Rode's Guide to New York City listed James Weston as the sole owner. Mother Asenath kept the brood intact until she died in 1857 at Saratoga Springs, while visiting a relative named George W. Weston, who owned an important mineral-water bottling plant there and maintained a house in Greenwich Village as well.

After their mother's death, the three surviving sons—Ezra, James, and Harding—gradually moved uptown to 8th Street, 14th Street, and 23rd Street, shifting with the center of population that was drifting ineluctably toward the perennially popular Upper East Side. James was a broker when he was not running a variety of businesses; Harding was usually an advertising salesman; Ezra tended to work for banks.

Then in 1858 Harding married a girl whose roots also stemmed from Worcester County—Mary Parker, the daughter of Mary Wadsworth and Hiram Parker. The ceremony was performed in the romantic up-river town of Peekskill some time during September 1858, according to Harding's papers of application for a military pension on file in the National Archives. Harding had trouble remembering the date in later years, since the marriage proved to be a fiasco. He wrote in 1909: "I have not lived with my wife in 40 years. I never got a divorce from her or she from me. I think she is in Boston if living." She was, in fact, at that point dead.

Since Harding lived on to be 92 years old, dying on February 9 of 1927 in the National Soldiers' Home at Hampton, Virginia, he was very much dependent on his pension to tide him through his later years. As he himself said in an application of April 2, 1915: "I am now upwards of 80 years old and cannot make ends meet." Apparently neither he nor Isabel—not to speak of Mary—ever made any attempt to restore the bridge that was broken in Nyack in the 1860s when he "socked" his lovable brother. It is doubtful that anyone ever visited his grave.

After January 13 of 1860, which the New York City Ledgers listed as the birth date for Isabella Pound, Harding was taken by military fever as the Civil War was brewing. According to friends who testified on his behalf to help him gain his pension, Harding dressed up in military garb and walked the streets of lower Manhattan recruiting for Company G of the New York Cavalry. He became widely known as "Cap'n Weston." His difficulty in gaining his pension stemmed from the fact that his record on the field of battle did not quite match his performance on the streets of New York. He served only from December 2, 1861, to February 17, 1862—not quite the three-month minimum. It took a great deal of personal pleading to finally obtain the stipend. When he was asked for an official explanation for the brevity of his service, Harding wrote the following: "A general quarrel in the Regiment. There were only 2 English companies. The rest were German. My Co. petitioned [Colonel Dickel] to be made a Co. of Artillery" from cavalry; the Colonel temporarily agreed, but then withdrew his offer and made matters worse by appointing a Captain Ten Eyck over poor Harding. It was another fiasco in a life full of failures.

James, unlike his brothers, remained in New York City during the war, running a Metallic Artificial Legs and Arms Business at 491 Broadway that was remarkably successful in a grotesque way. But by 1867 all three Westons were home. Ezra had resumed his duties as a broker for a bank, working at a building at 42 John Street in the financial district, while Harding was selling ads for newspapers. By 1870 Ezra had developed a very strong yearning to return to his farm roots, and so with the help of his two brothers, he decided to abandon his financial career and open up a large hotel in Nyack-on-the-Hudson. This hostelry would cater to refugees from the business world, since a new railroad line had just been completed from the ferry docks at Hoboken northward, and to the kinds of people whom Ezra Brown Weston found most interesting: artists, writers, and appreciators of The Beautiful.

At this point, Aunt Frank enters the scene. Probably born in Westchester County across the river from Nyack in 1832 (she gave a different birth date, usually younger, at every census report), she had supposedly married a man named Freer, who apparently died. Our only grounds for this are various undocumented glosses on Canto 22 that say that Pound, when visiting Gibraltar in 1908, was approached by a shady dealer in currency who called him by this name, which he had apparently borrowed from Frances during his sabbatical year earlier:

And a voice behind me in the street.
"Meestair Freer! Meestair . . ."

Pound says in *Indiscretions* that Frances had a husband before Uncle Ezra, but he gives no details, and her obituaries are silent. Since she was fond of dancing at the inaugural balls of presidents and she visited Washington often, it would seem that Ezra may have met her there before or after the war.

Uncle Ezra was doubtlessly drawn to Nyack because of his wife, who had several Wessells relatives there, as well as across the Hudson in Westchester County. But their dream of establishing a hotel for people dedicated to The Beautiful was doomed from the start. They were too idealistic and too kind. Ezra wanted to escape from Wall Street, and in so doing he left his good business sense behind. They also did not have enough personal contacts among artists to make such a venture work—such as Pound would have later in Rapallo.

Another problem was that Uncle Ez was surrounded by numerous eccentrics who had attached themselves to him and were relentlessly holding him back. Pound describes two of them in this way in *Indiscretions* (pp. 19, 20):

One of them resembled Rosa Bonheur; she pursued a career of masterly inactivity until the age of 87; never wholly parasitic, she made small and neat sketches in lead pencil, and was intermittently employed on "accounts". . . .

The most adhesive . . . was Mary Pinker. As housekeeper she remained till his end, whereupon she went into deep mourning: she desired to wear a veil. This luxury of grief was denied her, and this inhibition so injured her finer feelings that in the ensuing complications she suspended immediate contact with the family, appearing only on more formal occasions. She was, however, present at my great-aunt's third wedding. . . .

Pound says, in short, that he could not imagine his Uncle Ezra without his minions around him, and these minions gradually destroyed his dream.

In addition to these parasites, there was Brother Harding, with his constant attempts to borrow money to finance his impossible schemes. After Harding "bopped" Ezra on the head, the rest of the family dropped him—except for Ezra, who saw him on the side and doubtlessly continued to lend him small sums of cash. In his autobiography Pound mentions the emotional impact of all this on his mother, who "had seen the [Weston] star at its zenith, with the Nyack place and her uncle's intention to be a country gentleman and a patron of the fine arts; she can't have liked the collapse, she can't have liked either the strain—if any—before the hotel was decided upon, or the early stages of its progress" (p. 27). And so when Homer appeared shortly after the debacle, the family, which might have once scorned him as a Wisconsin bumpkin, was not wholly indisposed to welcoming him into its fold (p. 8).

The "invisible" grandfather, Harding Weston, is a fascinating character. He weaves in and out of the city directories of New York for about a half a century, always living in questionable if not downright sleazy milieux. Following is a brief sample of his movements during the post-Nyack period:

1881–83   Broker: 148 West 10th Street (home and business)

1884–89   Disappears (records show he lived for a time in Mineola, Long Island)

1890–94	Clerk: 20, then 26 Greenwich Avenue (dangerously near the Jefferson Market Prison, now library)
1899–1900	Patent medicines: 234 Sixth Avenue (but not there at 1900 census time)
1902–03	Agent: 25 East 14th Street
1904–07	Prime outlet for "Shakers" Toothache Pellets at the preceding address
1909–11	Patent medicines: 144 West 23rd Street (when Pound was in New York during this period, he thought that his grandfather was dead.)
1920–21	Patent medicines: 131 West 23rd Street, Room 22

This was Harding's last address before he went off to live in a series of veterans' hospitals for the last decade of his life: first in Bath, New York . . . then in Dayton, Ohio . . . and finally, for some inexplicable reason, in Hampton, Virginia, where he is buried in the nearby military cemetery in Gravesite 1366-A of Section E. The doctor who admitted him to the hospital in Dayton wrote: "Applicant presents a marked case of Senile Dementia with delusions and attacks of viciousness. He is very quarrelsome and requires a great deal of care." Another doctor described him as a man who seemed to have had visionary powers that had gone astray. He was, in short, a difficult case.

Pound, of course, was fascinated by his errant grandfather. In 1920, while writing *Indiscretions*, he said: "When I say that [Harding Weston] remained, the verb may be taken in all of its senses; he was at last report still remaining, invisible. A Sixth Avenue barber once asked me if I had seen him. For the first twenty years of my life I was led to suppose [him] deceased. It is not suggested that he had 'done anything,' but rather a sort of persistence in various forms of re-action rather connected, in the familial mind, with his 'having ideas'" (p. 20).

Back in Nyack, the United States Census Report of 1870 shows that Ezra B. Weston was living in a large, white, wooden

39

overleaf: Detail of a map of Nyack in 1873. Ezra Weston owned the large house at the corner of Clinton and Hillside while his wife "Frank" and ► her sister owned the two houses to the left along Hillside Avenue.

mansion three stories high on Hillside Avenue at the corner of Clinton Avenue, where his orchards lined the street. There were two smaller houses also on his Hillside block, which belonged to his wife Frances and her sister, Eliza Wessells. Ezra's house was worth $82,000, an enormous sum for that time, while those of the two women were valued at $5,000. Nearby, up the hill on Hillside Avenue were houses that belonged to a carpenter named John C. Wessells and his wife Sarah and their two children, Sarah and Charles. John was Aunt Frank's brother, and either the mother or the child is the Cousin Sadie whom Pound refers to in letters during his visit of 1910. Next to them lived Charles H. Wessells, a provisions broker from New York, who was also Frances' brother. He was quite wealthy, and would soon move to the city, where he would live during the turn of the century in a fashionable town-house in the West Nineties. Charles' and John's children were much beloved by the childless Aunt Frank, and she took them to Europe, just as she did young Ezra in the years to come.

For a few years, Nyack seems to have been a dream. To a businessman tired of the turmoil and hubbub of The City, the tree-shaded town at the majestic bend of the Hudson with its sweeping views north and south was an Earthly Paradise. But by 1876 the insolvency of the hotel venture was already apparent. The *Rockland County Journal* reported that Ezra Weston and his family had removed themselves to Washington (where they lived at 203 East Capitol Street, not far from the Capitol Building, where Congressman Thaddeus Pound was orating). They returned to Nyack for the summer season in 1877, but by 1880 the property had been surrendered to the Metropolitan Insurance Company, which had issued the mortgage. The lot was broken up into a series of small parcels, and middle-class homes were erected on the site. They in turn disappeared when the New York State Thruway cut a broad and merciless swath through the town as it sped to cross the Hudson at Tappan Zee.

Back in the city against his will, Uncle Ezra made the best of what many called a ruined career. But he was neither totally bankrupt nor despairing. He had money enough to start up the boardinghouse on 47th Street, which was quite profitable and increased in value after his death. He also engaged in the cattle-feed business with his brother James at 170 Bleecker Street, which became the site for the Mills Hotel, where the venerable eccentric Francis George Train died. With the help of his wife Frances, Ezra once more assembled a little world around him, including the fatherless Isabel and husbandless Mary. During his incarceration in the camp near Pisa, Pound reflected back on this lively world of the boardinghouse with its memorable characters:

> and as for playing checquers with black Jim
>   on a barrel top where now is the Ritz-Carlton
> and the voice of Monsieur Fouquet or the Napoleon 3rd
> barbiche of Mr Quackenbos, or Quackenbush
> as I supposed it,
> and Mrs Chittenden's lofty air
>   and the remains of the old South
>   tidewashed to Manhattan and brown-stone
>   or (later) the outer front stair
> leading to Mouquin's
>   or old Train (Francis) on the pavement in his
>   plain wooden chair
>
> (Canto 74, p. 447)

Some of these people can be documented authoritatively, while others have totally disappeared, thanks in large part to the destruction of the U.S. Census Report of 1890 in Washington and the vandalization of pages of the 1890 New York City Police Census Report. In my article "Ezra Pound's New York" (see Documentation section), I explained the process of identification with all of the difficulties involved. Mr. Q. is Abraham Quackenbush, who ran a real estate business in the Yorkville section of New York around the turn of the century. He lived in the boardinghouse for years, along with his wife Elizabeth. In *Indiscretions* (p. 34), he is described as looking like Napoleon III, and his goatee or small beard is singled out. Pound says that Quackenbush was an old bore who was always placed at the head of the second long dining table in the back parlor, so that his dull remarks would not interfere with the flashing repartee between Uncle Ezra and his great friend, Monsieur Fouquet.

John D. Fouquet was another of Ezra's partners in the hotel at Nyack, and he continued to be a friend even after the debacle.

Pound describes him in *Indiscretions* (p. 34) as having a drooping nose, and looking like Chauncey DePew of the New York Central Railroad with his bald head and his silvery mutton-chops. John was an architect who had an office in the upstairs level of the old Grand Central Depot, which had a Moorish rather than a Greco-Roman design. Pound describes his voice as having a "shrill, high, normal tone . . . ascending to pure Punch and Judy or drooping to a false double-bass (it is just possible that this was done for my benefit and that he did not use it in 'ordinary conversations,' but I doubt this hypothesis)". Pound calls him "Monsieur" Fouquet because John hailed from old French stock in New Orleans. Yet, despite this rather aristocratic ancestry, John was first and firmly Democratic, egalitarian, and even on the side of the notorious Tammany Hall in local politics.

The boardinghouse, Pound makes clear in his autobiography, was the scene of many heated political debates. Writing in 1920, Pound obviously could not remember very much specifically of what he had heard from the ages of five to seven, but he clearly heard a lot. If Monsieur Fouquet was a Democrat who always argued for the people, Uncle Ezra was an old-line Republican who represented the traditional values of New England. It was south-western populism transferred to the city against agrarian conservatism. Uncle Ezra subscribed to the Tammany publication *Judge* —but only to make fun of it. Apparently these arguments had raged for a good thirty years—long before Baby Ezra appeared on the scene. But with the child there, both older men had even more inspiration to put on a show.

The important thing to be mentioned here is that very early in his life, Ezra Pound was exposed to politics, with the issues handled in a sane if impassioned manner by men who, despite their personal antics, knew perfectly well what they were arguing. When Pound was placed under observation in St. Elizabeths, his various obsessions and willful assertions of the self were treated as end-products of a spoiled childhood in which he was the only youthful member of the family. That was the world of Wyncote— but it was just one of Pound's youthful worlds. For as correspondence and memoirs make clear, young Ezra was in New York constantly, since the Pounds never seem to have developed the kinds of friends in Philadelphia who could rival the vivacious Westons.

Another factor to be noted here is the very important statement in *Indiscretions* that is almost lost in the forest of detail about Fouquet: "I adored both him and my great-uncle." The statement is strong and meaningful. It seems clear that at this time young Ezra felt that his namesake was a surrogate father, since his own father Homer was very much indebted to Ezra Senior for his daily sustenance. In describing the relationship between the placid, homespun Homer with the always jovial Ezra B., Pound suggests that Homer may have found Ezra's "chuckle and 'haw' somewhat alarming, this series of prodigious pop-guns of good humour. 'An' I bet him a dollar an' the first thing I knew in the morning was a fellah yelling hurrah for Grover [Cleveland], and running off with my ash-barrel,' plus bubbles and gurgles of merriment. Or possibly Homer's puzzlement was only that usual to the long parallelogram object when confronted with the stubbier, stockier form of humanity" (p. 28). Pound would later adopt this voice himself in his role as "Uncle Ez."

Pound also informs us in *Indiscretions* (p. 28), in a passage that many people find startling, that he remembers throwing his baby rocking chair across the room at the age of six on hearing the unfavorable results of a national election. That would have been in November of 1892, when Grover Cleveland, the alcoholic imbiber, won, with the support of Thaddeus Pound. Pound explained this childhood reaction as a result of economics: "I was genuinely oppressed by the fear that my father would lose his job and that we should all be deprived of sustenance. It was in the days before 'Civil Service,' and an appalling percentage of Government employees were almost automatically 'fired' as a 'natural result' of every change in administration; fired after perhaps thirty years' service and with no prospects of a pension." So politics and economics were intertwined in a way that would have a direct bearing later on his intellectual growth and eventually even his poetry.

Because of the loss of valuable documents, there is no way to identify definitively many of the other occupants of the rooming-house even though some have tried. Mrs. Chittenden with her airs is forever lost (she may have been a musician named Kate Chittenden) along with black Jim (no servant named James is listed in available records). It is probable that the "Mr. Bohun" mentioned in *Indiscretions* as an oil man and long-term resident was one Oliver Dow, and the faithful "Mary Pinker" who was denied the funereal veil may well have been a Mary Egleton, but there is no point in pressing for details here. A look at the existing census reports shows a wide variety of people, ranging from a southern "literary writer" to some students from Columbia to a host of black servants from Virginia and the Carolinas. It was truly a little self-contained world.

On their return to New York, the Pounds moved into this house on 47th Street rather than with Grandmother Weston because her establishment at 52nd and Lexington was filled with many fresh, young, middle-class girls whom she mothered when she was not assisting Dr. Bird, who had his office on the ground floor, or another practitioner. As a result, Baby Ezra became almost *de facto* the child that Aunt Frank and Uncle Ezra never had. If Uncle Ezra had not died in 1894, he might well have made his namesake an heir to the considerable amount of money that he and Frances were amassing with their successful new operation. But instead, Aunt Frank got the money, and she then tried to open a fancy new hotel . . . but that sad story can wait.

In the spring of 1888, when Pound was two and a half years old, his parents and Grandmother Weston took him to the fashionable resort of Newport for a time, near Hopkinton, the hometown of Mary Weston. There they enjoyed a lovely season by the sea in the company of some of America's wealthiest citizens. About this time, the child received his most memorable toy, a miniature elevator, as he reported in his essay "Henry James" (*Literary Essays*, p. 303). In fact, it is James who seemed to set the model for Pound's writing of his autobiography, since James in *Washington Square* was "'putting America on the map,' giving us a real past, a real background'" (p. 312). In the fall of '88, when Pound was now three years old, his parents and Grandmother Mary Weston again took him on a trip; this time to Wisconsin, to the great mansard-roofed house in Chippewa Falls, where he encountered the beard of Grandfather Thaddeus. There he also encountered

Great-Grandfather Elijah and his brother Joel, whose years were fast approaching those of Methuselah.

Back in New York in 1889, Homer Pound decided that it was finally time to stop mooching off his affable brother-in-law and to settle into some kind of job for his life. Since his experience was in the field of minerals, he applied for work with the United States Mint in Washington, but there were no openings there. Actually, for spans from April to June of 1881 and from February of 1882 until May of 1883, Homer had found employment at the Mint branch in Philadelphia, as an assistant assayer. Suddenly a job opened there, and he leaped at the chance. In no time, the bags were packed, and the family of three was off to the City of Brotherly Love.

Despite the departure, New York City would always be a part of Pound's beloved past. This affection shows clearly in the little poem written after the visit of 1910 and published in *Personae* (p. 62) under the title "N.Y.":

> My City, my beloved, my white! Ah, slender,
> Listen! Listen to me, and I will breathe
>   into thee a soul.
> Delicately upon the reed, attend me!
>
> *Now do I know that I am mad,*
> *For here are a million people surly with traffic;*
> *This is no maid,*
> *Neither could I play upon any reed if I had one. . . .*

Still, the poet goes on to repeat his desire to turn the cacophony of the metropolis into true music.

New York's own music was something that did not escape the growing boy, who went back to 47th Street constantly over the next twenty years. He speaks of the sounds and the colors of the neighborhood in this affectionate way in *Indiscretions* (p. 42): "And at the end of the street jingled the small horse bells of the Madison Avenue horse-cars, bobbing down toward the white-washed tunnel, and . . . beyond that the tracks from the 'Grand Central,' invisible because of the wall and the Express Company; and beyond that was 596 Lexington Avenue—with the cable cars." This is transformed into verse in Canto 74 (p. 447):

or a fellow throwing a knife in the market
past baskets and bushels of peaches
                at $1. the bushel
and the cool of the 42nd St. tunnel   (periplum)
white-wash and horse cars, the Lexington Avenue cable
refinement, pride of tradition, alabaster

Pound used to go down to the Washington Street Market to shop
for the boardinghouse meals with Uncle Ezra and, after his death,
with Aunt Frank. There in the sea of pushcarts and temporary
stands that stretched for miles with fresh fruits and vegetables,
his relatives and he would select the finest foods for the day. It
was during one of these visits that he saw a man throw a knife at a
darting figure, and the vision of potential death clung in his mind
during his own incarceration in the camp north of Pisa.

When they were not eating in the house, Aunt Frank liked to
take the boy to Mouquin's Restaurant—the branch located at
Herald Square on Sixth Avenue. There Pound was exposed to
genuine French cooking, although the black cooks in the boardinghouse doubtlessly knew something about the "receipts" of
Charleston or the delicacies of Monsieur Fouquet's New Orleans.
Through his aunt and his uncle especially, Pound early developed
a taste for exquisitely prepared food, and that taste would stay
with him throughout his life—especially since his wife Dorothy
steadfastly refused to cook until World War II came. Pound's
veneration for food and for famous eating places goes on into the
Pisan Cantos:

> Sirdar, Bouiller and Les Lilas,
>   or Dieudonné London, or Voisin's . . .
>   the cake shops in the Nevsky, and Schöners
> not to mention der Greif at Bolsano . . .
> Mouquin's or Robert's 40 years after

(Canto 74, p. 433)

There is also the surprising line in Canto 110 (p. 780): "That war is
the destruction of restaurants."

When Uncle Ezra died in 1894, young Pound was present at
the funeral, which he describes in *Indiscretions* (p. 20) as an event
with much weeping and wailing and gnashing of teeth. The ser-

vice was held in the large front parlor of the boardinghouse, and all of Ezra's many friends were there. Aside from the paid advertisements that ran in the local papers, the *New York Daily Tribune* issued this following tribute on Tuesday, December 11, at its own expense:

> Ezra B. Weston, one of the old residents of this city, died yesterday, after a lingering illness, at his home . . . He was sixty-seven years old, and had retired from active business twenty years ago. Prior to that time he had been connected with several of the city's savings banks, but met business reverses, and had led a life of quiet and seclusion for a number of years. His wife survives him.

Even the commercial papers were moved by his death.

It must have been a long, arduous journey following the horse-drawn hearse across the Williamsburgh Bridge and out Jamaica Avenue to the Cypress Hills Cemetery on the Queens-Brooklyn boundary line. Ezra had purchased a large plot of land there back in 1853 to bury his eldest brother, George, and here he was finally laid to rest beside his mother Asenath, his sister Elizabeth, a sister-in-law, and the ashes of a nameless person—probably brother James Wheeler Weston, who disappears from New York in 1888 (the ashes were deposited there in 1889). Two decades later, Uncle Ezra would be joined by his wife, Frances Amelia, even though she remarried after his death. For Aunt Frank's heart, like that of young Ezra, was always with the lovable, affectionate, mirthful "Uncle Ez."

♦ THREE

MA WESTON'S CHILDREN'S HOUR: THE WADSWORTHS AND ALL THAT

When young Ezra was not with the Westons on 47th Street, he was only eight blocks away at 52nd Street and Lexington with Grandmother ("Ma") Weston. It has already been emphasized (just as it was to the child) that, although Mary Weston was legally a Parker by birth, she chose to ignore that connection in lieu of the fact that she was a Wadsworth through her mother. After all, the Parkers were mere common laborers—men who made their living by making shoes—while the Wadsworths were rich and powerful bankers and brokers. There was no romance or family tradition related to Hiram Parker of Hopkinton, and romance and tradition were things that Mary found essential, especially after her unfortunate coupling with Harding Weston. And so when she was not superintending her boardinghouse at 596 Lexington, with twenty-eight young ladies and three gentlemen and Dr. Arthur Bird on the ground floor across from her quarters, she regaled the young child with stories about his rich family past.

Mary's Bible was a compendious work known as *Two Hundred and Fifty Years of the Wadsworth Family in America*. It had been written by one H. A. Wadsworth and published in Lawrence, Massachusetts, in 1883, one year after family members had staged a massive reunion in Duxbury, one of their prime points of origination. Mary's mother attended this reunion, along with some wealthy relatives from New York whom Ma Weston assiduously cultivated. The Wadsworth history is full of the lore that delights genealogists. It tells how the family is believed by some to be able to trace its roots all the way back to a Duke Wada of Northumbria in the remote 800s, and to a semimythic castle-builder named Wade, who constructed a famous highway known as Wade's Way in Yorkshire. There were also attempts to make the obvious Saxon name Norman-French. Most of this detail was purely imaginary, but the family did have one proof of a long-standing past: a coat of arms. This consisted of three silver fleur-de-lis, stalked and slipped, on a red background. The design suggests that the ancient Wadsworths helped the English forces defeat the French in some remote battles, and since no one was allowed to draw up a coat-of-arms after the Battle of Crécy in 1346, the Wadsworths could rightly trace their origin at least to the time of Geoffrey Chaucer.

There were two male Wadsworths who came to America early: William, on the *Lion*, which docked in Boston on September 16, 1632, twelve years after the *Mayflower*, and Christopher, who shows up in Duxbury one year later. Although there is no clear connection between these two men, it seems logical that they were related, given the relative rarity of the name and the fact that there were only about 1,000 white settlers in eastern Massachusetts in those days, and they came in religious and family groups.

Although Mary Weston was related to Christopher's strain of the family, it was to William's side that she looked for one of the men who seemed most illustrious to her and to her other relatives: the Connecticut patriot Captain Joseph Wadsworth. His lineage can be unravelled as follows: William's group of emigrants soon moved from Boston to Newtown (later Cambridge), where they were joined a year later in 1633 by the famous religious reformer Thomas Hooker. These men were all Puritan refugees who had fled England because of their nonconformist beliefs about religion, going first to Holland, then to America (often with the assistance of men like Thomas Weston, already cited in the previous chapter). Unlike some of the earlier settlers, they were for the most part well-to-do and well educated: Hooker himself had attended Cambridge with Oliver Cromwell, the great Puritan reformer who had successfully deposed kings. Therefore although the modern world tends to find the term "Puritan" distasteful, with

The coat of arms of the Wadsworths.

The Wyllys Mansion and the Charter Oak, where Captain Joseph Wadsworth hid the Connecticut Charter from the British.

its connotations of sexual conservatism and general fanaticism (and Pound himself was not partial to Puritanism), we have to remember that they were also fiercely democratic, anti-aristocratic, and strongly supportive of commonwealth forms of government, as well as human rights. It is this positive side of the early family history that Mary Weston stressed, and that Pound found interesting.

In 1636 William Wadsworth, Thomas Hooker, and several others left the Colony of Massachusetts to strike out on their own, establishing a settlement in the verdant Connecticut Valley, on the site of modern Hartford. William owned a large tract of land on what is now the downtown area of that insurance center, bounded by Asylum, Trumbull, West Pearl Streets, and the river. William married twice: first, to a woman whose name is unknown and who died young; second, to Eliza Stone, who gave him five children, among whom was the future Captain Joseph Wadsworth of Charter fame, who was born in 1648 and died in 1729. Pound was enormously proud of this man—especially during his years of confinement in St. Elizabeths—because he felt that the Captain stood for the individualistic values of free speech that he had thought he was expressing over Radio Rome, against a government such as that of Franklin Delano Roosevelt which (so Pound believed) had meddled with the Constitution in an attempt to pull the nation out of the disastrous Depression:

> Will they get rid of the Rooseveltian dung-hill
> And put Capn. Wadsworth back in the school books?
>
> (Canto 97, p. 671)

Even an impartial viewer has to respect Captain Joseph, since he and Hooker and others helped to frame the Connecticut Constitution in 1638–39, which established a type of commonwealth government with elected legislative officers. This has been called the oldest political constitution in America—and the first to directly produce a governing body standing for democratic principles. Following the disastrous Battle of Worcester (England) in 1662, King Charles II actually granted this charter to the Americans in the hope that he could win their sympathies. Therefore, the Charter was established by law. However, when James II ascended to the throne after Charles, he immediately tried to renege on these dangerous promises, seeing them as still another (and legal) channel open for the subversion of the monarchy. Through an ardent loyalist named Sir Edmund Andros of Massachusetts, James demanded that the Charter be returned—and hence revoked. When the Connecticut Assembly refused to comply, Andros was dispatched to Hartford to seize the document and enforce the King's will.

At this point, Joseph Wadsworth becomes the central figure in the drama. Andros was received in a Hartford inn, where he was flatly told that the local residents would not surrender their hard-won and quite legal rights—the "local power" so dear to the American populists, Confucians, and Ezra Pound. Andros got up to seize the paper, but somebody doused the lights; Captain Joseph grabbed the document instead, ran out the door, mounted his horse, and sped off to the southern edge of the town, to the mansion of the governor, George Wyllys, who happened to be out of town on business. Mrs. Wyllys received the Captain and, knowing that the King's men were in pursuit, suggested that he stash the paper in the large, spreading oak that stood on the front lawn of the house. This was a very fabled tree; it had lifted its massive foliage for years there on the banks of the Little River, serving as the official meeting-place for the sachems of the Suckiac and other local Indian tribes. Joseph took her advice and hid the Charter in a crevice inside the ancient oak, then ran off into hiding. In this way, the Charter was saved.

To understand the importance of the incident to Pound, we must read his recounting of it in *Indiscretions* (p. 6):

> It is one thing to feel that one could write the whole social history of the United States from one's family annals, and vastly another to embark upon any such Balzacian and voluminous endeavor. Hence my great-aunt [Frances Weston] in parenthesis; hence Joseph Wadsworth, who stole the Connecticut charter and hid it in Charter Oak, to the embarrassment of legitimist tyranny; picturesque circumstances, candles snuffed out with a cloak which popular art has represented as cavalier rather than round-head. . . .

Clearly Ma Weston's readings had their effect. One can see that the writer passionately cares about his material; he has even suggested that Captain Joseph may have doused the candles—which most histories neglect to mention. In addition to literature, Pound was also exposed to objects of art to reinforce his understanding of his family's history: heraldic ornaments out of the Longfellow volumes . . . coats-of-arms . . . India ink drawings supposedly made by the Loomises . . . a fire-bucket from Barre (which is mentioned in Canto 74, p. 447). In short, Ma Weston was a complete and thorough educator, and the fact that she made Wadsworth history American history is underscored here. Her teaching would have a profound effect on Pound throughout his life. Whether among the poets in Chelsea or the Fascists in Rome, Pound always thought of himself first and foremost as an American—a fearless pioneer like Thomas Weston (who lived briefly in Massachusetts) or Thaddeus Coleman Pound or Captain Joseph Wadsworth. No matter where he turned, he encountered the archetype.

The Connecticut Charter lay dormant until the 1690s, when it was brought back to light and reinstalled; it lasted as a legislative force until the 1880s, but the lovely old Charter Oak fell mysteriously and suddenly to the ground on August 21, 1856. As a result, when young Ezra visited Hartford with his parents to examine this famous tree in the 1890s, all that was left was the legend. Still, legends, as we have already seen, can be powerful formative shapers, and Pound celebrated his heroic ancestor's acts by recording in his Later Cantos (written in St. Elizabeths) a gift given in "resentment" (kind sentiment) to Joseph by the local government:

> 20 shillings to Wadsworth
> "in resentment." Town house in Hartford.
>
> (Canto 111, p. 782)

Another more extended passage incorporates the language used by King Charles in granting the charter to the Colony of Connecticut:

> "In grateful resentment to Wadsworth, 20 shillings
> May 15th
> Town House in Hartford

Charles, God's Grace, '62
Brewen, Canfield,
a Body politique
and meere mocion
Ordeyned, heirs, successors, Woollcott, Talcot, perpetual
Seal, Governor, Deputy and 12 assistants

(Canto 109, p. 773)

The passage goes on to paint the New World in terms suggesting
the paradise that men believed would come:

and not hinder fishinge
for salting
by Narrowgancett
and on the South by the Sea
Mynes, Mynerals Precious Stones Quarries
As of our Mannor East Greenwich

Everywhere that Pound looked in his family past, he could see
these paradises that somehow never came to fruition, whether in
Idaho, Wisconsin, or the Connecticut Valley. Whose fault, he
undoubtedly asked himself, was that?

One last anecdote about the Captain should be recorded here,
since it was imprinted on young Ezra's brain. In 1693 Colonel
Fletcher of the Colony of New York visited Hartford in an attempt
to enforce a royal commission against Captain Joseph for com-
manding the local militia without the King's sanction. Actually,
this was an early attempt by New York to gain control over the
fledgling colony. Every time that Fletcher began to speak, however, Captain Joseph would order his drummers to drown out the
man's words. This happened again and again, until finally Captain
Joseph said (in effect): "If you interrupt us once again, I'll make the
daylight shine through you in a single flash!" Mary Weston
drummed such stories as these into her grandchild—stories about
fierce individualism and standing up for one's rights—and they
would have an effect later, both for the better and for the worse.

To return to the origin of the Wadsworth branch that was
actually closest to Pound, we find the already mentioned Christopher Wadsworth appearing in Duxbury on Cape Cod Bay in
1633, although he may have arrived a year earlier with William.

Very quickly he was chosen as the first constable of Duxbury—a high honor, considering that he was competing with the Aldens, the Standishes, and the Brewsters, who had gotten there before him. During his lifetime he held every major office in the town, from deputy to surveyor. He lived in a house that was still standing during the reunion of 1882, near Captain's Hill, with property running down to the bay at Morton's Hole. This remained in Wadsworth hands until 1855. We do not know Christopher's birth date or the name of his father, but we do know that he married a woman from Duxbury by the name of Grace Cole. Before his death, the date of which is also unknown, he and Grace created a family that had at least four mature members: Joseph, Mary, John, and Samuel. We should keep John in mind for later developments, because it is through him that we find the Longfellow connection.

Proceeding on Pound's line, we encounter Samuel Wadsworth, who became a great colonial hero. We do not know when he was born, but he was a taxpayer in 1655–56, owning land near Milton, where he became the captain of the local militia. During the 1670s, the Indians were making their last great stand in eastern Massachusetts against the incursions of their white invaders. They were led by a chief from the Wampanoag tribe who was called Metacom, and whom the white people dubbed Philip. During this so-called King Philip's War, the natives used terrifying guerrilla tactics—with sudden raids and secret ambushes and nightly scalping parties—to cause panic throughout the entire area. It took a great deal of courage—or obstinacy—to hang on.

In 1676, after a particularly hair-raising attack on the town of Marlborough, Captain Samuel took his band of fifty men to reinforce the depleted garrison. The Indians cleverly allowed him to penetrate their lines, drawing back until they lured him to a mound called Green Hill. Then some five hundred suddenly swooped down upon the gallant little band. Samuel and his men made a ferocious stand, clambering up the hill and doing their best to beat the Indians backward, but they were gradually outnumbered and overcome, and reinforcements—unlike those programmed in Hollywood—arrived moments too late. Samuel was hacked down there on the bloody hill.

Captain Samuel Wadsworth's actions were praised by all the whites. A monument was eventually erected on Green Hill in commemoration of his bravery, and the money for this was raised by one of his sons, Reverend Benjamin Wadsworth, who went on to become famous as the ninth president of Harvard College—a school whose name recurs repeatedly in the Wadsworth annals. Lest we expend too much sympathy on the tragic fate of the Captain, we should consider what the fanatic Cotton Mather said in his *Marginalia* about the unlucky handful of Indian prisoners who were taken: the white men forced them to run a gauntlet and "then they threw hot ashes upon them, and cutting off collops of their flesh, they put fire in their wounds, and so, with exquisite, leisurely, horrible torments, roasted them out of the world" (quoted with not too much disapproval by the author of the Wadsworth history, H. A. Wadsworth, p. 60). If Ezra Pound tended to tease William Carlos Williams because of his hybrid blood (Jewish, English, and Spanish), Williams retaliated beautifully with his masterfully understated attacks on the Puritans in his *In the American Grain*, a book that Pound, despite certain reservations about style, admired greatly.

Before Captain Samuel's death, which was said to have come in his forties, he had married Abigail Lindall (who died in 1687), and they had a sizable family that consisted of a girl named Abigail and six sons. Besides the future President of Harvard, Benjamin, these included:

EBENEZER WADSWORTH (born in 1660). With his eldest brother, Christopher, he helped to found the town of Milton, where his people already owned land. The oldest grave in the Milton Burial Ground belongs to Christopher (d. 1687), while Ebenezer (d. 1717) lies nearby. Ebenezer was married, but we do not know the family name of his wife, Mary. They had four children, including a son who was named:

RECOMPENSE WADSWORTH (born in Milton in 1688 and died there in 1729). He married Sarah Morey, and they had four children, of whom the third was:

DAVID WADSWORTH I (born in Milton in 1720). He began the steady westward migration of the family by picking up stakes and moving to Grafton, southeast of Worcester, where he died young

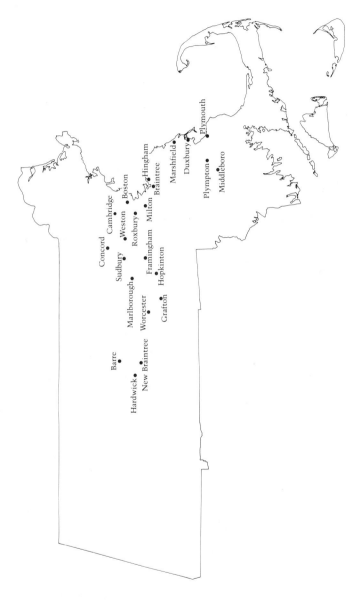

Eastern Massachusetts, showing the sites which were most important to the Wadsworths and the Westons.

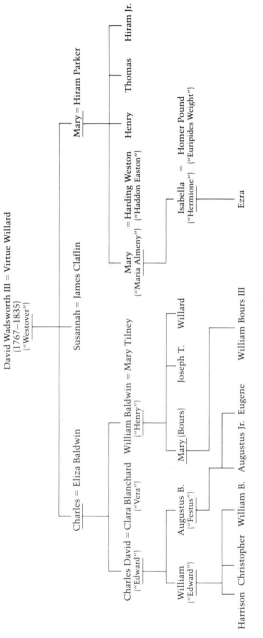

Recent generations of the Wadsworths.

at the age of 29 in 1749. Before that, he married Hannah Paul and had four children, of whom the oldest was:

DAVID WADSWORTH II (born in Grafton in 1741 and died there in 1821). His wife was Elizabeth Whipple (1744–1827), who presented him with a family of ten children, of whom the oldest again was:

DAVID WADSWORTH III. This man, born in 1767, is a pivotal figure, because he moved to the town of Barre, where the Westons were living at this time, along with the Hows. Here all three families' paths cross. David Wadsworth III took for his wife a woman named Virtue Willard, who probably came from Sudbury. In the Homer Pound scrapbook at Yale, there is a photograph of a large, imposing grandfather clock with the inscription "Ben Willard Clock" from "Sudberry" (Homer's spelling), which once stood in the Wayside Inn and later in Homer's house in Wyncote outside Philadelphia.

Before David Wadsworth III died on May 5, 1835, he fathered a large family of eleven children, who formed the eighth generation descended from the first "Xtofer Waddesworth of Duxbury." This group includes three people who were important to Pound: his great-grandmother Mary Wadsworth, who was born in Barre in 1808 and was the youngest member of the brood; her brother, Charles, who was born in 1805 and is the ancestor of the New York bankers whom Mary Weston admired so much; and a sister named Susannah, who was born in 1793 and married James Claflin of Hopkinton. Through Susannah, Mary Wadsworth met Hiram Parker of Hopkinton, and this resulted in their marriage and the birth of Ezra Pound's maternal grandmother, Mary Parker Weston. Susannah Claflin also had a daughter named Susannah, who shortly will be mentioned in a quotation from *Indiscretions* for being a monument of good New England sense.

Before we take the Wadsworths to New York City, it is time to pause and pick up the Longfellow connection before it recedes totally from view. Pound's kinship with the poet stems back to Christopher Wadsworth of Duxbury, who fathered John I, who fathered John II, who fathered Peleg I, who fathered Peleg II, who married Elizabeth Bartlett of Plymouth; in 1778 they had a daughter named Zilpah, who married Stephen Longfellow and then gave birth to the poet in Portland, Maine, in 1807. This side of the family moved in a Maine–New Hampshire orbit that was somewhat removed from Mary's Massachusetts–New York branch. But still the connection was quite real, and Mary's people strongly felt that "one should deal gently with the reputations of members of the family, especially if their endeavors have been recorded in Westminster Abbey" (*Indiscretions*, p. 27), where Longfellow's bust stands in the Poet's Corner with the great figures of British literature. This may explain why, although Pound later vehemently disagreed with Longfellow's notion of creative writing, he kept substantially silent about him—especially when other family members were around.

Pound makes clear in *Indiscretions* that Ma Weston constantly read him the poems of Longfellow. In addition to *Tales of a Wayside Inn*, she recited "Paul Revere's Ride" and other bits of Americana, so that the child early felt a kind of fascination with the "simple versification of Longfellow" (p. 8). Mary's text was doubtlessly the beautifully illustrated 1886 Houghton Mifflin six-volume edition of *The Poetical Works*. Among the illustrations is a lovely drawing of Old North Church in Boston. Pound recalls that during the 1890s on a trip to that city with his parents to attend one of their many Christian Endeavor conventions, he climbed the steps of Old North Church—and was terrified by the sudden clangor of the bells. On the same trip or possibly another he visited Hartford and Sudbury.

Pound describes his grandmother as follows in *Indiscretions* (p. 19): she was "a confirmed romantic; she began to read me Scott's novels in the seventh year of my age; she conserved more illusions—if, indeed, romanticism be an illusion! I give it up. She was 'a monument of good sense' *à la* New England, exceeded therein only by her cousin Susannah. I suppose Scott himself was a 'monument.' Her mind may have been like his, minus the narrative urge, and tempered by romantic timidity befitting the feminine nature of a now somewhat legendary era. Her timidity was as egregious as it was unaffected." This timidity manifested itself in Mary Weston's appearing in very few public documents. We do not know the exact date of her birth (the 1890 New York Police Census lists 1845, but that seems too recent). Dr. Jerome

Kavka's report on Pound in St. Elizabeths says that she "continued to 'pump romantic Colonial history' into him until the time of her death [when] the patient was twelve years of age." She is buried in Hopkinton with her family.

Pound, of course, quickly outgrew the simple versification of H. W. L. In fact, one might view Pound's whole career as an attempt to slough off the obvious and embarrassing poetic techniques of his own ancestor, as well as other Victorian poets. Free verse and a lack of rhyming were merely the more obvious ways in which this was done. Still, what is perhaps ultimately more important is the similarity between both men in two respects. First, both writers stood in awe of Dante Alighieri, the great Italian author of the *Divine Comedy*, a work that can safely be said to have haunted almost every writer of the later twentieth century because it offers a coherent world-view that no one can offer today. Longfellow translated the work and Pound played off it in a highly original way in constructing his *Cantos*, an epic about history employing subjective judgments, precisely as the *Comedy* itself does. Secondly, both Longfellow and Pound refused to confine themselves to the narrow strictures of their own national literatures, and in this sense even Henry Wadsworth can be said to be modern. His *Tales of a Wayside Inn* range from Norse and Greco-Roman mythology to Arabic and American sources; and he taught "Comparative Literature" at Harvard while the name was still being coined in Germany. Pound's *Cantos* are, of course, notoriously multilingual, and he essentially studied Comparative Literature at both Penn and Hamilton before the formal name existed (and got into trouble by doing so, since he therefore put himself outside the easily controlled channels surrounding national literatures). Both men abjured provinciality and sensed the one-world drift of the future. It is perhaps for this reason—or else that he did not want to pick on an easy whipping boy—that Pound seldom criticized his famous forebear.

Returning to David Wadsworth III in Barre at the start of the nineteenth century, we find the Wadsworths beginning to make a major move with many other Americans: from the farm to the city, from agriculture to trade. David, in fact, was already partaking in the Industrial Revolution by establishing a profitable business as a manufacturer of scythes. With his profits, he sent his son Charles, brother of great-grandmother Mary, to college—to Brown University in Providence, where he graduated in the Class of 1827 and then moved on to New York State. He remained a bachelor until his forties, when he married Eliza Baldwin, who presented him with two sons: Charles David (the "Edward" of *Indiscretions*) and William Baldwin Wadsworth (the "Henry"). The father is listed in the Doggett City Directories of the late forties and early fifties as being a "builder," while the rather unreliable alumni records of Brown say that he was a banker. In any case when he died in his sixty-first year in 1866, Charles Wadsworth had prepared his sons for successful lives in the New York financial world, where he himself had played a role. These sons were close friends of Ma Weston, knew Pound fairly well without being intimate, but otherwise remained a bit aloof from the other members of Pound's family, such as Uncle Ezra, whom they considered a failure, and Aunt Frank, whom they (along with Mary) judged as a bit gauche.

Of the two sons, Pound's favorite was Charles David Wadsworth, who was born in New York City on February 4, 1847. He attended the old Spencertown Academy in Columbia County (southeast of Albany) before moving on to Williams College for a stint and then to the Wadsworths' favorite place for matriculation, Harvard. He graduated in the class of 1867 and then returned to New York, where, as Pound puts it in *Indiscretions* (the source for the quotations that follow), he took "the Exchange as a bore and an imposition; it had bored him for forty years; he has, I presume, never had enough money" (p. 26). Clearly Charles David had intellectual ambitions, but his desire for cash finally caused him to follow his younger brother, William, who had bypassed college and immersed himself in the brokerage business while he was still in his teens.

There was a firm called Wadsworth & Co. at 32 Broad Street in the financial district as early as 1869. In the 1880s, it was called Wadsworth & White at 44 New Street, and later Wadsworth & Wright. When Charles David died on February 16, 1942, at the age of ninety-five, he was the second oldest alumnus of Harvard and one of the oldest retired members of the New York Stock Exchange. As Pound said in 1920, the two Wadsworths "have been on the Exchange for so long that their seats are almost a patent of nobility" (p. 26).

In 1871 Charles David Wadsworth married Clara Blanchard, the daughter of a Brooklyn merchant. She is called "Vera" in *Indiscretions*, where it is noted that Ma Weston (perhaps jealous) did not thoroughly approve of her because she "went in for society," but when the poet revisited America in 1910, he renewed his acquaintance with the couple and found them "perfectly simple people untroubled by this form of desire" (p. 27). It is perhaps worth mentioning here that, of all of Pound's relatives, these two, with William Baldwin's family, were the only ones who were in a position to hobnob with the Astors, the Vanderbilts, the Rockefellers, and the other leading members of New York society.

Charles and Clara had two sons, who are also mentioned in *Indiscretions* with a certain amount of pride. One was a doctor called "Festus," who was actually named Augustus Baldwin. He began his career with the determination to starve in New York rather than be driven for any reason from the metropolis. Graduating from Massachusetts Institute of Technology in 1892, Augustus showed every sign of becoming a builder like his father, but he reversed his field suddenly and graduated from the Columbia College of Physicians and Surgeons to enter a very successful career in medicine. He specialized in immunology and, aside from his lucrative personal practice, held several important professional offices, some for the State of New York in Albany. It was at his house there that his father died in 1942. Augustus himself died at the home of his daughter, Caroline, in 1954, leaving two sons to assist her in carrying on the family name.

His brother was named William, but was referred to in *Indiscretions* as "Edward," a man who "has somewhat drifted about the professions—in a charming manner" (p. 26). It is true that William Wadsworth (born June 18, 1882) seems to have been as bored by business as his father. The 25th Reunion Class Report of the Harvard Class of 1904 quotes William speaking with ennui about his career in law (he also got an L.L.B. from Harvard in 1907 aside from his B.A. in 1904). In the Report, he narrates how he gave up the helter-skelter life in the Big City in 1918 (when he was only thirty-six years old) and moved in semi-retirement to a gentle-man's farm in Kinderhook, Columbia County, while still main-taining an interest in banking with the Shawmut Trust Company. He had six children—two of whom also attended Harvard to become architects—and so once again, the line went on.

Pound liked Charles David Wadsworth and his two sons precisely because of their detachment from the great wealth that they made. Charles David was first and foremost a gentleman, who was famous throughout New York for his beautiful and colorful cravats. In his various homes—in Plainfield, New Jersey, or in the fashionable part of the West Fifties in New York, or in exurban Chatham, where he retired before dying in nearby Albany—Charles David would, on entering a chilly room, not light a fire immediately, the way his brother William Baldwin would; he would either sit and wait for his servants to do it or finally do it himself in such a way that made one think that the servants had done it. In short, he was aristocratic and European. He was also, from his studies at Harvard, mildly interested in literature; at his table it was "felt that conversation should include literature, limited" (p. 26); and so, Pound freely confessed, he tended to gravitate more to Charles David's circle than to William Baldwin's during his visit of 1910. Earlier, of course, he went wherever Ma Weston took him. Various letters at Yale concerning the 1910 visit mention Charles acting very "decorative," while "Madame" Vera was cordial, and son William was going on and on about how he really wanted to end his days on a farm.

The other side of the family, William Baldwin's, was more material: "This is an American businessman. One would discover on examination that he was, is, a gentleman" (p. 26). At his death on April 24, 1934, *The Plainfield Courier* eulogized William Bald-win Wadsworth, a longtime resident of that town, in this way:

> Mr. Wadsworth was born in Spencertown, New York, June 25, 1849, and at the age of twelve started to work in New York City. At the age of 20 he joined the New York Stock Exchange, of which at the time of his death he was the oldest member.
>
> His career of more than 60 years on the Exchange carried him through all the depressions and booms of the so-called modern times during which the United States saw its greatest growth . . .
> His interest in charitable work was keen, but what he did was

DR. A. WADSWORTH, BACTERIOLOGIST, 81

Director of Laboratories for State Health Department, 1914 to 1945, Is Dead

Dr. Augustus Baldwin Wadsworth of Manchester, Vt., director of laboratories and research for the New York State Department of Health from 1914 to 1945, died Tuesday in the home of his daughter, Miss Varoline D. Wadsworth, 111 East Eightieth Street. His age was 81.

Dr. Wadsworth was graduated in 1892 from Massachusetts Institute of Technology and four years later from the College of Physicians and Surgeons, Columbia University. He served as alumni fellow of the college from 1899 to 1905, Alonzo Clark scholar from 1905 to 1910, instructor in bacteriology and hygiene from 1899 to 1908, associate in bacteriology in 1908-9, and assistant professor from 1909 to 1913.

The educator was American representative at the International Conference on Standardization of Serum and Seriological Test, Health Section, League of Nations, held in Paris in 1922. The same year he received the Order of St. Olav from Norway. In 1953 he received the Herman Biggs Memorial for outstanding service in public health in New York State.

Dr. Augustus B. Wadsworth

The obituary of "Festus." (*Courtesy of the* New York Times)

The mansion at 452 West Eighth Street in Plainfield, where William Baldwin Wadsworth lived from 1893 to 1909. (*Courtesy of Ruth Cochrane*)

without ostentation. He lived quietly and wanted no credit. Coming of old stock, he never was ill until two weeks ago, and his friends and acquaintances united in considering him a remarkable man.

In short, his was the classic American success story. Unlike the Pounds and the Westons, who had big dreams that they somehow never could make come true, William Baldwin Wadsworth saw his dreams fulfilled. The importance of a man such as this to someone like Mary Weston was inestimable. Aside from the heroes out of faded books, she could point to this hard-working and diligent broker as a model for her grandson.

Pound's own assessment of William Baldwin tended to agree with the obituary: he saw the man as a successful millionaire, but one with a heart. The material side is clearly reported in *Indiscretions* when Pound notes that at William's dinner table in Plainfield the talk "ran to motor cars (when I knew it)—the family seemed to require several each—and to supplementary motorboats, and to the Exchange, merits of still and unstill market" (p. 26). In short, unlike his more cultivated brother, William Baldwin "had taken the Exchange seriously." Still, Pound also comments on William's generosity: "he was reputed to have 'stood by' the family connections to such remote degree and so often that 'one shouldn't really appeal.' He even did me a turn once, who, being the grandson of a cousin, couldn't decently have been supposed to be in the running" (p. 26).

Pound's Wadsworth connection, documented above and in the many carbon copies of letters created by D. D. Paige for his *Selected Letters* (now housed at the Beinecke Library in Yale), should lay to rest two misconceptions that various people have about Pound. Because many people read the famous Usura Cantos and little else in Pound's major work, they sometimes get the idea that Pound was opposed to all forms of finance. This is not true. Pound was opposed to crooked manipulations of money—not the diligent, hardworking creation of it. Capitalism was never, *per se*, an evil to him, but he felt that capitalistic endeavors had to be tempered with a sense of "distributive justice" and certainly with patronage of the arts. This explains why the Harvard-educated Charles David Wadsworth had more appeal to the poet than his brother.

63

The other important misconception about Pound is that he was a kind of stranger in paradise, an outsider looking in at the riches of capitalism who was denied them and who therefore turned to eccentric economic reforms and Fascism as ways of subverting the system. This is again absurd. Through Ma Weston, Pound was always in touch with these very important relatives who were in the forefront of the investment system of America, the heart of what makes capitalism tick. Over William Baldwin's table at 452 West Eighth Street in Plainfield or in Charles David's many elegant townhouses in New York Pound was close to the "secret heart" of the country. It was precisely because he knew so much—not so little—that Pound became a critic, not just of American capitalism, but of the majority of economic systems throughout the world, where too few people are properly fed and too much money is controlled by an oligarchy—John Adams' distrusted "few."

William Baldwin Wadsworth married a Canadian girl named Mary M. Tilney, who died rather young in 1908. But before that, she gave him three children who survived: Joseph Tilney (1876–1952), Willard (1881–1959), and Mary (1882–1958). Mary married a gentleman named William Alsop Bours, and they had a son who was named for his father, and who carried on the family line. William, his wife, and children are all buried together in the beautifully maintained Hillside Cemetery of Plainfield, in the shadow of a large granite tombstone that says quite simply: WADSWORTH.

Before leaving them, we should say something about William's wonderfully eccentric son, Willard, who died a bachelor in Florida, where the family tended to winter. He shows that kind of originality that one encounters again and again with Pound's relatives, who were never afraid to express their individuality:

Broker Who Used '41 Car
Left $2.7 Million Estate

ELIZABETH, N.J. Nov. 11 [1963] Willard Wadsworth, a Plainfield stockbroker who drove a 1941 Ford, left an estate of $2,785,494, according to an accounting filed here. . . .

The executors of his estate, the Bankers Trust Company of New York and his nephew, William A. Bours 3d of Wilmington,

Del., filed the accounting at the office of the Union County Surrogate. Among his assets were the Ford, listed at $50, and a seat on the New York Stock Exchange valued at $155,000.

Pound was right when he said that he felt that he could write the whole social history of the United States from his family's annals. Certainly the Wadsworths, better than any of the other perhaps more colorful branches, exhibit the change from a Puritan theocentric commonwealth to a capitalistic democracy; from a rural society based on the farm to a society based first in cities, then in suburbs, and finally, in Charles David's case, in exurban communities that resemble their very beginnings; from people who make their livelihood by working the soil, to those who develop small crafts or trades (scythe-making), to urban vocations such as construction, and finally to the heart of the capitalistic system—stockbroking and banking. Is it any wonder that economics should have fascinated Pound so much, when his father was involved in the physical act of making money and his relatives like the Wadsworths were so important in its distribution? And so, when Homer Pound got the call to return to his work with the Mint, his own close relation to money continued as he moved his little family to Philadelphia.

♦ FOUR
GROWING UP AROUND PHILADELPHIA

Ezra Pound grew up in a wooden, three-storied house at 166 Fernbrook Avenue in Wyncote, a suburb of Philadelphia located ten
miles north of the city on the Reading Railroad. The train station
there is marked Jenkintown, since that community occupies the
eastern side of the Tacony Creek Valley, with Wyncote taking the
west. Fernbrook Avenue is located on a fairly high hill just two
blocks away from the station, so that Homer had no problem in
his commutation to the Mint. He could take one of many com-
muter specials that glide very swiftly into the central terminal on
Chestnut Street. From there, it was an easy walk down Chestnut
to Juniper Street, the site of the old Mint.

At night when Homer came home, Isabel would meet him at
the station according to reports gathered by Carl Gatter, a later
occupant of the house. Since Gatter inherited a place that attracted some attention, he did extensive research on Pound's early
days, and many of the details that follow are taken from that
work. The house itself, thanks to Gatter, was still in fine shape
when Pound visited it in 1958, on his release from St. Elizabeths.
During his incarceration, Pound had written to Gatter often,
asking about details of the place.

The house was entered from a front porch with a door on the
left, opening on a small entrance hall that led on the right to a
front and back parlor and, straight ahead, to the dining room and
kitchen. On entering, one saw the Ben Willard Clock, the case
clock that had once stood in The Wayside Inn. The front parlor on
the right was furnished in the extremely plush, late Victorian
style of the day. A Ming Dynasty vase was quite visible, and there

67

were Chinese calligraphic objects on the parlor table that seem to have had a later bearing on the writing of the famous Seven Lakes Canto (49), as Hugh Kenner has shown in his *Pound Era* (p. 265). These objects had been given to Hiram Parker by a Chinese merchant when Hiram was a seaman before turning to shoemaking. Chinoiserie was very popular in this period among the middle classes, so that when Pound got around to developing his Confucian interests a decade later, he would feel quite comfortable in that milieu:

> The old swimming hole,
> And the boys flopping off the planks,
> Or sitting in the underbrush playing mandolins.
>
> (Canto 13, p. 58)

India prints tended to cover the chairs, and in a corner stood a piano that Isabel was fond of playing, which was recalled vividly later by such visitors as Hilda Doolittle and William Carlos Williams.

In the back parlor or study was a fireplace, with a portrait of Uncle Ezra above it. This room was appropriately filled with books, and it was here that young Ezra (with or without the assistance of his mother) continued the reading initiated by Ma Weston. The walls of this room also contained portraits of Mary Wadsworth Parker (Pound's great-grandmother) and Hannah How Weston (Pound's great-great-grandmother) done by the artist William Page. The adjoining dining room had a large, circular table in the middle.

As a visitor ascended the staircase past a landing with a stained-glass window, he or she found in the front tower a guest room, and beside that another bedroom that was used by Homer and Isabel. Behind these was a side bedroom that was occupied by Susan Angevine Pound at various odd times when she was not living with her daughter, Florence, the music teacher, in North Philadelphia on Estaugh Street. There was another small room and then the maid's quarters in the rear, with a private bath.

The top floor belonged to young Ezra. When he was not sleeping in the tower room, he slept in the other two bedrooms

166 Fernbrook Avenue, with the tower room to the left.

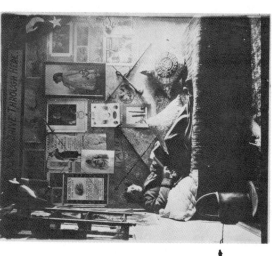

Young Ezra in the tower room, called the "Den" in Homer Pound's Scrapbook in Homer's writing. (Courtesy of the American Literature Collection, the Beinecke Rare Book and Manuscript Library, Yale University)

that occupied this floor. A photograph is included here showing Pound lying bespectacled in his "den," as Homer's handwriting labels it, with the fire bucket from Barre that is mentioned in the *Pisan Cantos.* "Paying guests" were sometimes put here, as well as free ones. Even after Pound departed for Europe, Isabel kept his room looking roughly the way he had left it: with two foils and a fencing mask thrown into a corner and a small 6" by 5" water color done by William Brooke Smith, who will be mentioned shortly, on the wall.

In sum, it was a much-too-large house for a family that never went beyond three, but the extra space came in handy for hosting the many guests that Homer and Isabel acquired during their active church work at the turn of the century. It was a typical upper-middle-class house in a suburb that seemed to be roughly divided into two segments: the moderately well-off, like the Pounds, and the extremely wealthy, like John Wanamaker, who built his palatial "country house" above a nearby private lake. This manor, called Lyndenhurst, was a typical monstrosity of the period, with countless towers and turrets and hidden recesses— like some gigantic cake with cupolas and crenellations. When it burned to the ground in 1907, Homer and Ezra, who was just back from Europe, rushed over to the other hill to try to save some of Wanamaker's "priceless art," which Ezra later pronounced to be largely fake. In the nearby areas were also the wealthy Wideners and the Bergers.

If the Westons in New York lived in the shadow of the wealth of the Jewish Helen Gould, the Pounds lived very close to the Christian nouveaux riches in the Philadelphia suburbs. Even today, although Wyncote has sunk in desirability with the passage of time, a visitor senses in the streets and at the train station that he or she is moving in a privileged world. This sense increases as one speeds into the heart of the city, past the depressingly similar houses on the North Side. Homer was not the least bit blind to this social injustice, as we shall see; and neither, of course, was his son. In many ways, both of them had their hearts back in the metropolis—not out in the country-club green. But here the presence of Isabel Pound surely makes itself felt. Having suffered Hailey, she was tired of roughing it, and wanted the big, suburban house that her long-suffering mother had been denied through the vagaries of Harding Weston.

On arriving in Philadelphia, Homer Pound obviously had two primary objectives in mind: he had to find a decent home for his family, and he had to batten himself down in his job, to provide security for them. Actually, finding a home proved to be the harder of the two tasks. The first place that they took on arriving was a three-storied, brick row house at 208 South 43rd Street, which was still standing a century later. This was on the western edge of the city at that time. It is now in a rather run-down section behind the expanded University of Pennsylvania campus, and is clearly earmarked for renovation. Back in the 1890s, the Pounds could sense already that this was simply not the right neighborhood, and so, like many other white Anglo-Saxon families, they fled to the suburbs.

Their first move north of the city was to a wooden house at 417 Walnut Street in Jenkintown, Wyncote's sister across the railroad tracks. The local *Hatboro Public Spirit* announced on March 22, 1890, that Mr. Pound of Philadelphia had moved into George W. Tomlinson's new house that Friday. The Comley family lived nearby, and in Canto 28 we find the following reference to one of its members:

> Az ole man Comley wd. say: Boys! . . .
> Never cherr terbakker! Hrwwkke tth!
> Never cherr terbakker!,

(p. 136)

For some reason, known perhaps only to the fastidious Isabel, this house was not satisfactory, and so two years later they shifted to another place. The same Hatboro newspaper announced on April 2, 1892, that Mr. Pound had taken Mr. Burrough's house on Hillside Avenue. But once again, this house did not quite fit the bill, and so, at some unannounced point in 1892, the Pounds moved to Fernbrook Avenue. This house would serve as Ezra Pound's legal residence for many years, until he established himself in London. It would be the basic home for Homer and Isabel until 1930, when they decided to extend their long vacation on Homer's retirement to a permanent residence in Rapallo with their son. With the help

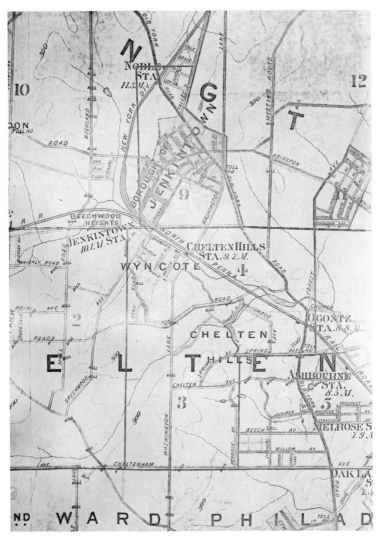

Map of Wyncote showing Fernbrook Avenue. (*Courtesy of Special Collections, the Van Pelt Library, the University of Pennsylvania*)

Portrait of Isabel Pound, whom Ezra called "Hermione" in his masked autobiography, *Indiscretions*. (*Courtesy of New Directions, Inc.*)

of friends, the house was then put up for sale, and most of the furnishings were auctioned off—except for the silverware and the paintings, which were shipped off to Italy. These finally resided with Mary de Rachewiltz in the castle at Brunnenburg, except for the portrait of Uncle Ezra, which was sold in the 1950s to Henry Ford, who was trying to fix up his Wayside Inn in an authentic fashion, and which is believed to have disappeared in a fire that ravaged the inn in the 1950s.

The cost of the house on Fernbrook Avenue was $6,000, and since Homer began his job at the Mint making only $5 per day, being promoted to the position of Assistant Assayer in 1891, when he made $2,000 a year, the price was rather steep. After all, they had a maid, and Ezra would have to be educated for a time in private schools because of the paucity of public-school education in the suburbs, and the Pounds were accustomed to a highly civilized life style. This is where Grandmother Weston stepped in. Pound told Dr. Kavka, the psychiatrist at St. Elizabeths Hospital, that Mary Weston supplied the money for the purchase, and that would explain why, on land maps, the property is listed as belonging to Mrs. Homer L. Pound—a very anomalous occurrence for the time. The psychiatrists, of course, saw all this as still another example of the strong matriarchal control of the family exerted by Mary and Isabel. It is true that Pound himself lamented the domineering behavior of Isabel. She tried to control what he wore, which tended toward the dandified, and she interfered constantly in his daily routines. On the night of June 27, 1958, Pound, free of the madhouse, lay on the sofa in the front parlor of the house that he had grown up in, conversing idly but passionately with the man who now owned it. He spoke openly about his adoration of his father (a love that is not openly expressed in his writings), but he said about his mother: "I never appreciated her until she was dead." He also told Dr. Kavka: "I was my father's son in opposition to my mother . . . far removed from the Oedipus complex."

Sometimes, to help make ends meet, the Pounds took in paying guests. Usually they were religious people, such as their local preacher, William Barnes Lower, who stayed with them from 1900 until his marriage in 1902. He was a poetaster, who published his poor offerings widely in the local newspapers and church organs, and it is extremely doubtful that Pound liked him as much as his predecessor, Reverend Carlos Tracy Chester. Then, while Ezra was away at Hamilton, the Pounds took in Mrs. Mary Lovell and Miss Margaret Whitechurch, who were both ardent temperance speakers.

The Pounds soon settled into the middle-class life in Wyncote, becoming friends with many of the neighbors. Homer is mentioned in the local papers for being active in dramatic groups, and the couple hosted musical events and lectures in their commodious house. There were other people living in the community who were intimately concerned with publishing, as Pound would be. One was the famous Cyrus Curtis, whose Curtis Publishing Company put out the world-renowned *Saturday Evening Post*. Mr. Curtis was an occasional dinner guest at the Pound home. Then there was his friend and assistant in publishing, George Horace Lorimer, who sometimes took shortcuts through the Pounds' back lawn in order to get to his own house. In the camp at Pisa, Pound remembered a scene when his father was working in the backyard of the house and stopped to chat with Lorimer about an interview that he was trying to get with Senator Albert J. Beveridge of Ohio (later a strong opponent of the Nelson Aldrich Plan that created the Federal Reserve System):

> and George Horace said he wd/ "get Beveridge" (Senator)
> Beveridge wouldn't talk and he wouldn't write for the papers
> but George got him by campin' in his hotel
> and assailin' him at lunch breakfast an' dinner
> three articles
> and my ole man went on hoein' corn
> while George was a-tellin' him,
> come across a vacant lot
> where you'd occasionally see a wild rabbit
> or mebbe only a loose one
> AOI!
> a leaf in the current
>
> (Canot 81, p. 519)

Although Pound is praising Lorimer here, in other places—such as in *Guide to Kulchur*, written in the thirties—Pound associated his old neighbor with the worst aspects of American popular publication: "Lorimer honestly didn't know that there ever had been a civilization" (p. 89).

It is now time to confront the suggestion made by Pound in an interview with Allen Ginsberg (written by Michael Reck) that his anti-Semitism was something he acquired in the suburbs. Obviously it is difficult to pin down the starting point of anyone's feelings, and it is rather foolish for a biographer to challenge his subject when the subject speaks with conviction and authority. It is very clear that Wyncote, from the hermetic nature of its composition, was a perfect breeding ground for xenophobia of all types. The local newspapers, for example, rather boldly printed the following notices:

> *April 18, 1891:* "The new proprietors of Beechwood announce that hereafter no Jews will be taken to board there. In previous years the Hebrews have been plentiful."
>
> *May 30, 1896:* "Just no more Italians in Wyncote. Is our budding hope that this place will be entirely aristocratic squelched?"
>
> *June 5, 1897:* "All Italians but two families have moved away."
>
> *October 9, 1897:* "The Italians have moved back into their old quarters in Frank Mayo's buildings"

One early Wyncote resident (the population was only 1,608 in 1890) said that anti-Semitism there was like the dust—nowhere visible on the surface until there was a slight rustle or disturbance, and then it was swirling all around. Given this background, it is hard to understand how anyone could have escaped without some of the same feelings.

And yet we have to consider the opposite behavior of Homer Loomis Pound, who underwent a deep religious conversion after buying his house in the Philadelphia suburbs. In opposition to the general will of the community, Homer, who had converted to Presbyterianism while living in Jenkintown, freely invited many Italians and Jews and other "foreigners" from Philadelphia to his home in Wyncote. Later, Homer confessed that he had been reared in an almost irreligious way by his father, a backsliding Quaker who was so immersed in politics that he had not paid due respect to his soul.

Once they settled in Wyncote, the Pounds became a bastion of the Calvary Presbyterian Church, which they helped to found, and which was eventually located only a block from their house. Homer rose quickly to become the President of The Young People's Society of Christian Endeavor, a nationwide group that was zealously promoting a socially enlightened form of Christian action. Isabel became the Vice-President of the Women's Union of the church in 1892. A notice that appeared in the *Jenkintown Times-Chronicle* on May 8, 1897, said: "H.L. Pound, secretary and treasurer of the Children's Institute, last Wednesday evening, during the prayer meeting in the Presbyterian church at Ambler, spoke on the work among the children in the Italian settlement in Philadelphia." Despite her Brahmin roots, Isabel journeyed with her husband into the slums of South Philadelphia to plunk away on a piano as Homer tried to persuade the Italian immigrants to surrender their Catholic creed for Presbyterianism. In fact, he helped to found the First Italian Presbyterian Church in the city, as well as the College Settlement House for the poor.

Homer took this work so seriously that, after he returned from a trip abroad with his family in 1902, which included Italy, he resided for a period in the city, and it was only in 1903 that he finally decided to return to the suburbs. During a similar stretch from 1910 to 1911, when Pound returned to the States from London, his parents were living in town to be closer to their Christian Endeavor work and the job at the Mint. In many ways, clearly, Wyncote was more of a hindrance than a help. In any case, we can see two important things here: one, Pound did not learn anti-Semitism or any other form of xenophobia from his parents; two, his parents took upon themselves the Herculean task of trying to convert the Italians to their faith, while—more than ironically—their son would veer in the opposite direction, and they would freely elect to live out their days in the land of the unconverted.

Actually, Pound never really blamed Wyncote for anything. He simply called anti-Semitism a stupid, suburban prejudice, and although there was obviously a great deal of this among his neighbors, there is no trace of it in Pound's letters at this time.

Homer in his retirement in 1933 on a balcony in Rapallo, Italy.
(*Courtesy of the Free Library of Philadelphia*)

The old Philadelphia Mint at the corner of Juniper and Chestnut Streets, where Homer Pound worked as an assayer. (*Courtesy of Special Collections, the Van Pelt Library, the University of Pennsylvania*)

Only in the teens, after his acquaintance with economists like Major C. H. Douglas and Alfred Orage do anti-Semitic comments appear. What becomes apparent is that anti-Semitism, like Pound's many other passions, was an intellectually generated phenomenon. Pound did not hate the Jews *per se* and said so often, proving it early by his friendship with the pianist Katherine Ruth Heyman and later with Louis Zukofsky and others. It was in London, when Pound was studying international banking and its pernicious effect upon social harmony, that the poet concentrated upon the influence of the Rothschilds on world finance, directed to a large part by Orage and Douglas. The notion that he might have acquired this prejudice against Wall Street bankers and Jewish financiers from populist sources has to be viewed with doubt, since there is little indication that either Homer or Ezra Pound was favorable in the 1890s toward populism—a political philosophy that was far from anything advocated by Uncle Ezra Weston or Thaddeus Coleman Pound.

In short, we might blame Wyncote for any number of things, but Pound's later anti-Semitism does not seem to be one of them. Still, we are all subject to influences in our childhood from forces that we can barely understand, which often show themselves later in our development. I would suggest that what Pound acquired in Wyncote was more a dislike of the Establishment, the rule of the privileged rich (like Wanamaker and Curtis), than a dislike for any ethnic group. Then and later he adored Italy and the Italians, even though, as we have seen, the rest of his neighbors considered them pariahs. Here again, the Western liberality of the father has to come into play, exerting itself over the stern and rigid class distinctions of the mother. Despite the psychiatric opinions of St. Elizabeths, Homer Pound made his presence felt. If Isabel spoke in a "high-society voice" (as certain neighbors complained), Homer drawled on with his "dangeds" and "darns," and the two seem to have balanced each other out. Homer twice sublet his home to W. B. Hackenburg, the President of the Jewish Hospital Association, in a move that probably made several of his neighbors either furious or uneasy, but there was a pioneering courage to this toiler in the Mint. He gave his son a warm, open home and—against the cowardly behavior of his neighbors and friends—acted with true Christian love toward the world. What more could one have asked for?

As for Ezra's own religiosity, he formally professed his faith in Christianity on March 24, 1897, at the Calvary Presbyterian Church, and he officially clung to it until his death in Venice in 1972, being buried with Protestant rites on the island of San Michele, in a place reserved for non-Catholics. Of course, unofficially, Ezra Pound was anything but a standard Christian—especially a Presbyterian. He admired Confucianism for its ethics, Neoplatonism for its cosmogony, and Italian Catholicism for its way of coping with the everyday affairs of life. In St. Elizabeths, he told Dr. Kavka that he was an "earnest Christian" until he was sixteen, and from sixteen to twenty-four, he came under the influence of mysticism: he described himself as being, thereafter, "an aesthetic pagan."

The pastor of the Calvary Church during the middle nineties was Reverend Carlos Tracy Chester, who was a close friend of Ezra's during his childhood—so close that Pound dedicated *Exultations* to the man from London in 1909: *"longaevitate amicitiae"* (in long-lasting friendship), and the poet was visited by the Reverend's son Hawley in Paris during the twenties. Pound admired the pastor for his literacy, since Chester wrote many stories and articles for local newspapers and served as an editor for at least three publications. Clearly Chester encouraged the young man in his literary pursuits. He was also the person who suggested to the Pounds that their son should transfer to his own alma mater, Hamilton, when things were not going well at the University of Pennsylvania.

As for Pound's "aesthetic paganism," this developed through his intensive study of the Latin poet Ovid and through his long friendship with Hilda Doolittle, whose passion for classical lore is well known. Pound soon believed that the only way to escape from the stifling morality of the Victorian period lay in the creation of a new pagan renaissance. He embarked on his Latin readings in his early schooling, at the very same time that he was imbued with Christianity at the church down the street and over Homer Pound's dinner table.

Pound's early schooling was conducted in the almost informal, casual manner of the day in a series of small private schools that were present everywhere. Public schools at this time were quite limited, and it was Homer Pound, in fact, who was helping to establish them. Pound's first formal place of education was a little school in Jenkintown that was administered by one Miss Elliott. When his family moved to Wyncote, he entered the Chelten Hills School, which was run by the influential Heacock family out of a nearby house. Then in 1894, at the age of nine, he transferred to Miss Florence Ridpath's school, which was only a block from his home, in anticipation of the building of a public school for the community. He remembered Miss Ridpath later with love and affection, comparing her well with his favorite teachers in college. Then when the Wyncote Public School finally opened in 1895, he transferred there. The records for all of these schools are lost, and one suspects that if they did exist, they would simply show an intelligent, but not brilliant, student.

Since there was no public high school at this time in Wyncote (although Homer was working on establishing one), Pound was forced to continue his high-school training elsewhere. The *Jenkintown Times-Chronicle* said on September 11, 1897: "Thomas Cochran, Bert Stinson, Ray Pound and Fletcher Hunter will attend the Cheltenham Military Academy this year. The academy opens on the 22nd" As we can see by the notice, Ezra had become Ray (sometimes spelled Ra), simply by detaching the last syllable of his first name. He told Carl Gatter that this name was thrust upon him by others, since Ezra sounded too biblical. Later, of course, he would adopt a variety of pseudonyms, just as he was constantly changing his middle name or names. He liked to shift his name in the same way that he liked to change the voice or persona through which he spoke in his poems. And he was fond of made-up names for others, especially his beloveds, as we shall see.

From the age of twelve to sixteen, since he had proceeded through his early education swiftly, Pound decided to finish his classes at the Cheltenham Military Academy in nearby Ogontz. The academy was set on imposing grounds, and had a variety of large houses to serve as dormitories, but Ezra walked there daily. The students had to wear uniforms, and drill was compulsory.

The academy has long since closed its doors—put out of business by the public high schools around it—and therefore, once again, no record exists for Pound's work. However, a bulletin issued by the school indicates that the boys were given a solid grounding in Latin, history, and mathematics. A letter written from the school on June 10, 1898, tells his parents that he was beaten in the high jump by Skinny Dayton, and how difficult it was to keep up with the assignments in history, spelling, English, arithmetic, and Latin, as well as declamation. There is no mention of Greek, which was a part of the Classical Curriculum, and even though Pound's Greek was always a sometime thing, as he himself confessed in letters to Anne Lebeck and others, he nevertheless picked up a smattering at some point. Pound refers to a shadowy character in Canto 80, p. 512:

> and it was old Spencer (,H.) who first declaimed me the Odyssey
> with a head built like Bill Shepard's
> on the quais of what Siracusa?
>   or what tennis court
> near what pine trees?

It has been assumed that this man, whose name is spelled Spenser on page 145 of *Guide to Kulchur*, was a teacher at the Academy, but the existing bulletin mentions no such person attached to the school, and no digging around in the census rolls of Wyncote and vicinity has unearthed anyone with this name. However, since *The Cantos* begin with an English translation of a Latin translation of Homer's Greek, we see the importance of the event described—especially since Pound emphasizes the spoken value of poetry, not the written artifact; but the fact that Pound translates from a Latin version is meaningful too, not only for what it says about his own educational weakness, but about a great weakness for the whole of Europe over the centuries, where people tended to get their Greek classics by way of the Romans.

The teacher who made the greatest impact on Pound at this point was one Frederick James Doolittle (no relative to Hilda), who taught the young man Latin. The boys called Mr. Doolittle by the Shakespearian name of "Cassius," because he had a lean and hungry look, but he was solid—"a fine bit of old oak," as most

An early class photograph showing Ezra Pound to the left of his mischievous friend Tommy Cochran. (*Courtesy of Special Collections, the Van Pelt Library, the University of Pennsylvania*)

Bespectacled young Pound (center) in the military dress of the
old Cheltenham Academy, where he prepared for college.
(*Courtesy of Special Collections, the Van Pelt Library,
the University of Pennsylvania*)

people said. Pound praises Doolittle in a letter written on January 18, 1898, to his parents, and he confided to Donald Hall in his *Paris Review* interview: "I got into college on my Latin; it was the only reason they *did* take me in" (p. 32). It was also Latin that helped him get into Hamilton, despite an otherwise mediocre record. Yet even given his long-standing interest in the Greco-Roman classics, he would write home in June of 1898, like any other twelve-year-old:

> no more Latin, no more Greek
> no more smoking on the sneak

Two pictures of him in military garb survive from the Cheltenham days. One shows a bewildered-looking, bespectacled boy peering out of a group of mesomorphic military types. Pound constantly wore glasses in childhood, suffering from acute astigmatism, although he finally cured this ailment through a Dr. George Gould of Philadelphia to whom he later referred James Joyce. But Joyce's condition was too far advanced at that time for the doctor to be able to help. All in all, Pound was not the neurasthenic type of sensitive adolescent described by Joyce in his *Portrait of the Artist as a Young Man*, although he would gradually appear to be that as he progressed. At Cheltenham, he seemed to be "one of the boys." He competed in fencing and tennis, at which he was quite good, and he would continue these sports at Penn, where he also ushered, for pleasure and profit, at the football games of the Pennsylvania Quakers, who were then one of the terrors of the East. Although there were already rumors (collected years later by Gatter) about Pound's dressing in a dandified manner with a cape and a cane, these were muted. Several fathers of pretty girls seem to have distrusted Pound greatly, as Hilda Doolittle's father would do, but that also is to be expected. The major thing that Pound resented in these days was the military tenor of the life that he had to lead—especially the drill—and he was very eager to graduate, which he did at the premature age of fifteen in 1901.

After establishing a home for his family, Homer Pound then proceeded to accomplish the second phase of his mission: to acquire what amounts to tenure in his job as Assistant Assayer at the Mint, which was then housed in a Greco-Roman temple of a building just a stone's throw away from the highly ornate City Hall with its Victorian gingerbread. In *Indiscretions,* Pound says, "I remember the Greek 'temple' façade, if not 'in,' at any rate indebted to the taste that built Monticello" (p. 46). He goes on then to say that if

> the old Mint didn't exactly show the results of Jefferson's inquiries for the exact proportions of La Maison Carrée of Nîmes, it at any rate had a moderate number of sensible columns, and a reposeful chunky appearance, befitting the deity of coinage rather than the harpies of fluctuation. In the rotunda one found various derelicts of the G. A. R., sitting in wooden arm-chairs, with some obsolete weapons in the vicinity. These poor old bulwarks of the Union were, I believe, generally shaken up when the 'Demys' came into office. At other times they must have run through considerable small talk and consumed a fair deal of chewing tobacco (as, say, from the years 1865–95).   (p. 47)

Young Pound was a constant visitor in the Temple of Money. Even at that tender age, the whole mystique of money—its making and distribution—seemed to work a hypnotic spell over him. He describes how his father "would be standing by a highish shelf-table before a window, and part of the window obscured by a black-board divided into small squares. He would squint through the remaining cylindrical bottles seriatim, and write the due proportion of thousandths in the square assigned to the bottle" (p. 47). Homer was the Master Alchemist, with his myriads of gold strips, filaments, coin discs, and other magic appurtenances. Out of his temple came money, the life-blood of the society around them.

In his interview with Donald Hall, the aged Pound reminisced about the way that men once heaved silver coins with huge shovels into machines where they would be melted and recast: "This spectacle of coin being shovelled around like it was litter—these fellows naked to the waist shovelling it around in the gas flares—things like that strike your imagination" (p. 40). Indeed, it struck the young man's imagination so vividly that in Canto 97, in a passage based on the scholar of money Alexander del Mar (one of Pound's favorite minds, whom he discovered in his St. Elizabeths years), he would say:

> 371¼ grains silver in Del's time
> as I have seen them by shovels full
> > lit by gas flares.

(p. 673)

In many ways, the making of money seemed to be a metaphor for the making of literature. Both processes required skill, training, precision, and care. He said to Hall:

> Then there's the whole technique of making metallic money. First, the testing of the silver is much more tricky than testing gold. Gold is simple. It is weighed, then refined and weighed again. You can tell the grade of the ore by the relative weights. But the test for silver is a cloudy solution; the accuracy of the eye in measuring the thickness of the cloud is an aesthetic perception, like the critical sense. I like the idea of the *fineness* of the metal, and it moves by analogy to the habit of testing verbal manifestations.

(p. 40)

These words clearly show how economics and literature merged in Pound's mind, both late and early. Thoroughly opposed to the romantic notion of composition that was dominant in the nineteenth century, Pound insisted that every word had to be weighed and examined with great care in the process of creation, precisely the way his father assayed the metals. A brilliant maker or distributor of coins was a kinsman to a brilliant artist. Both were concerned with keeping society alive—the minter with his coins, the artist with his words. To be sloppy in either case was inexcusable. There is no doubt that Pound saw the false manipulators of money as the true traitors to any society, along with the polluters of language. Unlike the other seven who were indicted with him in 1943, Pound never argued that he had spoken out in criticism of the United States; he merely insisted that it was his duty to do this, in defense of what he considered the economic and political muddleheadedness of the American government of that time. A deeper treason would have lain in silence.

81

The youthful trips were taken to the Mint in an atmosphere of fun, even though the highly serious Isabel was often along to make sure that her son thanked anyone who gave him an odd nickel. Homer's fellow workers were fond of teasing visitors by telling them that they could claim any sack of money that they could carry. Of course the sacks were all unliftable. Homer also liked to indulge in a game called "weighing your name." He would ask a visitor to write his or her name on an envelope that had already been weighed, and when this was done, he would place the envelope on a finely tempered scale that would quite literally weigh the letters of the name. When Ezra and his father visited the British Mint on their European tour of 1902, they found none of this levity. The Philadelphia Mint was a pleasant place to work in, even though the eye of the director Abe Bickersteth was constantly upon his charges.

And so life drifted along during the childhood of Ezra Pound. There were all of the usual activities: sledding on the Wanamaker hill or skating on their pond; riding in a buggy belonging to Levi Bean; swimming in the Tacony Creek or hiding in the caves along its banks; playing tennis on the innumerable courts that dotted the suburban green. During his confinement in Washington, Pound thought often of those happy days of his youth, and asked Gatter for any information he could come up with about the youngsters whom he had grown up with there: a pretty girl named Adele Polk whom he had once dated; he wondered why she had never gotten married . . . and Ned Heacock, who went on to the University of Pennsylvania with Pound and was a good friend, but then died suddenly, tragically in a canoeing accident on a river in British Columbia in 1907 . . . and the unforgettable Tommy Cochran, whose dark, brooding eyes peer out of a photograph of classmates at Miss Ridpath's school, standing next to Pound. In his letters to Ingrid Davies, Pound frequently mentions what a delightfully mischievous boy Tommy was, and how he paid for his mischief by having to attend about five schools. Pound, on the other hand, attended only three before college. To the Pound of Pisa, Tommy's face came back to haunt him in those dark days of despair, but he thought not of the glowering eyes that Tommy had in moments of pensiveness, but the way that his whole face lighted up when he was happy; this reminded Pound of a sculpture he had seen of Can Grande, the great patron of Dante: "Can Grande's grin like Tommy Cochran's pleno d'alegreça" (Canto 91, p. 615).

In short, Wyncote was a typical American suburb that afforded Ezra Pound a very typical childhood. There is no sign during these youthful days of the brilliant personality who would set the literary world of London aflame, who would change the course of twentieth-century literature in freeing it from many of the strictures of its nineteenth-century past. Pound told Carl Gatter that the first poem he ever published appeared in one of the local papers. The prime nomination for this honor was a piece of doggerel titled "Ezra on the Strike," in which some provincial persona named Ezra is commenting on a coal strike in 1902. I shall quote only the first few lines:

Wal, Thanksgivin' do be comin' round,
With the price of turkeys on the bound,
And coal, by gum! thet were just found,
        Is surely gettin' cheaper.
The winds will soon begin to howl,
And winter, in its yearly growl,
Across the medders begin to prowl,
        And Jack Frost gettin' deeper.

The suggestion that this abomination was written by William Barnes Lower, who was living with the Pounds in 1902, is far preferable—especially since Pound told Dr. Kavka that his first opus was "On the Defeat of William Jennings Bryan" in 1896 and—"For God's sake, don't look it up!"

When Pound's wearisome stay at St. Elizabeths ended in 1958, one of the first places that he headed for was Wyncote. It was as if the Philadelphia countryside offered a sheltering shade from the naked light of publicity. Besides, his long and friendly correspondence with Carl Gatter made him want to meet this man who had come into possession of his house and who knew its every corner now better than he did. Pound arrived on a hot June night from Richmond in a car driven by one of his most faithful disciples, David Horton. Imbued with Pound's own notions that the American government had fallen into the hands of people who were selling it down the drain, Horton had issued Pound's hand-picked classics in his Square Dollar Series. He was accompanied by Mrs. Horton, the tired and aged-looking Dorothy Pound, and a lovely young girl from Texas named Marcella Spann (later Booth), who had appeared at the "Ezuversity" at St. Elizabeths and would accompany the poet and his wife to Italy. Marcella helped Pound edit the anthology *Confucius to Cummings*, and is mentioned in a beautiful sequence in Canto 113:

> Yet to walk with Mozart, Agassiz and Linnaeus
> 'neath overhanging air under sun-beat
> Here take thy mind's space
> And to this garden, Marcella, ever seeking by petal, by
> leaf-vein
> out of dark, and toward half-light
>
> (p. 786)

Everyone was extremely tired, since Horton, not knowing the intricacies of the suburban turnpikes, had gotten hopelessly lost.

Immediately on entering, Ezra noted that the place seemed "dolled up" a bit, but he acted as if he had just come back for a weekend from Hamilton, and made himself at home. After examining the lower floor, he ascended the stairs, pointing out an oak finial on the railing that was still detachable fifty years later, as well as a crack in the stained-glass window on the landing that he had made years before with an errant tennis swing. On the second floor he inspected the bedroom occupied by his parents, and on the third the tower room, the place where he had read so many classics and studied so many languages. Outside, he wanted to see the fruit trees planted by his father.

As the group ate the somewhat overcooked roast, Pound noted that it had been an even fifty years since he had visited the house, because on his return in 1910 his family was living in Philadelphia, deeply engrossed in their missionary work. At last the tired guests climbed the stairs to bed, and Pound, who chose to sleep downstairs, and his host were left alone. Over the surrounding chorus of crickets, the old poet talked on and on about his youth: about the Sheip boy next door who was constantly bragging that his father manufactured cigar boxes; he walked away with all the academic laurels at the Academy . . . about the kindly Miss Ridpath and her brood of scholars . . . about the elflike Tommy Cochran—what had ever happened to him? (Gone to the Navy) . . . and Adele Polk (he would talk to her over the phone the next morning) . . . and Ned Heacock, who had died in that freakish accident. With the exception of Adele, they were all gone.

Finally Pound said that he wanted to sleep. Gatter went upstairs, leaving Pound to himself. But as soon as Gatter had disappeared, there was a click at the door, and Pound was passing outward into the now cool summer night, into the heavy chorus of crickets.

From his upstairs vantage point, Gatter watched the old man make his way south on Fernbrook, examining all of the houses, as if he expected the doors to open and the Sheip boy to come running out.

Pound walked slowly, meditatively down toward Bent Road, where the Calvary Presbyterian Church, founded by his father and mother, sits on the corner. He stood staring at it for a long time.

Then he suddenly remembered something. He and a buddy in his youth had planted a tree once behind the church, and the planting of a tree is to Pound a sacred act:

Said Baccin: "That tree, and that tree,
"Yes, I planted that tree . . ."
                    Under the olives
Some saecular, some half-saecular
            trees, conduits

(Canto 88, p. 581)

He decided to trespass upon the church grounds and find that act of creation from his youth. It seemed somehow important.

Yet, as he stepped on the lawn, something pulled him back.

It was as if he suddenly realized that this tree was no more regraspable than were the phantoms of his childhood or the town of Hailey or the laughter of Ezra Brown Weston. They had once been alive. Now they were gone.

85

He walked slowly, quietly, back to the old homestead and went to bed.

The next morning Pound was up and ready to depart—for New Jersey, New York, and ultimately Italy, the country that Pound had adopted over the years as his second home. As the car pulled away from Fernbrook Avenue, the pain of the last decade was still too great for him to welcome back the world of his Wyncote past. Eventually, of course, he would do that. But now he needed that country that he had discovered back in 1898 under the tutelage of his beloved aunt from New York. We turn now to the vivacious Mrs. Weston, who first showed Ray Pound the world.

♦ FIVE

AUNT FRANK AND THE WORLD AT LARGE

The first half of the Gay Nineties was not a particularly happy period in the otherwise happy life of Frances Amelia Weston. During the first few years, her husband Ezra was extremely sick from his heart ailment and required constant tending. Given his debilitated condition, Aunt Frank had to keep the boardinghouse going—and this she did with great expertise. Finally, however, on December 9 of 1894, Uncle Ezra succumbed, and after a funeral attended by young Ezra and his family, Aunt Frank entered a period of mourning.

For the next few years, she was joined in the boardinghouse by Ma Weston, who gave up her place on Lexington Avenue. The first surviving letter of Ezra Pound in the carbons prepared by D.D. Paige for his *Selected Letters* is dated on April 28, 1896, and is written to "Pa" from his son visiting at 47th Street. Young Ezra mentions that his mother went to some sort of meeting (presumably a church meeting) with Miss Dow, an occupant of the establishment, and that Ma Weston did not want to come back with them to Philadelphia. Other letters show other visits on frequent occasions.

When the young man was in New York, Aunt Frank took him everywhere with her. Being childless herself, she constantly favored either him or her niece from the Wessells, Sarah (Sadie), or her nephew Frank. On Sundays Ezra and Frances would go either to St. Bartholomew's Church at 44th and Madison or, more commonly, down to the Madison Square Presbyterian Church of Dr. Parkhurst, which Pound referred to as a "Palladian gem" in

Patria Mia (p. 17). Both Ezra and Frances were always extremely moved by the famous preacher's rhetoric.

Charles Henry Parkhurst was born in Framingham, Massachusetts, on April 17, 1842, and he studied at Amherst before assuming his duties as pastor of the church in 1880. When he died, the *New York Times* of Sept. 9, 1933, called him a "militant New York crusader of the Nineties" and the moral leader of a generation of men. He had died the day before in a freakish accident at Ventnor outside of Atlantic City by falling off his front-porch roof while sleepwalking—despite the presence of a posted guard.

Parkhurst became famous in New York because he stood up fearlessly against the vices of Tammany Hall, the Democratic machine that was running the city. In this sense he shared the views completely of Ezra Brown Weston and his wife. One of his books, *Our Fight With Tammany* (1895), makes his position very clear. In February of 1892, without anticipating any trouble, Parkhurst delivered a passionate but controlled sermon in which he condemned the city's administration for being a "damnable pack of administrative bloodhounds, polluted harpies, and a lying, perjured, rum-soaked, and libidinous lot"—a rhetoric that sounds strangely familiar to any reader of Pound's more acid prose or Canto 14.

This sermon got picked up by the newspapers, since Parkhurst's church was a center for intellectuals. When Tammany Hall heard about it, the graft-ridden politicians were frightened and furious. They made an extremely bold move by having Parkhurst hauled into court on the charge of libel. When the Reverend could not back up his assertions with facts, he was told to either produce evidence for his charges or to withdraw them. Parkhurst was not about to withdraw anything. Now fighting mad, he used his parishioners and himself as private detectives and began to organize a massive investigation of police corruption. Going down into the Bowery and the Tenderloin District, Parkhurst gathered evidence firsthand by interviews with all sorts of people. He then took his findings back to the court, demanding that a formal investigation be launched by the city. The city was forced to comply, and so there were trials and convictions of policemen and

Chas. H. Parkhurst.

The famous New York eccentric George Francis Train, talking to his beloved children and birds on his favorite park bench in Madison Square, across from Dr. Parkhurst's church.

politicians alike. As a result, William L. Strong was elected as a reform candidate for mayor and Theodore Roosevelt with his "big stick" was brought in to direct the city's police force. This was the start of Teddy Roosevelt's successful political life.

Aside from being a hyperactive idealist, Parkhurst was also a scholar—and this side appealed to the studious Pound. Parkhurst knew Sanskrit so well that he wrote a treatise called "Forms of the Latin Verb Illustrated by the Sanskrit." A gifted orator, he coined the expression "Hell with the lid off" to describe New York politicians, and it became a part of the English language. He also had a good sense of humor. When the vengeful police closed down a brothel and sent the girls out into the streets in a driving snowstorm, they told them to go to Dr. Parkhurst's residence at 133 East 35th Street in Murray Hill, since he was the man who was responsible for their expulsion. The prostitutes milled around in the street outside the Reverend's house, screeching insults, until the Doctor and his kindly wife went out and invited them in for tea and cookies. Once the women were inside, Parkhurst and his wife explained that they were not the enemy, and they sent the women back to assail the pimps and the police with fresh vigor. In addition, Parkhurst was always opposed to any form of Prohibition, and this anti-puritanical philosophy was an attitude that the later Pound could admire. Canto 2, which celebrates the triumph of the wine god Bacchus over his enemies, shows a similar feeling.

Another vigorous idealistic type who was very evident around New York in the Gay Nineties was George Francis Train, who was referred to in a passage cited earlier from Canto 74. Pound always remembered Train sitting on a chair out on the pavement, although he was just as commonly sitting in the later days of his life on a park bench in Madison Square, where he would converse only with children and birds. After the fashion of St. Francis of Assisi, he was known as "The Sage of Madison Square."

Born in Boston in 1829, Train lost most of his family to cholera in New Orleans while still a child. He had to go to work for a relative in Boston, where he then founded Train & Co., which sent first-class clipper-ships to California during the Gold

Rush of '49. This made him rich, and he compounded his wealth by financing the building of the Union Pacific Railroad from 1862 to 1869. Always fiercely individualistic, Train ran as an independent candidate for President in 1872, losing to Grant, at whose inauguration ball Aunt Frank danced.

Like Parkhurst, Train was a brilliant and fiery orator who would assail any institution that he thought was evil. In 1872 he was arrested on Wall Street for attacking the American government in a speech that the famous blue-nosed attorney Anthony Comstock found offensive. But Train was undeterred. He traveled several times around the world—once in eighty days, thereby supplying much of the fact for Jules Verne's fiction; and in 1870 in Marseille, he delivered rousing speeches on the downfall of Napoleon III, thereby endearing himself to the French Communists, who proclaimed him a member of their "Red Republic." Out of his many travels he wrote *An American Merchant in Europe, Asia, and Australia* (1857) and *The Downfall of England* (1862), a title that doubtlessly lingered in Pound's mind, even though Pound declared in *Indiscretions* that he was not quite sure what Train stood for in the way of principles.

Before dying at the age of seventy-four in 1904, Train was a fixture either in Madison Square or down in Greenwich Village, where he sometimes sat outside his final residence, The Mills Hotel for single men, where he died a pauper. Train began his last autobiography, *My Life in Many States and Foreign Lands* (1902), by saying, "I have been silent for thirty years." It is true that during those last years he seldom tried to communicate with anyone except his beloved children and animals. His long act of noncommunication may have suggested to Pound a way of reacting to an unresponsive or hostile world, since Pound himself became silent during his later days. Train ended his work with words that also sound as if they could have issued from the poet: "I was born into a slow world, and I wished to oil the wheels and gears, so that the machine would spin faster, and withal, to better purposes" (p. 339).

It is true that Parkhurst seemed to have diminished in value in Pound's mind with the passing of years. In the poem "L'Homme

Moyen Sensuel," written in 1917 and published in *Personae*, Pound describes the Reverend in this following satiric couplet:

> These, and yet God, and Dr. Parkhurst's god, the N.Y. *Journal*
> (Which pays him more per week than The Supernal).
>
> (p. 238)

Still, there is no doubt that the visual impressions of the two men and the rough energy that they represented stuck in the poet's mind. Often in the Later Cantos there are laments to the effect that strong, vigorous men of action are no longer around. Parkhurst would take on City Hall and Train would attack the Washington Establishment. Where, Pound would ask in the 1950s, had such men gone? They were, indeed, part of the great American tradition of spokesmen for the people, taking risks to speak out against the corrupt politicians and bankers. They were definitely *not* part of a world

> where the dead walked
> and the living were made of cardboard.
>
> (115, p. 794)

Finally by 1898, after four long years of widowhood and seeing her sister-in-law Mary Weston safely laid to rest back in her native Hopkinton, Aunt Frank decided that a change of atmosphere might be in order. Always a great traveler, she booked passage for a three-month stay in Europe, and she invited Ezra Pound, going on thirteen, and his mother to accompany her at her expense. Although Isabel went along, she is seldom mentioned as a participant on this momentous voyage. Pound would always remember it as his own voyage into the world with his beloved aunt.

The actual details of the trip became clouded over the years, as the sights seen on this tour merged with the sights seen on others. When Pound was writing *Indiscretions* from Venice in 1920, he described his first journey in this way:

> Let it therefore stand written that I first saw the Queen of
> the Adriatic under the protection of that portentous person, my
> great aunt-in-law, in the thirteenth year of my age; and that my

European inceptions had begun a few weeks earlier with the well-donkey at Carisbrooke Castle, and very large strawberries served with "Devonshire cream" at Cowes, and that the chances are I had "seen" Paris, Genoa, Rome, Naples, Florence, and probably the leaning towers of Bologna (these last from the train) in the interval. Or it is possible that I had not "seen" Paris, but Brussels, Cologne, Mainz, Nuremberg. The exact order of these impressions, seeing that I was to revisit half of them four years later, is now somewhat difficult to recall; and I do not know whether I have been twice, or been only once in Pisa.

(p. 5)

He was, as he knew, a very lucky boy, for not many young men were given an opportunity like this.

As Ezra and Isabel prepared to depart, Homer moved over to the nearby suburb of Meadowbrook for the summer. Mother and son took the train to New York, where they prepared themselves for the steamship by helping Aunt Frank pack her voluminous bags: "a vast collection of valises, suit-cases, hold-alls, handboxes, and heterogenous parcels . . . I know that for three months' travel there were ninety-seven little tissue-paper parcels of green tea prepared in advance and distributed throughout her multifarious luggage—ever since the painful occasion when they had all been found together on the top of *one* suit-case, to the amazement of a *douane* official" (p. 9). Aunt Frank believed in traveling prepared. She took along her own properly packaged tea so that the locals, with their various addictions to beer and to wine, would not interfere with her private rituals.

Only one letter survives, to Homer, showing their progress. On July 5, Pound wrote his father from the Grand Hotel de Suisse in Brussels. They had left London, which they had used as a base for touring British castles, and had crossed over to the continent. They had seen London Tower, St. Pauls Cathedral, Warwick, Kenilworth, Stratford, and other usual tourist sights. On the second page of this letter, in the form of a postscript, young Ezra shows his already developing interest in politics by crowing about an American victory in the Spanish-American War: "Hurrah, Santiago has fallen"—which is underlined. One other letter, dated

September 6, 1898, is written from the German steamship *Königin Luise*, and announces that they will be home soon.

We have to go to the *Pisan Cantos* to get a more accurate tour plan, although it is still very surrealistic:

> coloured photographs of Europa
> carved wood from Venice venetian glass and the samovar
> and the fire bucket, 1806 Barre Mass'chusetts
> > and the Charter Oak in Connecticut
> > or to begin with Cologne Cathedral
> > the Torwaldsen lion and Paolo Uccello
> > and thence to Al Hambra, the lion court and el
> > mirador de la reina Lindaraja
> orient reaching to Tangier, the cliffs . . .
> Mr Joyce also preoccupied with Gibraltar
> > > and the Pillars of Hercules
> > > > (Canto 74, p. 447)

Here, after a few American mementoes, we have the souvenirs of a voyage that began with the old Orient Express route out of London to Brussels, Cologne, down the Rhine to Lucerne, which has the Danish sculptor Torwaldsen's statue of a lion; then on to Italy. We know that Pound visited Venice, and then he would have seen the Uccellos in Florence; after a possible excursion to Rome, the party would have skirted the Riviera and gone all the way south to Gibraltar, a place that Pound visited many times later. There the company took a side-trip to Tangiers, where Aunt Frank—voluminous clothes and all—mounted and rode a skinny mule to the delight of all except the animal. Elsewhere, Pound mentions seeing a fakir blowing fire upon straw that had been ignited by the bite of a snake on his tongue (Canto 74, p. 432), but that may have occurred during a later visit.

In 1898, the three voyagers would probably then move on to the great Moorish palace in Granada, which has the Chamber of Queen Daraxa, though Pound mentions the mirror of Queen Lindaraja. The party would have next journeyed northward over the Pyrenees Mountains to Paris, and finally boarded their German ship for home. Whatever the order, it was truly a Grand Tour, including almost everything that Pound would visit again and

again for years to come—especially the French and Italian segments. For a time, especially during his graduate work at Penn, his
interest in Spain would be strong, but that would fade. He never
penetrated Scandinavia or eastern Europe, and he seldom showed
much interest in Greece as a place to visit. It was southern France
and northern Italy that would dominate his consciousness—and
he saw these first through the eyes of his lovable aunt, who,
although she disliked overusing the adjective "beautiful," "continued to use it with apologies" (p. 6) all over the place. "And her
wide and white-bodiced figure—as for example perched on a very
narrow mule in Tangiers—is an object of pious memory as she
herself is of gratitude. Without her I might not have been here.
Venice struck me as an agreeable place—as, in fact, more agreeable than Wyncote, Pa., or '47th' and Madison Avenue. I announced an intention to return. I have done so. I do not know
quite how often. By elimination of possible years: 1898, 1902,
1908, 1910, 1911, 1913, 1920."

Aunt Frank did something for young Ezra that nobody else
was willing or able to do: she showed him that there was more to
life than the safe, snug suburbs of Philadelphia or his family
history in New England. She showed him the world, and the
impression that this made on him and his later writing is inestimable. Never now could he dream of writing the tale of Hiawatha
or the story of Evangeline. If he told any story at all, it would have
to deal with the world at large. It would have to tell "the tale of the
tribe."

SIX

PENN AND THE APPARITION OF A DRYAD

Now begins a part of Pound's academic career that can be documented with authority. In the 1960 interview with Donald Hall in Rome, Pound said that he knew that he wanted to be a poet as early as the age of fifteen, when he was graduating from the military academy. He said, in fact, that he aimed to enter college "to get out of drill at Military Academy" (p. 31), meaning that he could have prolonged his stay at the preparatory school if he had so desired. When Hall asked him how he arrived at the decision to become a poet, he replied: "My grandfather on one side [T. C. Pound] used to correspond with the local bank President in verse. My grandmother on the other side [Mary Weston] and her brothers [Hiram Parker's three sons] used verse back and forth in their letters. It was taken for granted that anyone would write it." The surprising part of this statement concerns the poetizing of the three young men who worked with shoes in Hopkinton; but since no correspondence from any of these people survives, except for T. C. P.—and his contains no verse—we must take Pound's words at face value. Clearly in the latter part of the nineteenth century, the line between poetry and prose was not as clearly drawn as it was later, when Pound would issue his famous dictum that poetry should be at least as well written as prose. To write poetry was natural; but to play the role of "the poet" was something else, not quite so natural.

When we consider the fact that Pound went to college without the slightest discussion on the part of his parents, we have to acknowledge the important part that Homer Pound took in this decision. After all, not every young man went to college in the early 1900s. Many of them were forced into jobs to support themselves. Pound made it very clear in a letter written to Ingrid Davies on March 30, 1955, that he owed his education to his father, who was willing to go to the Mint day after day while his son buried himself in books in preparation for a career that would almost always keep him close to the starvation line. Pound told Davies that he survived on two pounds in London before World War I when everyone insisted that five pounds was the absolute minimum that one could live on. So despite the psychiatrists of St. Elizabeths, who persistently saw Pound under the influence of his mother (who did, in fact, push him), his father was very much a part of the family picture. If Homer had not been so sympathetic, the whole course of modern poetry might have been different.

As for Pound's selecting the University of Pennsylvania as his school, the choice was dictated to a large part by economics. Homer was not a rich man. Having already cut expenses by having Ezra commute to the academy, he felt that the family could save more much-needed money by having the young man commute to college too. It seems strange that the Pounds did not consider two other schools: Harvard, which, because of the Wadsworth connection, might have been able to help the young student with a scholarship; or Columbia, which was just up the street from Aunt Frank's boardinghouse.

With the wisdom of hindsight, we can see now that the selection of Penn was wrong. First of all, because Ezra was forced to live at home the first year, he was denied the kinds of close relationships that develop in dormitory living. This provided him with a double handicap, because he was two years younger than most of the other students, and age differences can be crucial in later adolescence. Another difficulty was caused by the closeness of parental control. It is at this point that we first see signs of Pound behaving like a rebel. Perhaps the greatest disadvantage to Penn was the fact that it was an urban school, and like most city institutions, faculty–student relationships were not closely cultivated. Since Pound was beginning to have difficulty relating to people who were not intellectually motivated, he was almost automatically thrown upon the faculty for discourse—yet that faculty tended to remain aloof.

In a brief vita that Pound wrote for the anthologist Louis Untermeyer in 1932, the poet claimed to have had tremendous self-assurance during these early years:

> Entered U.P. Penn at 15 with intention of studying comparative values in literature (poetry) and began doing so unbeknown to the faculty. 1902 enrolled as special student to avoid irrelevant subjects. 1903–5 continued process at Hamilton College under W.P. Shepard, "Schnitz" Brandt and J.D. Ibbotson. 1905–7 at U. of Penn. Chiefly impressed by lack of correlation between depts. and lack either of general survey of literature or any coherent interest in literature as such (as distinct for example from philology).
>
> *(Partisan Review, 28, 18)*

Although the youthful wisdom proclaimed here may seem a bit inflated, there is reason to believe, from what both Hilda Doolittle and William Carlos Williams said about this period, that Pound was indeed extremely self-assured and very much in command of his destiny. Naturally this was frightening to many people—his teachers as well as his peers. Inevitably, of course, this attitude would create major problems.

The family prepared their son for his entry into the university by treating him to a two-week vacation at Ocean City, Maryland. Then, in September of 1901 classes began. In those days at Penn, as at most other schools, there was a yearlong initiation period for incoming students. It appears from several sources that one particular student had a hard time with the hazing process. When all freshmen were forbidden to wear loud socks, Master Pound appeared the next day in extremely brilliant footwear. The local *Jenkintown Times-Chronicle* reported the outcome anonymously but gleefully: "The U. of P. students haven't any use of loudness in half-hose. They compelled one of their number to adopt Nature's own 'flesh colour' en route to our village. The temperature registered about forty degrees. He is doing well." The date of this notice is April 19, 1902, showing how late in the academic year such strictures were practiced.

Hilda Doolittle described the event this way in her *End to Torment*, written in the 1950s: "he wore lurid, bright socks that the older students ruled out for freshmen. The sophomores threw

97

him in the lily pond. They called him 'Lily' Pound" (p. 14). Pound himself mentioned the incident almost triumphantly to Ingrid Davies on April 28, 1955: "Haven't been in a frog pond since my freshman year. . . . Naturally if frosh were forbid to wear red sox—" then he would wear them. And so the shy, bespectacled boy from the Cheltenham class photo suddenly became the daring rebel who would stand up and assert his rights. Pound went on to brag to Davies that the very next day after his dousing, he appeared with the same footwear. The psychiatrist E. Fuller Torrey described this act as a "baptism" in his psycho-biography of Pound, and in many ways it was. In this somewhat ludicrous event, we still see in the young man the first overt signs of his willingness to stand up against the Establishment and assert his rights. Ezra Pound and Society had collided head on—and neither was totally willing to yield.

For the reasons already cited, Pound's record obviously had to suffer. He was working on a Bachelor of Science track (which exempted him from Greek) and he was classified as a regular student, although he would later shift to a special category. He received Distinctions (modern A) in only one course: Solid Geometry. If this sounds surprising, we should remember that Pound always emphasized precision in any form of thought, and he doubtlessly acquired some of his skill with numbers from his father. Yet paradoxically, his two Failures that year were in Algebra and Trigonometry. Did the teachers have something to do with this? Pound was always very susceptible to the personal influences around him.

His achievements in the subjects that one might have expected him to excel in were disappointing. He received a mere Pass in two terms of English Composition and in one term of English Grammar, American Colonial History, Principles of Government, Public Speaking, Elementary German, as well as in two terms of Latin, where he read Livy and other basic authors. His marks of Good (modern B) were received in the second terms of Public Speaking, Algebra, Elementary German, English Grammar, and two terms of a Latin course in which he read Horace's *Odes*. This was hardly a distinguished record, and it certainly did not please his parents, but the Pounds did not panic—yet.

As for teachers during these first two years at Penn, Pound was not in any sense as impressed with them as he would be with those at Hamilton. He studied history under one Herman Vandenberg Ames, and he would write a tribute to the man in 1936 when the University was publishing a memorial volume in his honor. Some of his Latin and English teachers he would get to know much better when he returned to Penn for his Master's degree, and so they are best left for that later period discussed in Chapter 9.

Since he had no close friends among the students or the faculty, Pound had to seek companionship elsewhere. He found it in the city—especially in a handsome, sickly, brilliant young painter named William Brooke Smith. A year older than Ezra, born on April 3, 1884, Smith studied art at what became the Philadelphia College of Art and then maintained a studio near the downtown area, where he often served as host to Pound either alone or with a company of budding artists—verbal and visual alike. His address from 1904 to 1908 was 839 North Franklin Street.

Our most complete portrait of Smith comes from a passage in H.D.'s *End to Torment* (pp. 13–14):

> There is the first book, sent from Venice, *A Lume Spento*. It is dedicated to William Brooke Smith. Ezra had brought him to see me. He was an art student, tall, graceful, dark, with a "butterfly bow" tie, such as is seen in the early Yeats portraits. Ezra read me a letter he wrote; this is under the lamp at our sitting-room table. The letter was poetic, effusive, written, it appeared, with a careful spacing of lines and unextravagant margin. . . . The boy was consumptive. His sister had just died. He waved to us from the car once. I wondered what he was doing on our West Chester turnpike. It seemed his sister was buried near West Chester. It seemed far from Wyncote. Or do I dream this?

In her extravagant manner, always hovering in and out of reality, Hilda manages to present the ethereal boy in the correct "unreal" light.

The fact that Smith made a strong impression on Ezra is revealed in a letter written by Pound to William Carlos Williams from France in 1921. It appears that Williams had never met the young man, and asked Pound who he was. Pound replied:

Any studio I was ever in was probably that of some friend or
relative of Will Smith, who avoided a very unpleasant era of
American life by dying of consumption to the intimate grief of his
friends. How in Christ's name he came to be in Phila.—and to
know what he did know at the age of 17–25—I don't know. At
any rate, thirteen years are gone; I haven't replaced him and shan't
and no longer hope to.

(*Selected Letters*, p. 125)

The poignancy of Pound's feeling about Smith's untimely
death in 1908 is revealed in the dedication of his first book of
poems, published that same year in Venice:

This Book was

LA FRAISNE
(THE ASH TREE)

dedicated

> to such as love this same
> beauty that I love, somewhat
> after mine own fashion.

But sith one of them has gone out very quickly from
amongst us it is given

A   LUME   SPENTO
(WITH TAPERS QUENCHED)

in memoriam eius mihi caritate primus
William Brooke Smith
Painter, Dreamer of dreams.

In this elaborate, Edwardian dedication, Pound uses for a title part
of line 132 of Canto 3 of Dante's *Purgatorio*, in which the remains
of Manfred, the son of the Holy Roman Emperor Frederick II, are
carried from his place of death "with tapers quenched" because he
was considered a heretic by the Church. The dedication suggests
that, like Manfred, Smith (as well as Pound) was an artist who was
considered an outcast by the rest of society. This role of the
"different" and despised artist, made famous during the Romantic
Age and perpetuated during the Aestheticism of the 1890s by
people like Walter Pater and Oscar Wilde, was obviously one that
Pound found intriguing. In London, he would successfully play
the part of the eccentric *artiste* who shocks the bourgeoisie with
his sometimes outrageous clothes and extravagant manners.

Clearly he was already cultivating some of this behavior in Philadelphia with his friend.

What was it that William Brooke Smith knew at this time that made such an impression on the young poet? That we shall probably never know for sure, but the answer is not hard to guess. Somewhere along the line, and definitely not in any formal university classes, Pound acquired a keen appreciation for the work of artists. In fact, art was drawing him toward the Renaissance as a center for study, and it was constantly attracting him to Italy more than to any other region: "the eyetalian peninsula," as he playfully calls it in Canto 80 (p. 510). Obviously it was Smith who first taught him:

> all that Sandro knew, and Jacopo
> and that Velásquez never suspected
> lost in the brown meat of Rembrandt
> and the raw meat of Rubens and Jordaens
>
> (Canto 80, p. 511)

Even in his own work, Pound always emphasized the "thing seen," what the Italian poet Guido Cavalcanti called the *veduta forma* in his *Love Song*, where he says that all love

> Cometh from a seen form which being understood
> Taketh locus and remaining in the intellect possible
> Wherein hath he neither weight nor still-standing,
> Descendeth not by quality but shineth out
> Himself his own effect unendingly. . . .
>
> (Canto 36, p. 177)

In the sense that both the ideal poet and the artist work from "seen forms" rather than gross abstractions, they are kindred. If Smith's water colors survived, doubtlessly they would be comparable to Pound's early poetic efforts, with a strong line and sharply visible forms. It would be foolish to suggest that Pound was saying in Smith's studio in 1902 what he would say to Hilda Doolittle and Richard Aldington in the British Museum tearoom in 1912, but one is tempted to believe that at least some of the ideas of the Imagist platform were already being voiced.

The other important person whom Pound met in his freshman year was a young woman whom he often called Dryad, but who was born with the rather unattractive name of Hilda Doolittle—which he would later change. From the beginning, they had a great many things in common. For one thing, they both had a strong veneration for the Greek and Roman classics, and this would bind them closely for their entire lives, even though they would physically be apart. In her one year at Bryn Mawr before the first of many nervous collapses, Hilda spent five of her fifteen hours of study per term on Latin, reading Horace and Livy, and engaging in Latin composition; she spent another five hours on English literature, and the last five on Chemistry. Greek, though not really emphasized by either, still exercised an extremely strong attraction for both. It became, in fact, almost a secret language for them, the way the troubadours of southern France composed hermetic verses of love that sought to shut out the masses. English literature was also obviously an obsession with both, and even if Hilda was not yet writing poems the way she would in 1912, when he renamed her H. D. as he pronounced her an *imagiste*, she was still very sensitive toward the poems that he was creating. Eventually (we are not sure when), he would present her with a hand-made anthology entitled *Hilda's Book*, which has been printed in part at the end of her *End to Torment*, a memoir about their early affair. The majority of these poems were written from 1902 to 1907, before he met Mary Moore, and when he still believed that marriage with Hilda was a distinct possibility.

The details of their meeting in 1901 are recounted by Hilda in a book of testimonies written on Pound's behalf by many celebrities such as Eliot, Joyce, Hemingway, and others in 1933, when *The Cantos* did not seem to be attracting much interest and Pound was rather depressed by his reception in the intellectual community:

> I first met Ezra at a Hallowe'en dress party in Philadelphia when I was 15 and he was 16. He was dressed in a green robe. He said it was not Chinese. He had got it on a trip he had made with a wealthy cousin or aunt some years before. In Tunis, I think. This robe was much discussed. I suppose it was something Indo-Chinaish. It went with Ezra who had Gozzoli bronze-gold hair and the coat caught up with his hair and odd eyes. I had a friend

whose favorite sister was suffering from stupid nerve-specialists. Ezra was terribly upset about it and wanted something to be done. The girl herself was desperate and Ezra one day said: "Don't you think Matilda might like that green coat?" Matilda came to see me one day when Ezra was there. He insisted on her accepting the priceless robe—just to cheer her up. He did not bring one flowers but armloads of books—Ibsen, Maeterlinck, Bernard Shaw. Shaw was then considered shocking in Philadelphia and Ezra had a great row with one of the most important dons of the English department of the University. He said out loud: "Shaw is greater than Shakespeare."

(*The Cantos of Ezra Pound*, p. 17)

In her typically disconnected way (but not differently from the memoir technique of William Carlos Williams or even Pound himself at times), Hilda merges the first encounter with events of later years, since Pound shocked Prof. Felix Schelling, the Shakespeare specialist, during his master's years. But Ezra was always one continuous and cohesive personality to her—whether the Ezra of Philadelphia or London or Rapallo or even St. Elizabeths; he was always that one unforgettable individual who had profoundly influenced her whole life.

It is clear that Hilda always loved Ezra Pound to some degree from the first, and she says quite clearly in *End to Torment* that she regretted that she had never been able to bear him a child. The fault was not so much theirs as her father's. Hilda's father was Charles Leander Doolittle, the leading professor of astronomy at Penn and the director of the Flower Astronomical Observatory in the western suburb of Upper Darby, where the Doolittles also lived. The Doolittle family in Pound's day consisted of Hilda and five brothers and Mrs. Doolittle, the professor's second wife, who was Hilda's mother. The mother was extremely religious, having been brought up among the Moravians of Bethlehem, Pennsylvania, where Hilda was born on September 10, 1886. Father Doolittle was first and foremost a scientist who spent most of his waking hours in his observatory or private study. He seldom seemed to focus on anything closer than the moon—except when the extravagant Mr. Pound was around, and then his focus was quite close and quite discerning.

It is also clear that, for a time at least, Pound was very much in love with Miss Doolittle. William Carlos Williams discusses this affair in his *Autobiography*, where he also chronicles his infatuation with Hilda, although, in his often cantankerous manner, he describes her as a tall, willowy blonde who had a long jaw line and blue eyes and a somewhat disconcerting giggle. But he saw something "natural" in her, precisely as Pound did: "There was about her that which is found in wild animals at times, a breathless impatience" (p. 67).

Hilda herself imagined that she had a direct connection with nature. As she says in her eccentric novel, *HERmione*, which tells the story of her love affair with Pound in masked terms:

> Pennsylvania. Names are in people, people are in names. Sylvania. I was born here. People ought to think before they call a place Sylvania.
>
> Pennsylvania. I am part of Sylvania. Trees. Trees. Trees. Dogwood, liriodendron with its green-yellow tulip blossoms. Trees are in people. People are in trees. Pennsylvania.
>
> (p. 5)

In one of his poems in *Hilda's Book*, Pound already voiced this motif:

> She hath some tree-born spirit of the wood
> About her, and the wind is in her hair
> Meseems he whisp'reth and awaiteth there
> As if somewise he also understood.
> The moss-grown kindly trees, meseems, she could
> As kindred claim . . .
>
> ("Rendez-vous," p. 84)

And, of course, Pound also imagined himself a tree in a poem that appears in *A Lume Spento* (p. 54) and that has been reprinted at the start of the definitive *Personae* collection:

> I stood still and was a tree amid the wood,
> Knowing the truth of things unseen before,
> Of Daphne and the laurel bow
> And that god-feasting couple olde
> That grew elm-oak amid the wold.

An early photograph of Hilda Doolittle taken from the pages of Homer Pound's Scrapbook. (Courtesy of the American Literature Collection, the Beinecke Rare Book and Manuscript Library, Yale University)

FLEISHER (Capt.)   SCOTT   WILLIAMS
TERRONE (Coach)   FRICK (Mgr.)

William Carlos Williams in his fencing gear during his college days at the University of Pennsylvania. (*Courtesy of Special Collections, the Van Pelt Library, the University of Pennsylvania*)

They both had a strong pagan bent, and this would help them form a lifelong tie.

The fate of *Hilda's Book* is most peculiar. Hilda took it with her to Europe, and eventually gave it to her friend Frances Gregg—an American girl whom Pound disrespectfully called "The Egg." In *HERmione*, which was written in 1927 but not published until 1981, Hilda sets up Frances as an anodyne for the hurt suffered when she was abandoned by Ezra on his departure from Europe in 1908. Frances kept *Hilda's Book* and, though she was killed in the Nazi bombings of Plymouth, England, in 1941, the little handmade anthology with its specially written poems miraculously survived. It is now housed in the Houghton Library of Harvard.

In his *Autobiography*, William Carlos Williams tells how Pound and he used to catch a trolley on Market Street and ride out to Upper Darby, where the Doolittles lived (p. 67). There the three poets-to-be would "frolic with youthful abandon" over the unspoiled countryside. Williams remembered especially the profusion of violets and hyacinths in the meadows there. Students from local schools like Swarthmore and Bryn Mawr used to join them on these outings, with the girls wearing sweaters (then considered voluptuous) and dresses that reached only to the ankle. Hilda used to run ahead of them all, acting like a natural leader. She was then—or at least she seemed to be—an untrammeled spirit.

Some of the freedom of that period comes through in the poems of *Hilda's Book*. One, entitled "Era Venuta" (She Had Come), shows both the influence of the Romantic poetry of the nineteenth century and the Roman poet Ovid, whose *Metamorphoses* celebrate the oneness of things:

> Some times I feel thy cheek against my face
> Close pressing, soft as is the South's first breath
> That all the soft small earth things summoneth
> To spring in woodland and in meadow space . . .
>
> *(End to Torment*, p. 80)

The language is highly stylized and not a little archaic in the use of words like "summoneth," but there is a strong feeling in the poetry and an awareness of nature that would always be present in Pound's finest work.

Hilda's poems of that period did not survive; but her later poem "Evadne" answers Pound in its adoption of pagan divinities and rituals of nature:

I first tasted under Apollo's lips,
love and love sweetness,
I, Evadne;
my hair is made of crisp violets
or hyacinth which the wind combs back
across some rock shelf;
I, Evadne,
was mate of the god of light.

(*Selected Poems*, p. 38)

Sometimes Ezra and Hilda would go out into the meadows together, to get away from the prying mother and disapproving father, who is portrayed in *HERmione* as opposing any man as a mate of his only daughter. Often in the backyard, hidden from the family's eyes, they would read poems aloud, by Keats, Shelley, Swinburne, Browning, Yeats, and Whitman, whose Camden lay just beyond the tower of the City Hall. Pound had trouble at times accepting the Bard of Camden because of the slack and casual nature of his composition, but he would come later to see Walt as the apotheosis of the frank, accepting spirit of America, far superior to the self-conscious writings of the New England authors on whom he had been schooled by Ma Weston.

Hilda tells us throughout *End to Torment* that they read many unusual writers together, such as William Morris, whose medieval-sounding poems exerted a certain fascination upon them both . . . and Balzac's *Seraphita* with its transsexual protagonist . . . and Blake with his wild mysticism . . . and Swedenborg . . . and the iconoclastic Shaw. They also read books of Yoga, because even then, though Pound preferred the rational ethics of Confucius to the mystical immersion of Buddhism, he nevertheless was aware of the powerful way that Hindu wise men could exert control over their bodies. He told many novice poets to avoid all abstract theory and all philosophy after Leibniz, as well as Freudian psychoanalysis, because these pseudo-systems had lost any sense of the "magnetic body inside the meat."

The two young lovers also read Greek pastorals together, like Bion and the Andrew Lang translation of Theocritus and Moschus. These works would have a profound effect on Hilda, whose historical novel *Hedylus* portrays a world of ancient Hellas hovering between the actual and the divine. And they devoured the work of Dante Gabriel Rossetti—both his original poetry and his translations of Dante Alighieri. Later Hilda would always connect Ezra either with ancient Greece or medieval Florence. Pound was educating her, as he would do with others throughout his life, even in confinement. He would always maintain a love for this strange, tormented girl, with her beautifully haunted look, her sunken cheeks and her searching eyes, which resembled those of her astronomer father. Hilda's picture on the cover of *End to Torment* shows the patrician face of a Greek lady like the Hedyle who is a protagonist in her *Hedylus.* Her classically scissored bangs and arching eyebrows and chiseled features give her the appearance of a character out of Aeschylean tragedy as sculpted by a genius like Gaudier-Brzeska.

All her life long, Hilda would relive her early years in much of her fiction. *End to Torment* was written in 1958, the year when Ezra was finally sprung from his asylum prison. That explains the title. Hilda wrote it at the behest of Professor Norman Holmes Pearson of Yale, who wanted her to finally put down something lasting about the early part of her life. She did it to please him, and in the hope of ending some of her own perennial torment. Ostensibly she was convalescing from a fall at a clinic in Küsnacht, Switzerland, but during most of her life, Hilda was recuperating from one kind of fall or other—most of them emotional. In the thirties, she was analyzed by Siegmund Freud in a famous encounter which she described later in her *Tribute to Freud.* This analysis disgusted Pound, who believed that psychiatrists only turned people inward, and any hope for personal salvation lay in directing the mind outward toward ideals and goals. In 1958, as Hilda went back over her old association with Ezra, she was desperately trying to free herself from all her own suffering, past and present. Freedom would come for her three years later in the form of death.

Looking back over the chasm of fifty years, Hilda saw her early affair with Ezra as a kind of Golden Age of Youth. Williams testifies to the passion that Pound showed her, and how jealous Ezra became when he heard that Williams had had the temerity to date her. Meanwhile, Hilda had been jealous too. She heard many rumors about Pound's Don Juanlike behavior . . . how he had dated a certain Bessie Elliot . . . and one Louise Skidmore . . . and eventually there was talk about someone named Mary Moore from Trenton. But these peripheral affairs did not annoy her. Ezra called her his Is-hilda, his Isolde, and he was her Trist-an, her man of sorrow. Prophetic names.

In her seventies, Hilda could vividly recall events of a half-century earlier. They were sitting together in a crow's nest in a maple tree in her backyard, which had been built by her brothers to escape the ever-watchful eyes of her parents. Up there in the eyrie, they felt safe and snug. But time was ticking by, and Ezra had to catch the last cross-county trolley, or he'd never get back to Wyncote on time. Finally she told him that he simply had to go:

> "No, Dryad," he says. He snatches me back. We sway with the wind. There is no wind. We sway with the stars. They are not far.
>
> We slide, slip, fly down through the branches, leap together to the ground. "No," I say, breaking from his arms, "No," drawing back from his kisses. "I'll run ahead and stop the trolley" . . . .
>
> My father was winding the clock. My mother said, "Where were you? . . . Where is Ezra Pound?" . . . Why had I ever come down out of that tree?
>
> *(End to Torment, p. 12)*

Her prose is overly dramatic—unlike her poetry or her life. That was obviously a major part of her problem—constraint.

Behind Hilda there was always the stern, strict, professorial father and the zealous, religious mother who nevertheless entertained some social pretensions and was not the least bit happy that her daughter was in love with a poet. In her later fictional recreation of the events, where she called Ezra "George" and herself "Her," which is both short for Hermione and also the Eternal Female, she says:

... she wanted George to correlate her life here, life there. She wanted George to define and to make definable a mirage, a reflection of some lost incarnation, a wood maniac, a tree demon, a neuropathic dendrophil.

She wanted George to say, "God, you must give up this sort of putrid megalomania, get out of this place. . . ."

George was the only young man who had ever kissed Her. George was the only person who had called her a "Greek goddess." George, to be exact, had said ruminatively on more than one occasion, "You never manage to look decently like other people. You look like a Greek goddess or a coal scuttle."

(HERmione, pages 63–64)

She adored his directness. In a world that was otherwise "Anglo-shabby" or "Anglo-saccharine," he was real.

Once the always observant Papa Doolittle caught them snuggling together in an oversized armchair, and he asked Ezra summarily to leave the house. Another time, he said simply: "Mr. Pound, I don't say there was anything wrong this time. I will not forbid you the house, but I will ask you not to come so often" (Torment, p. 14). The general repressiveness was intolerable to both of them, and it would be just a matter of time before it was clear to both that they would have to go to Europe. Lady Fortune would help him to make his decision; she would follow eventually in his wake.

When Ezra actually did depart in 1908, Hilda was left behind, feeling desolate. This despair is beautifully voiced in a later poem in which she speaks as the nymph Callypso (her spelling), who has just been abandoned by Odysseus (one of Pound's favorite personae) on her island in the middle of the sea:

He has gone,
he has forgotten;
he took my lute and my shell of crystal—
he never looked back—

Odysseus (on the sea):
She gave me a wooden flute
and a mantle,
she wove this wool—

Callypso (from land):
For man is a brute and a fool.

("Callypso Speaks," *Selected Poems*, p. 61)

At first she tried to replace him with Frances Gregg, and this pattern would become typical. Whenever Hilda had a hard time with the men in her life—her husband Richard Aldington or her most passionate lover, D. H. Lawrence—she would turn to women for comfort. She was not afraid of being bisexual, the way he was. Until her death in 1961, she was accompanied by three faithful Lesbian friends: her primary lover, the millionairess Winifred Ellerman (better known to some as the novelist Bryher), who wore duck-bill haircuts and enjoyed being referred to by the pronoun "he"; Sylvia Beach, the Parisian bookseller and publisher of Joyce, who wore men's suits with bow-ties; and Sylvia's friend, the bookseller Adrienne Monnier, a robust French peasant type who was rumored to have bitten a man once when he persisted in making advances to her. These three ladies all detested Ezra Pound for his aggressive masculinity and the fact that they had to suffer the hardships of the Nazi occupation in France while Mr. Pound went on gaily "pounding" for Benito Mussolini over Radio Rome. Like her father, they always told her: "He's no good. Put him aside . . . put him aside."

But she could never put him aside. And he never forgot her either, even when he was in his asylum and she in her sanitarium. Both thought of the past with love and affection: *dove sta memoria,* "where memory stands," as Cavalcanti had put it. In Canto 113, back in Italy, he recalled the halcyon days of pre-war London and their conversation about Greek matters in a restaurant:

H. D. once said "serenitas"
                    (Atthis etc.)
        at Dieudonné's
                in pre-history.

(p. 787)

She was sure that many of the passages in *The Cantos* had been written for her, despite the nearness of Dorothy and the lover Olga Rudge. For example, in Canto 80, there was a passage that used the name Dryas (in Greek script); this was surely the "Dryad" of their youth:

[Dryás,] your eyes are like clouds . . .
[Dryás,] your eyes are like the clouds over Taishan
      When some of the rain has fallen
      and half remains yet to fall . . .
With clouds over Taishan-Chocorua
      when the blackberry ripens
and now the new moon faces Taishan
      Dryad, thy peace is like water
There is September sun on the pools

                  (p. 530)

Hilda confesses in *End to Torment* that they never physically consummated their affair, despite their passionate actions. She blamed him for that. But from the start (and this would color her interpretation of the seamy "Crawfordsville Incident"), he had always treated women as objects for veneration. In London, it would be said that he kept a candle lit before the picture of some woman around the year 1910—and nobody knew quite who. Hilda was always an ideal to him. That was why in the British Museum tea room he was ecstatic when he read her verses and saw that she had a genuine talent. She had fulfilled his ideal; she had become kindred—the way a troubadour makes his beloved assume a masculine guise in order to be equal to him. That was why he named her H. D. It was a fresh baptism, meant to shut out the profane, acting like a troubadour *senhal* or "secret name"; and it destroyed forever the silly name of Doolittle, the appellation of her forbidding father.

In Canto 79, written at Pisa, he had called her something new: a bassarid, a Thracian nymph devoted to the service of Bacchus-Liber. But the lines are more graceful and aesthetic than passionate:

Maelid and bassarid among lynxes;
      how many? There are more under the oak trees,
We are here waiting the sun-rise
      and the next sunrise
for three nights amid lynxes. For three nights
      of the oak-wood

111

and the vines are thick in their branches
      no vine lacking flower,
  no lynx lacking a flower rope
      no Maelid minus a wine jar
this forest is named Melagrana

                            (p. 491)

Poor Dorothy and Olga might think that those lines were written for them. . . .

By 1958, H. D. could see herself scattered throughout *The Cantos* like the *membra disjecta* of some dismembered Bacchant. Yet she had grown with time. She was no longer a tree-sprite rooted in the earth. In the lines above and later, she had become a priestess of Liber; she was liberated, free. In the beautiful Canto 90 he portrayed the ascent this way:

For the procession of Corpus
            come now banners
  comes flute tone
          hoi chthonioi
to new forest,
      thick smoke, purple, rising
bright flame now on the altar
            the crystal funnel of air
out of Erebus, the delivered,
      Tyro, Alcmene, free now, ascending . . .

                          (p. 608)

As she reminisced about those fields of old—of Upper Darby and Wyncote—Hilda thought that they had indeed danced together like wild bacchants—despite her father and her mother and all of the rest of them. Ezra and she had celebrated the magic of their youth in a love-dance in the City of Brotherly Love, which was actually the Prison of Bigotry and Hate, ruled inexorably by pent-up puritans. She and Ezra had always been maenads and bassarids. That is what had attracted them to each other from the start. They were rebellious revelers against all of the forces that repress and repel. At this point, not far from her death, she proclaimed from the enclosure of her sanitarium room: "I danced in the garden in the moonlight, like a mad thing. *Maenad and bassarid.* It is not necessary to understand" (*End to Torment*, p. 39).

SEVEN

ENTER "BILL" WILLIAMS— RIVAL AND FRIEND

> and as for the solidity of the white oxen in all this
> perhaps only Dr Williams (Bill Carlos)
> will understand its importance,
> its benediction. He wd/ have put in the cart.
>
> (Canto 78, p. 483)

During the summer of 1902, the Pounds took their son on another trip to Europe in the hope of helping him get on the right academic course. The places that they visited are not recorded authoritatively, but we know from mentions here and there that it was on this tour that Homer and Ezra visited the cheerless British Mint. They were also in Venice that summer when the Belltower collapsed, but fortunately they were not in the vicinity. Aunt Frank is believed to have been on the trip too—as the subsidizer.

As a corrective for poor marks, the trip was a failure. And, in fact, it may even have exacerbated Pound's situation among his peers, since few other boys his age had been to Europe so many times and seen so many things. Upon his entry into sophomore year, Ezra grandly added the name "Weston" after Loomis as a middle name. But there was a slight change for the better in that Homer and Isabel decided to let their son live in the dorms. Pound took up residence in a hall that had just been constructed, with the unattractive name of "P" (later it would be called Morgan).

Pound began to concentrate on Latin that year. His courses included the poetry of Catullus, a young Roman rebel who was as outspoken as Pound himself and whose epigrammatic style the American poet found highly laudable; Propertius, whom Pound would translate eccentrically but brilliantly in 1919, much to the irritation of hidebound scholars everywhere; Vergil, whose genius Pound played down because of his full-blown rhetoric and his toadying attitude toward the Caesars; and Ovid, who, as has already been noted, acted as a secret Bible in his *Metamorphoses* and a guide for realistic attitudes toward love in his erotic poems. This study of Latin would remain useful to him for the rest of his life.

Pound's major activities during that academic year were fencing, at which he was only barely adequate, if we can believe his sometime sparring mate, William Carlos Williams; chess, an activity in which he excelled, even though he lost a key match to his Princeton opponent in a contest between the two schools in March; and dramatics. Everyone that year was anxiously awaiting an undergraduate production of Euripides' *Iphigenia Among the Taurians*, presented in a translation by the Department of Greek, with music by Prof. Hugh Arthur Clarke of the local music department. Ezra garnered one of fifteen roles as a maiden in the chorus. After months of long preparation, the play was finally performed on the nights of April 28 and 29 at the Academy of Music on Chestnut Street. According to Williams' *Autobiography* (p. 57), Ezra, dressed in flowing white robes, with a blonde wig and an upholstered bosom, sang and swayed around the stage, heaving himself with passionate abandon. The play even drew Aunt Frank down from New York. She came with a new man in her life, one James Louis Beyea, a New York doctor whom she was now seeing regularly, and who would move into one of the houses of her expanding operation on 47th Street. In letters home to his parents, Ezra refers to him as "Uncle Jim" or "Uncle James."

After moving into the dorms, Pound at last became friendly with some of his peers. He took to ushering at the Quakers' football games, and during this work met a poor and struggling young philosophy student named Henry Slonimsky, who went on to study in Germany. In 1912, when Pound was at his zenith in London, Slonimsky stopped by on him returning from Germany, and the two reminisced about the old days back at Penn. Slonimsky brought out a work on pre-Socratic philosophers entitled

TRANSLATION

OF THE

IPHIGENIA AMONG THE
TAURIANS

OF EURIPIDES

AS PERFORMED AT THE ACADEMY OF MUSIC
IN PHILADELPHIA

APRIL 28TH AND 29TH, 1903

BY UNDERGRADUATES OF THE
UNIVERSITY OF PENNSYLVANIA

UNDER THE DIRECTION OF

THE DEPARTMENT OF GREEK

WITH MUSIC COMPOSED BY

PROFESSOR HUGH ARCHIBALD CLARKE
OF THE UNIVERSITY

Pound in disguise as a captive maiden in the chorus of
Euripides' *Iphigenia Among the Taurians*. (*Courtesy of the
Van Pelt Library, the University of Pennsylvania*)

Ezra Weston Pound,   Philadelphia, Pa.

"Ezra"

"Bib's" pride. Leader of the anvil chorus at the Commons. Oh, how he throws those legs! Peroxide blonde.

An entry from *The Hamiltonian* annual of 1905. (*Courtesy of the Burke Library, Hamilton College*)

Heraklit und Parmenides, which Pound found very intriguing. In Canto 77, he tried to capture Slonimsky's heavy accent:

"Haff you gno bolidigal basshunts? . . . .
Demokritoos, Heragleitos" exclaimed Doktor Slonimsky 1912

(p. 469)

It might seem strange for anyone to accuse Pound of not having any political passions, but that was in 1912, when aesthetics—not politics or economics—was at the forefront of Pound's mind.

Another friend of that time was Lewis Burtron Hessler, who would graduate from Penn and go on to teach rhetoric for a while at the University of Michigan when Pound was teaching at Wabash. Their interests were literary, and Pound wrote him letters from Indiana and then Venice which are important. Hessler would end his teaching career at the University of Minnesota, just as Slonimsky would go on to Hebrew Union College and hold various administrative positions in Jewish organizations in New York.

But the most important friend of this period was William Carlos Williams. He was two years older than Pound, pursuing dental studies, although he would wind up with a degree in medicine. From the start, Ezra and "Bill" had a lot in common. They were both wiry fencers and handsome: Williams was called a "dark Spanish beauty" in a student publication. They were both from comfortable homes in the suburbs. Williams hailed from Rutherford, New Jersey; his father was in the rum trade and the importation of goldwasser and various perfumes. Both had attended private schools for a time—Williams in Switzerland—and they had been brought up in homes where literature and art were constantly discussed and revered. Williams' father was an unnaturalized Englishman who had an uncanny knack for poetry and common sense. Williams recounts how, when Pound was visiting their house once, the young poet and the father got into a discussion of one of Pound's poems—especially the word "jewels," which Mr. Williams did not understand in the context given. When Pound replied that the jewels were actually books, Mr. Williams said in effect: "Well, why don't you say so then?" (*Selected Essays*, p. 8). Ford Madox Ford would make something of the same remark in Germany, rolling around on a rug and moaning. It would take

115

time before Pound got away from the precious and fabricated language of his literary predecessors and started to write in the language of the people—the *volgar eloquio* or "popular eloquence," as Dante had described it.

The main difference between the two young men lay in their family roots. Pound, as we have seen, was American to the core. Williams' father retained his citizenship in England, and his mother, whom Mr. Williams had met in his youth in the West Indies, had a mixture of blood in her veins: Spanish, French, Jewish. Her name was Raquel Hélène Rose Hoheb Williams. In his encomiastic essay "Dr. Williams' Position" (*Literary Essays*, p. 391), Pound noted these hybrid roots, but then added in praise: "At any rate he has not in his ancestral endocrines the arid curse of our nature. None of his immediate forebears burnt witches in Salem, or attended assemblies for producing prohibitions." But privately, so Charles Olson and others inform us, Pound said many less laudatory things about Williams' lineage, calling him names like "Dago Bill." Yet Williams was not without revenge, as his treatment of the Puritans in *In the American Grain* shows.

Their bond was based on something stronger than blood: the intellect. Both had a sincere and devout reverence for poetry that elevated it to the status of a religion. They were youthful priests of Poesis. Still, as their studies indicate, they were also radically different. Williams saw early that he could not make a decent living writing poems, and so he decided to become a doctor to pay his future bills. In this respect he was totally different from Pound, who hovered close to the poverty line for years in London and Paris, willing to take on that "Bohemian" life that Williams found silly and pretentious. Their intellects also created another bond: loneliness. Williams confesses in his *Autobiography*: "At Penn, aside from Ezra and Charlie Demuth, I had few close friends" (p. 60). Demuth, who would go on to become a well-known New York painter, attended Drexel Institute and lived in a rooming-house near the Penn campus.

It was hard for Williams, whose memory of the past was always a bit faulty, to recall the actual details of his early friendship with Pound and to distinguish between the various years. But it seems that they met in September of 1902, when a pianist named Morrison Van Cleve responded to Williams' violin-playing in Brooks Hall, telling him that there was a strange but interesting young sophomore around by the name of Ezra Pound, who was very much involved in the writing of poetry. This intrigued Williams, who was always eager to meet anyone who might share his interests. According to Charles Norman's *Ezra Pound*, Williams said: "Before meeting Pound is like B.C. and A.D. No beard, of course, then. He had a beautifully heavy head of blond hair of which he was tremendously proud. Leonine. It was really very beautiful hair, wavy. And he held his head high. I wasn't impressed but I imagine the ladies were. He was not athletic, the opposite of all the boys I'd known. But he wasn't effeminate" (p. 3).

From the start, their friendship was warm and heated. Williams, years later, was always willing to pay Pound his due. He freely confessed that the young sophomore was going "madly on, even to Yeats," while he was still pondering over the Romantic poets like Keats. Yeats, of course, was the man who drew Pound eventually to London. In short, Ezra was the pioneer and "Bill" followed. When Williams visited Pound in 1910 in London, Ezra insisted on dragging him to a poetry reading by Yeats. There they sat in hushed silence while the Master read. As they were leaving, Yeats rushed out of the room, calling Ezra's name after them. Williams, of course, was impressed, but perhaps not to the degree that Pound mentioned in a letter written thereafter: "I feel that Bill's mind has been duly benefited by his brief sojourn."

They met again in Paris in the early twenties, and Pound once again assumed the role of the cicerone for the kindly Physician of Rutherford, although the Doctor had managed to meet quite a lot of luminaries on his own. They did not see each other again until 1939, when Pound made his madly impassioned visit to America in an attempt to talk to some Congressmen about monetary reform and to pick up an honorary degree at Hamilton. During Pound's incarceration at St. Elizabeths, Williams remained loyal by writing numerous letters, and even then Pound was constantly suggesting that his friend should read Alexander del Mar or one of his many other new enthusiasms.

We might speculate at this point about other facets of their minds that drew the two together, especially as revealed in their later work. It is obvious that they both would go on to write a poetry that is strongly presentational, rather than representational, a poetry that emphasizes the direct image over the intermediary symbol or the vague abstraction. Williams' most famous line in *Paterson* is doubtlessly "No ideas but in things" (p. 6), while Pound is noted in his *Cantos* for continuing his lifelong campaign for things (*res*), not words (*verba*):

> and for all that old Ford's conversation was better,
> consisting in *res* non *verba*,
> > despite William's [Yeats'] anecdotes, in that Fordie
> > never dented an idea for a phrase's sake
> and had more humanitas

(Canto 82, p. 525)

Obviously the Pennsylvania students of 1905 were not the men that they would become. They were still far too encrusted with Victorian bric-a-brac that they could not slough off, with a dead and artificial system of rhetoric that had to be exposed to the naked light of observation in the same way that the scientists of the period were bringing things "out into the open" that had been covered over far too long.

When *A Lume Spento* was reprinted by New Directions in 1965, Pound was not at all happy about the event. He had always believed that any artist should discard his failures and juvenilia. He called his own collection one of "stale creampuffs," then added: "At a time when Bill W. was perceiving the 'Coroner's Children'." This suggests strongly that Pound, in retrospect, felt that his friendly rival was quite ahead of him during those days. If we compare one of Pound's ornate poems in *Hilda's Book* with the poem referred to, we can see that Williams' work (at least as we have it today) is far freer of archaisms, embellishment, and synthetic passions than is Pound's:

Hic Jacet

The coroner's merry little children
    Have such twinkling brown eyes.
Their father is not of gay men
    And their mother jocular in no wise,
Yet the coroner's merry little children
    Laugh so easily.

They laugh because they prosper.
    Fruit for them is upon all branches.
Lo! how they jibe at loss, for
    Kind heaven fills their little paunches!
It's the coroner's merry, merry children
    Who laugh so easily.

(*Collected Poems*, p. 30)

Yet Williams himself later dismissed his work of this time as mere Keatsian imitation.

Besides similarities, there were also differences. These came to the surface in 1919, when Williams rather insensitively published an inflammatory Prologue to his book of improvisations, *Kora in Hell*. Williams there defended the American Resident Poets against the Expatriates, and he suggested that both Pound and Eliot were too dependent on tradition, too "content with the connotations of their masters" (p. 26). Williams took sides with poets like Carl Sandburg, Alfred Kreymborg, and Maxwell Bodenheim. His attack culminated with the statement: "Ezra Pound is the best enemy United States verse has" (p. 28).

Pound was understandably quite upset. In three letters written to Williams in rebuttal on September 11 and 12, 1920, Pound accused Williams of making him bear the whole burden of leading a poetic revolution, while Williams and his friends lay back and did little to advance the cause of poetry. Pound was tired of seeing second-rate hacks like "the virile Sandburg" or that patron of trees Joyce Kilmer getting published easily, while he had to fight and plead with Harriet Monroe to get Eliot or even Robert Frost into her *Poetry Magazine*. Pound was especially hurt by this argument because it made him out to be un-American or even anti-American. He showed his continuing bond with Williams by saying: "The thing that saves your work is opacity, and don't forget it. Opacity is NOT an American quality" (p. 13).

Williams voiced their differences this way in *Paterson*:

P. Your interest is in the bloody loam but what
    I'm after is the finished product.
I. Leadership passes into empire; empire begets
    insolence; insolence brings ruin.

(pp. 37–38)

Here Williams is standing up for the "bloody loam" of Paterson, New Jersey, where he spent most of his life. He is accusing Pound

119

of being seduced by foreign empires which will inevitably topple into ruin, as Mussolini's did, and by "finished products," which are doubtlessly highly polished works of art conceived and executed with a strong sense of history.

Williams was not apolitical in the way that Wallace Stevens and Stephan Mallarmé were. At Penn, he and Pound argued constantly about the politics of the day: William Jennings Bryan's fiery speeches and the populist platforms . . . Teddy Roosevelt's "big stick" in the Caribbean or his defenses of the "little man" against the "malefactors of great wealth" . . . muck-rakers . . . coal-strikers . . . trust-busters . . . the "open door" to China. It was a great age of reform, and both young men were idealistic enough to want to see changes around them. Pound's parents (and sometimes he) went down into the Philadelphia slums, while a letter sent to Mrs. Williams from her son on February 12, 1904, says that William Carlos had also been down in the slums "helping the little bums." Both felt that there was something basically wrong—something economically wrong—with a system that could create gigantic wealth on one hand and abject poverty on the other. The difference lay in their solutions: Pound veered to the right out of respect for the tradition of his forebears, while Williams (and many of Pound's other friends later in life) tended toward the left, following the socialism that interested his father.

In later years when Pound attacked bankers as a primary cause of the economic and political rot, Williams listened attentively to everything that he said. That is why his *Paterson* contains lines like the following that sound as if they were lifted directly out of Pound's *Cantos*:

> Release the Gamma rays that cure the cancer
> . the cancer usury. Let credit
> out . out from between the bars
> before the bank windows

(pp. 182–83)

or the following:

> . . . the Federal Reserve Banks constitute a Legalized National
> Usury System, whose Customer No. 1 is our Government, the

richest country in the world. Every one of us is paying tribute to the money racketeers on every dollar we earn through hard work.

(p. 74)

But given these mutual concerns, the personalities of the two men led them down divergent roads. Williams would go on to establish a successful medical practice, living in daily contact with life and death, and seeing politics as merely one part of a grand design that is the real subject for poetry. Pound would run passionately after poetic and political causes, sacrificing himself if necessary, playing the part of a polymathic artist like Dante, who feels that all branches of knowledge lie within the ken of the poet. In his *Autobiography*, Williams voices their differences—as well as their love—more eloquently than any outsider can:

> I could never take him as a steady diet. Never. He was often brilliant but an ass. But I never (so long as I kept away) got tired of him, or, for a fact, ceased to love him. He had to be loved, even if he kicked you in the teeth for it (but that he never did); he looked as if he might, but he was, at heart, much too gentle, much too good a friend for that. And he had, at bottom, an inexhaustible patience, an infinite depth of human imagination and sympathy.

(p. 58)

When Pound and Williams were not arguing or reading poems to each other, they were often intent on picking up girls. Williams tells us in letters and in his *Autobiography* about the long walks with Hilda Doolittle and the Bryn Mawr girls out in the fields of Upper Darby. He also speaks about visiting Pound's house for parties, as in his letter of April 12, 1905, to his brother Edgar, when he first mentions Hilda's name. He also describes how Ezra once approached a girl on Chestnut Street and invited her to come to his room. The girl was horrified and cried out in the finest damsel-in-distress manner; "O sir, please go away! Please, sir! Please!"

Conduct like this could only have a bad effect on grades. In Pound's sophomore year, he did not earn a single Distinction. He failed one history course and got an Incomplete in another. He received merely Pass in three Latin courses and in single courses of American history, Logic, Philosophy, and English. His only grades of B were in two terms each of Advanced Composition and Latin, and a single term of Political Science. A change was clearly in order. But where?

In those days family preachers functioned as advisors, and their former pastor, Carlos Tracy Chester, with whom the Pounds were still in touch, recommended his alma mater, little Hamilton College in Clinton, New York. Clinton was also close to Durhamville, where Grandmother Pound had lived for a time, and so the place seemed somehow right. Pound traveled up to Clinton for a personal interview, taking the New York Central's pride and glory, the Empire State Express, which zoomed up the Hudson River Valley at speeds sometimes exceeding 60 miles an hour, and then cut across the Mohawk Valley to Utica, where a trolley could take him the remaining sixteen miles southwest to Clinton. Despite the map, the location was not as remote as it seemed.

Pound wrote a letter home on June 11, 1903, crowing about his great success with the president, Melancthon Woolsey Stryker, who was every bit as formidable as his name. The two hit it off extremely well, and there is every reason to believe that this personal accord helped Pound win some sizable concessions, since his record at Penn was hardly brilliant. Stryker took a gamble on the transfer, trusting Reverend Chester's words of praise and his own intuition and his respect for the young man's mastery of Latin. "Prex," as he was called by all the students, accepted all of the Penn credits except the failures and incompletes, admitting Pound as a candidate for the Bachelor of Philosophy degree. This exempted him from Greek—which, in the long run, was not especially helpful—but already Pound was concentrating on Latin and, from that, the Romance languages. Because of Stryker's generous welcome, Pound would be able to graduate right on time with the Class of 1905. Everyone was happy. A "new life" seemed about to begin and—almost miraculously—that was precisely what happened, at least as far as Pound's intellect was concerned.

EIGHT

HAMILTON AND THE EVOLUTION OF A DREAM

Hamilton College, perched on The Hill above the pleasant hamlet of Clinton, was a perfect antidote for Penn. There were no girls in the school, which was a tightly knit community consisting of about two hundred students and a small but excellent faculty. The college was focused on a main quadrangle that was flanked largely with buildings made of a golden-brownish fieldstone mined from local quarries. One of the dormitories was Hungerford Hall (since replaced by Old South), where Ezra Pound lived during his first year in Room 17. The following year, he would move to the brand-new Carnegie Hall, which was still under construction.

People who were students at this time have said that Ezra Pound appeared on the campus in the fall of 1903 with his mother in tow, and this aroused a stir of disapproval. To some, this was a sign of Pound's being a Little Lord Fauntleroy, and his clothing did not dispel the accusation. Then when he took a large suite on the ground floor of Hungerford (although the expensive suites were the only ones left for a transfer), his reputation for being a pampered rich boy grew. To some, this negative estimation never wavered, although others who got to know Pound through fencing or chess-playing ended up by thinking him a regular fellow.

Isabel probably made her brief stay in a charming hotel which stood at that time on West Park Row, along the village green, where the trolley from Utica came to its final stop. The only part of Clinton that is mentioned in *The Cantos* is a store run by the

Watson Brothers, specializing in stationery and books, that also stood on West Park Row. In that store Pound heard an ominous forecast:

> Entered the Bros Watson's store in Clinton N.Y.
>> preceded by a crash, i.e. by a
> huge gripsack or satchel
> which fell and skidded along the 20 foot aisle-way
> and ceased with a rumpus of glassware
>> (unbreakable as it proved)
>> and with the enquiry: WOT IZZA COMIN?

"I'll tell you wot izza comin'
>> Sochy-lism is a-comin'
>> (a.d. 1904, somewhat previous but effective
>>>>>> (Canto 77, p. 464)

Isabel stayed just long enough to look the place over carefully, to make sure that her son would not fall into any heathen ways, and then she returned to New York and Philadelphia. As the rail connections showed, Clinton was anything but inaccessible. Pound could slip down to New York for a weekend with very little trouble, and there was railroad as well as trolley service into Utica, where there were theaters, rather bawdy bars, and also church groups which constantly staged socials and dances. It was through a church group that Ezra encountered a very pretty girl (so described by William Carlos Williams, who later corresponded with and about her) named Viola Baxter. Pound dated her in his senior year and often went riding in the country with her. She later moved to New York, married a man named Jordan, and kept in touch with Pound in Europe. During the bleak days at St. Elizabeths she was one of Pound's most loyal friends, sustaining him with long, chatty letters about chocolate cakes and television programs and the kinds of everyday banalities that keep one in touch with reality. He was truly grateful later for her caring.

It is now time to confront the story of the Loomis horse thieves. Pound says, in an almost off-hand way in *Indiscretions*, that he first became aware of this connection through Grandmother Susan Angevine when he was at Hamilton: "Thaddeus, in first and legitimate espousals, took to himself [Susan Angevine] of the family Loomis, who were reputedly horse-thieves. That is to say, the family tradition . . . reported them to have been county judges and that like in Upper New York State; but an old lady whom I met in Oneida County said they were horse thieves, charming people, in fact, the 'nicest' people in the county, but horse-thieves" (p. 11). He adds: "I cannot recall that this grandmother has ever mentioned her family." Indeed, if Susan Angevine ever had, she would have said no such thing, since there is no provable link between her father, Nathan S. Loomis, and the notorious clan of George Washington Loomis, which is celebrated in *The Loomis Gang* and other popular works of fiction. The brigands died out in prisons and through bad breeding. The problem is that Nathan Loomis himself is difficult to pin down.

Years after *Indiscretions*, when Pound was being psychoanalyzed (if that verb applies) by Dr. Jerome Kavka in St. Elizabeths, he told quite a different and more plausible story. He said that Susan Angevine

> is a progenitor of one of the oldest homesteads in America, now known as the Loomis Institute, and located 'somewhere in Connecticut.' As a child, the patient knew this grandmother quite well (since she lived in Philadelphia until 1925). . . . Along with her mother, she moved to Montana, and despite the absence of hostility they lived in separate cabins two miles apart. The patient mentions this to convey the rugged individualistic character of his grandmother, who was of the "solid frontier type." . . . In summary, he states, "You could put that grandmother down as no fuss—no fuss about anything. It was my maternal grandmother that had a great deal of influence upon me."

From that first interview with President Stryker, Pound was fascinated by the man whom he (and everyone else) called "Prex." Even today Stryker's name is famous as one of Hamilton's greatest leaders, rivaling that of the founder of the school, Reverend Samuel Kirkland. "Prex" was famous for his colorful oration, an art that Hamilton prided itself on developing. Many people have suggested that Pound modeled his vitriolic prose style on Stryker's, but Dr. Parkhurst and some professors also exerted their influences. Every day Stryker would fulminate from the pulpit during the obligatory chapel sessions, and Pound would listen attentively, as his letters home reveal. Stryker was afraid of no one. He poked fun at "mighty Harvard" for allowing its students to select their own courses. He called President Teddy Roosevelt a pander to the people, who pretended to be interested in the common man while he was actually playing into the hands of his wealthy friends—roughly the same charge that Pound would direct against Teddy's relative, Franklin Delano.

When it came to religion, Stryker was a staunch Christian who approved of devotion before the great mysteries, but he also spoke out in no uncertain terms about the importance of doing something practical in life. Pound doubtlessly had Stryker (as well as Uncle Ezra) in mind when he wrote Canto 98, which discusses education in Confucian terms with a Yankee accent:

> And if your kids don't study, that's your fault.
> Tell 'em. Don't kid yourself, and don't lie.
> In statement, answer; in conversation
> > not with sissified fussiness . . .
> Dress 'em in folderols
> > and feed 'em with dainties,
> In the end they will sell out the homestead.
>
> > > (p. 705)

Stryker lingered on in Pound's mind until 1964, when the poet was publishing his *Confucius to Cummings* anthology with Marcella Spann. He included Stryker's translation of Martin Luther's famous *Ein feste Burg*:

> A tower of Refuge is our God!
> > A goodly ward and weapon.
> He'll help us free, tho force or fraud
> > To us may now mishappen.
> > > That old Arch-enemy
> > > Would our undoing be;
> > Gross might and vast device
> > His dreadful armor is.
> On Earth can none withstand him.
>
> > > (p. 120)

Despite the convivial atmosphere among the students at Hamilton, Pound did not make his peace with them there. On

August 14, 1943, when Pound's reputation from his broadcasts was at its height, *The New Yorker* interviewed a number of Pound's former classmates to learn what kind of a person he had been during his college days. The responses were largely negative. Most of those interviewed characterized Ezra as an eccentric, an individualist, a loner. His closest friend was obviously his roommate, Claudius A. Hand, who went on to enjoy a very successful career as a financial consultant on Wall Street. Hand and Pound were two of only three students who were not members of fraternities, and yet the choice seems to have been largely theirs. It was not hard to join a group in those days, although there were rumors that some of the fraternities from Penn had tried to blackball Pound from a distance.

Roommate Hand said that Pound used to wake him up late at night, offer him some beer (which he, the son of a Methodist minister, never drank), and would then insist on reading him some of his poetry. Hand would lie half dozing while his roommate went on and on, sometimes passionately and sometimes inaudibly. Then, when he finished a poem, Pound would ask: "Could you make anything out of it?" Hand would invariably say no, and this would cause Ezra to exclaim "O God!" and down the beer. Often he would tear his poems up, thereby practicing the stern judgment on his own creations that he expected others to practice on theirs. Hand also said that Pound did a lot of talking in those days about the future: He wanted very much to live his life abroad, and he imagined working in the foreign service. In short, Pound already seemed to have the intuition that he would leave this country and spend most of his life abroad.

Despite his relative unpopularity with other students, Pound's two years at Hamilton were a great success—for two reasons. First, he was blessed by having some excellent teachers who also became close friends; and second, he was already mulling over a design for a great epic that would occupy his later years. Once again, he seems to have had an extraordinary sense for prophesying his own future. One of the professors who influenced Pound greatly at this time was Herman Carl George "Schnitz" Brandt of the German Department. Pound quotes him spouting German in Canto 92, which, translated, means: "Hans Sachs was a shoemaker—and a poet too" (p. 621), thereby stressing the fact

127

that poets at one time in history were readily accepted by their societies. Brandt allowed Pound to move away from German prose, which bored him, into poetry, and it was his warm and adulatory letter that helped Pound to win his first (and only) teaching job at Wabash College. Pound's letter of thanks rests in the Burke Library at Hamilton, as well as a letter accompanying a book of Pound's poems, in which the poet asks his mentor to decide if the shoemaker or poet element dominates.

Another faculty friend, who was beloved by most of the students, was Arthur P. "Stink" Saunders. His nickname (*nomignolo* in Italian) was earned because of his work around chemicals in the Chemistry Department and not for seedy personal reasons. He is remembered fondly in Canto 87:

> That fine old word"
> > sd/"Stink" Saunders,
> > > "An independence."
> The nomignolo not reflecting on character
> but at that time, 1900 or thereabouts,
> applied to all professors of chemistry.

> > > > > > (p. 575)

Saunders' reverence for "independence" (which can mean a private income) was something that the individualistic Pound could easily sympathize with. Saunders was also important to Pound because he staged musical events in the school, and Pound was deeply concerned with music all during his life. When Saunders and his wife visited Paris in 1923 and saw the poet living on the brink of poverty, they generously gave him a check that was quite handsome for a professor's salary. Legend has it that Pound, in his own typically generous manner, then passed it on to someone who was needier than he.

Even more important as a teacher and friend was William Pierce Shepard, commonly called "Bill" or "Shep," who was Professor of Romance Languages and Literatures. It was he who made Pound familiar with Dante Alighieri in the original Italian and with a host of writers in French, Spanish, and Italian literatures, primarily from the Middle Ages. Shepard was well on his way to establishing an international reputation as a scholar in Provençal,

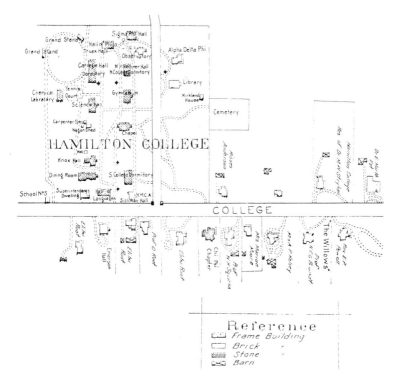

Map of the Hamilton College campus during Pound's days of
study there. (*Courtesy of the Burke Library, Hamilton College*)

WILLIAM PIERCE SHEPARD.
  A.B., Hamilton, 1892.
  A.M., Hamilton, 1893.
  Ph.D., Heidelberg, 1896.
  Φ B K ; Δ Υ.
Professor of Romance Languages and Literature, 1895.

JOSEPH DARLING IBBOTSON.
  A.B., Hamilton, 1890.
  A.M., Hamilton, 1894.
  Φ B K ; X Ψ.
Professor of English Literature, Anglo-Saxon and Hebrew, 1895.

ARTHUR PERCY SAUNDERS.
  A.B., Toronto, 1890.
  Ph.D., Johns Hopkins, 1894.
  Φ B K.
Childs Professor of Agricultural and of General Chemistry, 1900.

Three Hamilton professors who were close to Ezra Pound.
(Courtesy of the Burke Library, Hamilton College)

the old language of the South French troubadours, the first poets
of the modern world after the Dark Ages. These lonely creators—
little studied then as now and almost always greatly misunder-
stood—haunted both the young man and the old. Pound always
claimed that if someone was interested in modern poetry, he
should begin with its roots, which go back to these accomplished
composers of southern France.

Pound and Shepard were also fascinated by the private lives of
these poets, which descend to us in *vidas* attached to the song-
books containing their poems. These lives are almost entirely
mythic, but that, to Pound, provided a valuable link of these poets
with the original "makers" of Greece, to whom he saw them akin.
For example, the troubadour Peire Vidal dressed himself in a
wolf's skin to woo his beloved Loba, just as the Greek Actaeon was
changed into a stag after watching Diana bathe in the nude—and
both men were then attacked by dogs:

> Then Actaeon: Vidal
> Vidal. It is old Vidal speaking,
>   stumbling along in the wood,
> Not a patch, not a lost shimmer of sunlight,
>   the pale hair of the goddess.
> The dogs leap on Actaeon . . .
> Stumbling, stumbling along in the wood,
> Muttering, muttering Ovid . . .
>
>   (Canto 4, p. 14)

Shepard was known for his many articles on this poetry, and
in 1924 he would edit the poems of the troubadour Jausbert de
Puycibot (or Gaubertz de Poicebot, as Pound calls him). But earlier
Shepard was already discussing the man's strange life with his
protégé: the monk Poicebot leaves his monastery to become a
worldly poet and singer; he then becomes a knight in order to win
the hand of a lovely lady; after marrying her, he goes off to fight
for a time in Spain, and the feckless woman falls in love with
another man and abandons their castle; on returning to France
from Spain, Gaubertz accidentally encounters her leading the life
of a common whore and, despite himself, spends one last night in
her embrace before finally leaving her for good in the morning

after directing her to a nunnery. Pound would work this strange
tale into his Canto 5:

> Poicebot, now on North road from Spain
> (Sea-change, a grey in the water)
> > And in small house by town's edge
> Found a woman, changed and familiar face;
> Hard night, and parting at morning.
>
> > > > > > > > > > (p. 18)

In these vidas Pound could see the constant assertion of the love-
force at a time when mysticism was running rampant in the Dark
Ages; this cult of Eros was essentially what kept the race alive
when others were abandoning themselves to what Erich Auerbach
has called "vulgar spiritualism." The troubadours, as Pound saw
them, provided a "persistent awareness" beneath the mystical
tidal wave:

> > 2 thousand years, desensitization
> After Apollonius, desensitization
> > & a little light from the borders:
> > Erigena,
> > Avicenna, Richardus.
> Hilary looked at an oak leaf . . .
>
> > > > > > > > (Canto 92, p. 622)

It is doubtful that Shepard shared or implanted all of these ideas
in Pound's mind. His own work is conservative, treating the troubadours as forerunners of the highly Neoplatonic work of the
Italian poets who followed them, but there is no doubt that he
exerted a very strong influence on his precocious charge. The last
page of the Preface of *The Spirit of Romance* contains this para-
graph: "My thanks are due to Dr. Wm. P. Shepard of Hamilton
College, whose refined and sympathetic scholarship first led me
to some knowledge of French, Italian, Spanish and Provençal." The
very title of Pound's masterwork, *The Cantos*, has to be attributed
in part to Shepard's influence, since it was he who introduced
Pound to a formal study of Dante's cantos in the *Comedy*.

"Bill" Shepard was reputedly not an easy person to get to
know. In the Introduction to the Hamilton-produced *Letters to
Ibbotson*, he is described as a "tall cadaverous man . . . whose

squinting glance and sunken cheeks caused chills to run up and down" the students' spines (p. 3). He is reported to have said that he wished that the students had one collective head to go with their student body so that it could be the more conveniently lopped off. Obviously young Ezra shared those feelings completely. Despite Pound's warmth toward him, Shepard in his one surviving letter to Pound at Hamilton, thanking him for the just mentioned dedication, is very formal and reserved—but that was his nature. Pound's letters home show that he was even invited to Shepard's home on Bristol Road, at the foot of The Hill, where he and his wife entertained with the finest French cuisine and choicest wines. Young Pound, who had already developed a taste for gourmet food, enjoyed those rare evenings to the hilt, for it was precisely events like this that he had not had a chance to enjoy at Penn.

Pound's closest friend on the Hamilton faculty was Joseph Darling Ibbotson, a specialist in Anglo-Saxon and the Middle English of Chaucer. Ibbotson had the nickname of "Bib" because he once absentmindedly ran out of commons to the chapel without removing the napkin from his shirt (how seldom society forgives!). The 1905 edition of the yearbook, *The Hamiltonian*, carried a picture of Pound looking like a pre-Raphaelite dandy and bore a caption that said: "Bib's pride." So their affection was no secret. The caption also commented on Ezra's bellowing for food at the refectory and made two remarks about his personal appearance: his "Peroxide blond" hair and his lanky legs that he was accustomed to throwing around. Their mutually warm correspondence was published in the volume already cited, but only with letters from the years 1935 to 1952.

Professor Ibbotson lived in a beautiful white, green-shuttered mansion on College Street, about midway between the last trolley stop and The Hill. It is the kind of house that anyone who pictures a typical college town would imagine a beloved professor to be living in. In the famous 1960 interview with Donald Hall, Pound said that his whole idea for the undertaking of a poem like *The Cantos* began "about 1904, I suppose" (p. 23); elsewhere he said it occurred during talks with Bib. In 1955 during a radio celebration of Pound's seventieth birthday by the Yale Broadcasting Company, an anonymous letter (certainly written by Ibbotson) was read over the air waves:

> Dr. X [Shepard] and I saw him more frequently at our houses than did other members of the faculty. He came to my house rather often. Sometimes at a rather unusual hour. Thus one evening in his senior year, at 11:40, my doorbell rang, and there was Ezra. "Coming in from Utica, I saw a light in your study, the only welcoming light on [College] Street. May I come in?" We sat by the fire, and I had a lot of locust wood which burned with a blue flame, and we smoked and talked until nearly three o'clock. A good deal about Ossian. He had picked up an old German translation from the English of MacPherson and was enthusiastic, and the talk was of Anglo-Saxon poetry.

It is actually easy to pinpoint this occasion in Pound's letters to his parents. On March 5, 1905, he wrote home saying, "Going my homeward way at 10 P.M. I notices Bib's lights ablaze and knowing that he is still mostly college boy despite his family and professorship I dropped in and we smoked and ate and talked for an hour or two longer." This easy, cordial student–teacher relationship—as rare then as it is today—was precisely the thing that Pound was looking for at Hamilton. It mattered little that Pound excelled on the chess team or was excluded from a certain fraternity. Bill Shepard was laying the foundations for the future translations of that most difficult of all troubadours, Arnaut Daniel, while Bib was preparing the way for the controversial translation of "The Seafarer."

Pound's record at Hamilton was incredibly better than the one at Penn. It can be summarized as follows, using modern grades in an ascending order:

F: The Book of Job; Analytical Geometry.

D: Senior German; Trigonometry.

C: Psychology (did his antipathy toward this subject begin here?); English History; Beginning Italian; Junior French (two terms); Beginning and Intermediate Spanish.

B: Junior German; Junior French; Sophomore Bible (two terms); Intermediate Italian (two terms); English Literature; The Life of Christ; Senior French (three terms); Senior Spanish; Elementary Provençal.

A: In the Junior Year: Economics; Sophomore Bible (second term). In the Senior Year: Anglo-Saxon (two terms); Orations; Parliamentary Law; Bibliography; and Advanced French.

If the reader is wondering why Pound took so many courses, the answer is that Hamilton, like many schools of that time, operated on a trimester system from September to June, and also, of course, students worked much harder than they do today. Aside from this regular work, a letter in March of 1905 to Isabel said that he was engaging in "extra work with Bill next term in Provençal, 'The Troubadours of Dante.'"

If we scrutinize Pound's career at this point, we find that he already had an impressive array of foreign languages at his command: Latin, Anglo-Saxon, German, French, Italian, Spanish, and—to a lesser degree—Portuguese and Greek. Except for Chinese, there would be no more additions of any note. As for Sanskrit, Hebrew, or a variety of other languages that might have come in handy if one envisioned writing an epic about the world, Pound would sigh later: "There is no substitute for a lifetime" (Canto 98, p. 691).

At some time around 1904, as an inscription in a book of the verse of Thomas L. Beddoes shows, he met and fell in love with an older woman. She was a Jewish pianist named Katherine Ruth Heyman, whom he referred to by her initials or by the nicknames of "Kitty" or "the Kitty-mama." As the last name indicates, the affair was platonic. She was at least eight years older than he was, having been born in 1877 (some suggest an earlier date) in Sacramento, and she was extremely sophisticated—well on her way to establishing an international reputation as an interpreter of Scriabin, which she maintained until her death in 1944. In some ways, she was a prefiguring of Olga Rudge, Pound's long-standing lover and an internationally known violinist. Kitty was precisely the sort of steadying influence that the brash, often compulsive Mr. Pound needed. Although he could feel superior to his classmates and many of his teachers, he had to defer to her expertise and fame.

The details of their meeting are misty, but it seems that they probably met in Philadelphia, perhaps through the intermediary

William Brooke Smith. In her masked autobiography *HERmione*, Hilda mentions the sudden intrusion of an older woman into her world who threatened to take her beloved "George" (Ezra) away from her. The setting was either in the Pounds' house or in a recital room where the musical event had been arranged by Isabel Pound (we have to remember that Ezra's parents were extremely active in local dramatic and musical life):

> . . . a face emerged, emerged from the stir of notes and star-notes of notes . . . and a curious flat glass surface emerged, two flat glass surfaces that caught light, that dispersed light, that suddenly let light through her pince-nez and showed the smallish uninspired eyes of the musician. Her name is Stamberg, Jew or German or German Jew with a figure like that and wearing eyeglasses that have a tiny chain, a little rolled gold chain that fastened now behind her ear under her rat-tail untidy lean hair and that when she stops playing will be pulled off with a jerk and will fasten to a ridiculous little hook-in thing that is hooked in to the flat part above the protruding part of her odd humped front of drab cerise shirtwaist.

If Hilda was bitter, it is because she was jealous. She had heard the word "fiancé" mentioned about Ezra's relation to this woman. Then, as the woman began to play, Hilda watched her young beloved get drawn up into the music, and this led her to a very unfortunate perception: "George and this woman who is common, who is obviously Jew or German—have a secret, a power I haven't. Why haven't I ever *done* anything?" But fortunately for Miss Doolittle, "Miss Stamberg," or whoever she was, disappeared thereafter as her lover went on to other things.

In actuality, Kitty Heyman did not disappear at all. She died as a world-famous musician during World War II, as Pound learned later in St. Elizabeths, very much to his discomfort. For despite any anti-Semitic remarks he ever made, the strong bond between him and the performer was real. In fact, Kitty sealed their spiritual relationship by giving him a diamond ring that had belonged to her mother; she gave it to the young man "to keep until we're very old together." It was simply a symbol of their love for each other, and when Pound wanted to express his own love later for Mary Moore and did not have the funds to send her a ring that he had purchased on his own, he sent her Kitty's ring—quite honestly telling her how he had come by it.

Kitty Heyman would loom importantly in Pound's life at the time of his self-imposed exile from America, since she was in Venice during the spring of 1908. In fact, her presence there on a musical tour was obviously one of the factors that drew the young man there, in addition to his love of the City of Water. When he published *A Lume Spento* at that time, he included a long and sentimental poem entitled "Scriptor Ignotus" (The Unknown Writer, modeled after Robert Browning's "Pictor Ignotus," The Unknown Painter). It is dedicated to K. R. H. Using a Browning-like persona to speak through, Pound casts himself into the role of a certain Bertold Lomax, "English Dante scholar and mystic" who "died in Ferrara in 1723, with his 'great epic' still a mere shadow." Lomax apparently had a dream much like Pound's of writing a world-epic in honor of "an organist of Ferrara" whose name is unknown. Pound and his beloved pianist therefore serve as an analogy to Lomax and his organist, and both are subsumed under the famous connection between Dante Alighieri and Beatrice. If this triple analogy sounds complex, it shows that even in his youth, Pound's concept of poetry involved tradition in the finest sense—not in a Freudian uprooting of the past involving any "anxiety of influence." Lomax (or Pound) dreamed of writing a "great forty-year epic," and he ends his poem by making the same promise to his beloved that Dante did to Beatrice at the end of the *Vita Nuova*:

> Though sight of hell and heaven were price thereof,
> If so it be His will, with whom
> Are all things and through whom
> Are all things good,
> Will I make for thee and for the beauty of thy music
> A new thing
> As hath not heretofore been writ.
>> Take then my promise!

(p. 40)

This poem was omitted from the definitive collection of Pound's work, *Personae* of 1926, and it is easy to see why. It is pretentious and schematic, but certainly it shows, in the risk it takes, that

Pound's dream of writing a Dantesque epic was a reality before 1908, and his love for Miss Heyman was quite profound.

As his roommate Hand indicated, Pound was writing poetry all during his Hamilton years, but most was probably thrown away. His first serious published work appeared in the graduation issue of the *Hamilton Literary Magazine* for 1905. It is a translation of a bilingual dawn song, which he entitled "Belangal Alba." The heart of the poem is written in Latin, and there are Provençal refrains, which, he notes in a letter to his parents on May 3, 1905, are the "Oldest Provençal written." He also specifies that he gives three different versions of the refrain when it appears, since the original is very tortured and the exact meaning difficult to interpret. Here the careful scholar speaks in concert with the creator. Although the work is hardly comparable with Pound's later productions, it shows where he was at the start of his career:

Phoebus shineth e'er his glory flyeth,
Aurora drives faint light athwart the land,
And the drowsy watcher cryeth,
                    "Arise!"

REF:—
Dawn light, o'er sea and height, riseth bright,
Passeth vigil, clear shineth on the night.

They be careless of the gates, delaying,
        Whom the ambush glides to hinder
Whom I warn and cry to, praying,
                    "Arise!"

REF:—
O'er cliff and ocean white dawn appeareth,
Passeth vigil, and the shadows cleareth.

Forth from out Arcturus, North Wind bloweth
        Stars of heaven sheathe their glory
And, Sun-driven, forth-goeth
                    Settentrion.

REF:—
O'er sea-mist and mountain is dawn display'd,
It passeth watch and maketh night afraid.

The translation clearly shows a remarkable ability to handle difficult languages in poems extracted from remote periods of time. This was in many ways a strength, but it could also prove to be a weakness. The "show-off" side of Pound's nature is apparent in a letter that was written to his father on July 22, 1903. He opens with a German salutation ("Lieber Vater") and then passes through various linguistic changes, including the almost nonsensical "Nodding egzitemendz didding" (No excitement doing). In this letter the effect is one of humorous camp, but later the continual falling back on other languages to express himself would prove most annoying to many people. Of course there is a justification for much of it: if a poet is going to tell the "tale of the tribe," he has to acknowledge the fact that the tribe does not speak one language. Furthermore, some languages seem to possess various geniuses (possibly because of the writers in them) that others do not. But still, this love of difficulty for its own sake could be at times pernicious—simply a form of ostentation. In a letter written to his father on a Saturday in May of 1950, Pound bragged that he was graduating the youngest in his class and the "best read." Later, many of his colleagues such as Richard Aldington would ask if he was ever capable of giving one of his books an English title.

Because of the letters and the schoolbooks that survive, we know a great deal about what Pound was doing at Hamilton. For one thing, he was experimenting widely with the English language, trying to see what it could do with relation to Provençal. A letter written on an unspecified Sunday of 1905 says that he was trying to translate a debate poem by the troubadour Guiraut de Bornelh which used only five rhymes over sixty-eight lines. His marked-up copy of Sweet's edition of Anglo-Saxon poetry shows that he was deeply engrossed in that area, and Fred C. Robinson has demonstrated recently that, far from being the bumbling novice translator that the pedants tried to make him out to be, Pound's later version of "The Seafarer" not only usually makes sense, but shows the young man's daring (sometimes rash) tendency to emend and to select "difficult readings" over the more obvious ones adopted by the establishment. The copy of Swinburne that he had in 1905 shows an exhaustive reading; the poem "Anactoria" contains Pound's written gloss: "Sappho's ode outdone and passion torn in tatters." But Swinburne was one of the influences whom he would have to shake off.

By far the books that Pound seems to have pored over most are the three volumes of Dante's *Divine Comedy* published by the Temple Classics, which he later recommended to countless neophytes because of the notes and the ease of its bilingual organization. All three of his volumes bear the ink inscription: "E. P. Mar. 1904"—and are currently housed at the Humanities Research Center at the University of Texas in Austin. In thumbing through them, one sees instantly that Pound read Dante as if the Italian were an imagist writer. His marginal glosses, made with the same pen as the one that made the inscription, show that his thoughts in 1904 and 1905 were precisely those that he would put on paper in his first book of criticism in 1910, *The Spirit of Romance*. For example, in *Spirit* (p. 28), he praises Dante's verbal precision, for not referring vaguely to a river pooling itself, but "where the Adige pools itself," having a specific place in a specific river in mind. This is an essential part of Pound's poetic creed, and it formed the backbone of his imagist platform in 1912. It is also amusing to watch Pound improve on the Temple translator, who renders the Italian verb here, *stagna*, as "stagnates"; with a flourish Pound writes in the margin "pools itself." Even at age nineteen and twenty, Mr. Pound was never afraid of correcting his elders.

Perhaps the most interesting thing that we can observe by examining his schoolbooks is the way that Pound's mind was already functioning in a comparative literary way—far ahead of his time. For example, Dante's "oriental sapphire" of *Purgatory* Canto 1, line 13, is compared with Shakespeare's "Dawn in russet mantle," while other passages contain jottings linking them with the work of William Blake and St. Augustine and François Villon. Pound was also interested as much in ideas (what he would term later *logopoeia*) as in image-making (*phanopoeia*) and sound-making (*melopoeia*). Throughout Dante's *Paradiso* he could see relationships with Plato's notion of the heavens as contained in the *Phaedrus*, indicating that his interest in Christian Neoplatonism was already being strongly developed. It is believed that the poem "Plotinus" stems from this period. The Temple Classics also contained family charts that were useful for the future when

Pound would decide to incorporate parts of Renaissance history into his *Cantos*. The charts show the family lineage of the House of Este and the Malatesta families—both of which figure prominently in the first thirty cantos.

When Pound told Donald Hall that his idea of writing *The Cantos* evolved in his Hamilton days, he added: "It was a question of dealing with material that wasn't in the *Divina Commedia*" (p. 24). This same reverence for the Italian poet shows in an exuberant letter written to Isabel in February of 1905. Pound says that he has been discussing Emerson, but he considers Emerson and his ilk mere imitations of the great medieval mind of Dante. He says: "find me a phenomenon of any importance in the lives of men and nations that you cannot measure with the rod of Dante's allegory," and he goes on to pledge that he will "continue to study Dante and the Hebrew prophets." The first part of that promise was kept; the second—perhaps made piously to his mother—abandoned.

When we consider what he was studying in April of his senior year, we see that he was ahead of most modern graduate students:

In Old Spanish, he was reading *The Cid*, which he would adapt at the start of Canto 3.

In Old French, he was reading the *chansons de geste*.

In Old Provençal, he was studying the troubadours, especially the critic of the Church, Peire Cardinal.

In Old English, he was reading everything that he could.

In Middle English, he was reading Chaucer in the Pollard edition, and although he never emphasized Chaucer any more than he emphasized Shakespeare (feeling that the audiences for both were wide enough already), he dearly loved the Middle English author, as well as Sir Thomas Malory. Hilda Doolittle says in *End to Torment* that they read about the adulterous love of Lancelot for Guinevere in an unexpurgated edition—and the fact that there even were expurgated editions of *Le Morte Darthur* shows us how far away the world of 1900 is from us today.

But even if Pound had a vague idea of what he wanted to write during the better part of his life, he was still a long way away from it. As he told Hall: "The problem was to get a form—something elastic enough to take the necessary material. It had to be a form that wouldn't exclude something merely because it didn't fit" (p. 23). Without the "nice little road map" of the cosmos that Dante had at his disposal, Pound had to search, and this search would take a good twenty years before it would be fully realized. His idea of writing a work in three parts (with one in Dante's terza rima and the other two in dactyllic hexameters and iambic pentameters) was fortunately abandoned. He would finally settle on free verse as his mode of expression and "a journey of the mind," with its many sudden shifts and changes, as the mode of operation. As for general subject matter, he had not really begun to dent two of the areas that he would study voraciously a decade later: economics, where the editor A. R. Orage and Major C. H. Douglas would come into play; and Chinese or the Confucian element, which would be in part thrust upon him with the acquisition of the papers of the Oriental specialist Ernest Fenollosa. Of course, he had a long way to go. But back in 1905, as he graduated with a Bachelor of Philosophy degree from Hamilton College, he knew that, although the road was long and hard ahead, he was also somehow on the way.

♦ NINE

PENN AGAIN AND EUROPE

Pound's second formal association with the University of Pennsylvania was his last one. Although he would receive a Master's degree from the school in 1906, he would never be honored by it with an honorary degree, as he was by Hamilton. In fact, he would never even revisit the campus or recommend that anyone go there. His son Omar went to Hamilton, and when his grandson Siegfried de Rachewiltz asked him which college he should attend, Pound replied: "Go to an Ivy League school. But *not* to Penn. Go to Rutgers." The irony, of course, is that Rutgers is not a member of the Ivy League.

Given the earlier difficulties, the reader might wonder why Pound chose the school a second time. One answer seems to be that it simply was handy. Another is that Pound seemed to have matured and was therefore more able to cope with a school in an urban setting. Also, Penn had an excellent reputation, and a degree from it would be helpful in getting a job.

In an interview granted to the *Philadelphia Bulletin* on February 20, 1928, Homer Pound described the return of his son from Hamilton after a graduation ceremony that neither he nor Isabel attended. Ezra entered the living room and flung his degree onto a sofa, saying, "Well, Dad, here I am! Educated!" Homer replied, in effect: "Fine, Son. And what do we do now? You have to do something, you know."

Ezra was fully aware that his father was not going to support him forever. Letters written from Hamilton before graduation show that he was trying to land various jobs in a variety of departments in prep schools in the Philadelphia area—including

141

Cheltenham Academy. He also wanted to take some special courses at Penn on a part-time basis. A letter written to Isabel in March says that he had already been accepted at Penn for some courses with a welcoming note from the Dean, Dr. Clarence Child, whom he knew from his earlier studies in English. And so when other plans for employment fell through, it seemed only natural to return to the scene of his former disappointments. Still, with a good record at Hamilton behind him, Pound and everyone else felt that the second performance would have to be better than the first one.

Indeed, for that whole first year, it was. He was happy to be back in a city, far from the "tundra" of Oneida County, where he could stage musical events in his parents' house or entertain his friend "Bill" Williams or visit William Brooke Smith's studio near Franklin Square. Williams had decided not to be a dentist after all, and was working on the medical degree that he would receive shortly. Smith had just graduated himself with a Diploma in Applied Design from what is now called the Philadelphia College of Art. He won a $10 prize in modeling at graduation time and was setting himself up as a General Designer in the Philadelphia area. Hilda Doolittle, meanwhile, was preparing to enter Bryn Mawr College for her one, brief whirl through Academe. In short, the old friends were still around to make life pleasant.

It was probably at this time that Pound encountered someone with the initials "E. McC.," which he used as the title of one of his poems that appeared in *A Lume Spento*. This young man is further identified as someone "That was my counterblade under Leonardo Terrone, Master of Fence." The poem is essentially about risks taken in life and the constant possibility of death, and so several biographers have assumed that it is a memorial to one Eugene McCartney of Boothwyn, who, like William Brooke Smith, died young:

> Gone while your tastes were keen to you,
> Gone where the grey winds call to you,
> By that high fencer, even Death,
> Struck of the blade that no man parrieth;
> Such is your fence, one saith,
>> One that hath known you.

(p. 61)

The poem concludes:

> Thou trustedst in thyself and met the blade
> 'Thout mask or gauntlet, and art laid
> As memorable broken blades that be
> Kept as bold trophies of old pageantry . . .
> So art thou with us, being good to keep
> In our heart's sword-rack, though thy sword-arm sleep.

The problem with identifying the protagonist as Mr. McCartney is that Mr. McCartney was very much alive as late as 1936, as various documents show. There are numerous other candidates for the title, such as Eli McElheny in Pound's original Class of 1905, but the only one who could have died that young is one Ellis Reed McClure of the Class of 1907, who mysteriously disappears from Penn's records in about 1907. He seems to be the subject. In any case, the real person behind the poem is not necessary for making the work intelligible, and probably because the whole production smacks of blatant sentimentality, it was dropped from subsequent collections.

Pound was happy to see some of his old professors of English again, such as Felix Schelling, who specialized in drama; Cornelius Weygandt, a modernist; and the already mentioned Dr. Child, a medievalist. But in that first year of graduate work, Pound did not study with any of these people, who had rather ambiguous feelings about him from the past. Instead, he immersed himself in a study of Romance languages and literatures with the one man who made them work: Professor Hugo Rennert. Pound's only course away from Rennert's supervision was a Latin pro-seminar with another old friend from the past, Walton Brooks McDaniel, with whom he read the writings of the Roman poets Catullus and Martial. Pound often said in later years that these two Roman writers helped him to develop a sense of precision in language every bit as fully as the French novelist Gustave Flaubert did. In his essay "A Visiting Card," which was reprinted in *Impact*, he mentioned the value he gained by "copying a prose translation of Catullus by W. MacDaniel [*sic*]" (p. 57); but in the 1930s, he blamed the professor for being a part of a system that encouraged laziness and lack of originality:

143

Whether the nucleus of it is there in Prof. MacD's 'And besides, Mr Pound, we shd. have to do so much work ourselves to verify your results'?

Dated U. of Penn. 1906 when I suggested doing a thesis on some reading matter OUTSIDE the list of classic authors included in the curriculum, and despite the fact that Fellowships are given for research and that a thesis for Doctorate is supposed to contain original *research*.

(*Guide to Kulchur*, pp. 215-16)

The reading matter that Pound proposed and McDaniel rejected was doubtlessly a list of Renaissance authors whom Pound wrote about in "Raphaelite Latin," which was published in John Wanamaker's *Book News Monthly* in September of 1906, and M. Antonius Flaminius, whom he compared to John Keats in an essay published in the same place in February of 1908.

Clearly the key figure that year was Professor Rennert, who had written a well-received book on the life of Lope de Vega. With Rennert, Pound studied the following courses: Old Spanish, Spanish Drama, Spanish Literature, Old French, Provençal, Petrarch, and three-course-credit Special Work, the nature of which is unknown. We have an excellent portrait of Rennert from a note to *The Spirit of Romance*, where the professor is commenting on attempts by others to smooth out what appears to be the irregular rhythm of the Spanish epic *The Cid* into ten neat beats: "I can still see Dr. Rennert manicuring his fingernails in seminar, pausing in that operation, looking over his spectacles and in his plaintive falsetto, apropos someone who had attempted to reprint the *Cid* with ten syllables in *every* line: 'Naow effa man had sense enough to write a beautiful poem like this is, wudn't yeow think he wudda had sense enough to be able to keount ep to ten on his fingers ef he'da wanted tew!'" (p. 67).

Rennert also appears in *The Cantos* in three places. In Canto 28, he is conducting a class that is invaded by a tardy, disorganized girl:

> And old Rennert wd. sigh heavily
> And look over the top of his lenses and
> She wd. arrive after due interval with a pinwheel . . .
> She held that a sonnet was a sonnet

And ought never be destroyed,
And had taken a number of courses
And continued with hope of degrees and
Ended in a Baptist learnery
    Somewhere near the Rio Grande.
           (Canto 28, p. 135)

The other mentions of Rennert are brief. In Canto 20, he recommends that if Pound is interested in mastering the difficult language of a troubadour like Arnaut Daniel, he should take the trouble to go to Freiburg, Germany, to visit the renowned scholar and lexicographer Emil Lévy—a trip that Pound did indeed take, as the rest of the lines in the canto indicate. The other mention occurs in Canto 94, page 638: "We are the plant," said Hugo Rennert. The University of Pennsylvania was constantly admonishing its students and faculty to "take care of the plant." Finally, disgusted with the bureaucratic jargon and the crass disregard for the human, Rennert exclaimed one day in a way that would have appealed to Ovid: "But damn it, *we* are the plant." Pound liked the humanity of the remark.

It seemed for a time as if Rennert was going to replace Shepard and Ibbotson as the dominant mentor in Pound's career. The young man was already envisioning doctoral work in the Late Middle Ages and the Renaissance, with an emphasis on Lope de Vega and the Spanish theater, as well as on Latin treatises of the Italian Renaissance. When he distinguished himself in Rennert's classes and won a George Lieb Harrison Foundation Fellowship of $500 at the end of 1906, he selected Spain as the place where he would undertake the bulk of his summer research. However, affairs later took a turn for the worse and, as we shall see, Pound felt very ambivalent toward Rennert; then Italy replaced Spain as the center of Pound's interest once and for all.

On April 26, 1906, William Carlos Williams wrote to his brother Ed that Ezra was going away to Spain two days later "to study some old books there." Williams put Ezra's absence to good use by going to Bryn Mawr on May Day to watch Hilda, dressed like one of Robin Hood's merry foresters, cavort in the traditional spring rites (letter of May 6). A postcard from Pound to Viola Baxter indicates that Ezra sailed on the *König Albert* from New

York to Gibraltar, where he landed in early May. His memories of
The Rock in the *Pisan Cantos*, based on this trip and the later
voyage of 1908, indicate how parsimoniously he was trying to
live:

> Mr Joyce also preoccupied with Gibraltar
> > and the Pillars of Hercules
> > not with my *patio* and the wistaria and the tennis courts
> > or the bugs in Mrs. Jevons' hotel
> > > or the quality of the beer served to sailors
> > > > > (Canto 74, p. 448)

On both the visits of 1906 and 1908, Pound seems to have
come close to engaging in some shady financial deals that he
hinted at in a letter to Mary Moore. The agent of these doings was
a Jewish guide named Yusuf Benamore, who became a close friend.
Pound was apparently traveling under the assumed name of Mr.
Freer (which legend has it was a married name of Aunt Frank). In
Canto 22, Pound has Yusuf run up to him:

> And a voice behind me in the street.
> "Meestair Freer! Meestair. . ."
> And I thought I was three thousand
> Miles from the nearest connection;
> And he'd known me for three days, years before that,
> And he said, one day a week later: Would you lak
> To meet a wholley man, yais he is a veree wholley man.
> > > > (p. 103)

And so Yusuf conducted his friend to meet an Arab wise man who
did not seem to be wise or holy by any known definition. Pound
paints Gibraltar as a city of extremes: a sleazy fleshpot administered by the puritanical British. He quotes the reaction of a
typical American staying there:

> . . . And another day on the pier
> Was a fat fellah from Rhode Island, a-sayin':
> "Bi Hek! I been all thru Italy
> > An' ain't never been stuck!"
> "But this place is plumb full er scoundrels."
> > > > (p. 104)

Yusuf's cynical reply is:

> W'en yeou goa to some forain's country
> You moss be stuck; w'en they come 'ere I steek thaim.

Then Yusuf takes Pound to visit a synagogue. Since Pound has so often been accused of blanket anti-Semitism, this passage deserves special scrutiny. Written before the thirties, when anti-Semitism was an integral part of most right-wing politics in Europe, it shows a positive attitude toward the Jews. Pound stresses the sense of social camaraderie that he found in the temple. After the elders had taken some thumbfuls of snuff, they noticed the stranger in their midst:

> And then the rabbi looked at the stranger, and they
> All grinned half a yard wider, and the rabbi
> Whispered for about two minutes longer,
> An' the kid brought the box over to me,
> And I grinned and sniffed up my thumb-full.

(p. 105)

The actions then become more restrained:

> And then they got out the scrolls of the law
> And had their little procession
> And kissed the ends of the markers.

Pound succinctly sums up his attitude toward the experience much later in Canto 76:

> So that in the synagogue in Gibraltar
>   the sense of humour seemed to prevail
>   during the preliminary parts of the whatever
> but they respected at least the scrolls of the law
>   from it, by it, redemption . . .
> and there is no need for the Xtns to pretend that
>   they wrote Leviticus
>   chapter XIX in particular

(p. 454)

Two years later he told his mother in a letter written on January 11: "The only worship of god I can at the moment remember

147

having witnessed was in a little synagogue in Gibraltar & in San Pietro at Verona."

Pound went on to work at the Royal Library in Madrid, where he read widely in the works of Lope de Vega. There he met a young priest named Padre José Maria de Elizondo, whom he encountered after World War I in London. The priest was very helpful in getting a Cavalcanti manuscript for the young man, and Pound was extremely grateful to him. Although Pound was not especially fond of traditional Catholicism, he could see that Father Elizondo was a man who had some sense of the pagan roots behind the mass, and he also had an artistic sensibility:

> Padre José had understood something or other
> > before the deluxe car carried him over the precipice . . .
> learned what the Mass meant,
> > how one shd/ perform it
> the dancing at Corpus . . .

(Canto 77, p. 466)

Pound also thought that the Spaniard's analysis of the religious situation in Spain ("There's a lot of Catholicism here—and very little religion") and his forebodings about the future were all quite right:

> (Kings will, I think, disappear)
> That was Padre José Elizondo
> > in 1906 and in 1917
> or about 1917

(Canto 81, p. 517)

Pound seems to have stayed in a roominghouse in Madrid where the American painter John Singer Sargent once stayed, and where Sargent had painted Dolores Carmona, the sister of the proprietor:

> > and Dolores said: "Come pan, niño," eat bread, me lad
> Sargent had painted her
> > > before he descended
> (i.e. if he descended
> > > but in those days he did thumb sketches,

impressions of the Velázquez in the Museo del Prado
and books cost a peseta,
> brass candlesticks in proportion,
hot wind came from the marshes
> and death-chill from the mountains.

(p. 517)

As this passage indicates, Pound was fascinated by the paintings in the Prado Museum. He used to walk up and down in front of those by Velásquez, until he knew their order by heart. He recalled them from the distant past in this way in the *Pisan Cantos*:

and Las Meniñas hung in a room by themselves
and Philip horsed and not horsed and the dwarfs
> and Don Juan of Austria
Breda, the Virgin, Los Boracchos
> are they all now in the Prado?

(Canto 80, p. 493)

Pound apparently decided to leave Madrid when he witnessed an assassination attempt on the life of the young King Alfonso and his bride. At this point he visited Burgos, the home of The Cid, the Spanish hero whose epic he had studied so carefully with Rennert. On returning to Philadelphia, he would write an article called "Burgos: A Dream City of Old Castile" that would be published in the *Book News Monthly* issue of October, along with photographs of the sundial of The Cid, the Cathedral, and the coffin full of sand that The Cid pawned over to the Jews, who believed that it was filled with gold. These events figure in Canto 3:

My Cid rode up to Burgos,
Up to the studded gate between two towers,
Beat with his lance butt, and the child came out . . .
To the little gallery over the gate, between the towers . . .
And left his trunk with Raquel and Vidas,
That big box of sand, with the pawn-brokers,
To get pay for his menie . . . .

(Canto 3, pp. 11–12)

149

Reveling in his freedom from his parents' economic control—
a freedom that he would find difficult to repeat in the future—
Pound moved north through the mountains of southern France,
where he would walk many times in the future with his wife
Dorothy and Ford Madox Ford or T.S. Eliot:

> But to set here the roads of France,
> of Cahors, of Chalus,
> the inn low by the river's edge,
> the poplars; to set here the roads of France
> Aubeterre, the quarried stone beyond Poitiers . . .
>
> (Canto 76, p. 455)

Then, according to cards to Viola, it was on to Bordeaux, Blois,
Orleans, Paris, London, and 47th Street. We know from Letter
No. 15 to Mary Moore that he wrote "Capilupus to Grotos" in
1906 in Paris and the already cited "Scriptor Ignotus" (dedicated to
Kitty Heyman in London), and so the trip was a great succcess
creatively. Doubtlessly it confirmed his already strong feeling
that Europe was a place that was worth living in. Still, America
was his home, and he returned to face his second year of graduate
study with continuing high hopes.

TEN

A Troubled Winter, an Idyllic Summer: Aunt Frank and Mary Moore

By all rights, the fall of 1906 should have been a glorious time in Pound's career, and superficially it probably was. It is hard to judge because there are no letters from this period, since most of the people whom Pound was closest to were near him. "Doctor" Williams had just graduated, and was up in New York City interning at the French Hospital in the seamier quarters of the West Side, while Hilda Doolittle, who had dated him in Pound's absence, was now safely back in Ezra's tow, resting at home after her trying year at Bryn Mawr. There is no question of Pound's abiding love for Hilda—mixed with a pity for her inability to pull her life together. Although he continued to date her, he was also seeing other girls on the side—girls who might more conceivably make good housewives and mothers. His old girl friend Viola Baxter was moving to New York, and he would set Williams in her direction. Then, at the end of the oncoming academic year, he would meet the intriguing Mary Moore.

The change in Pound's second year from excellence to trouble is not hard to diagnose. During his first year, Pound had relied almost solely on Rennert for instruction and intellectual companionship. Now in this second year he continued by taking every course that he could with the man: the Sicilian Poets, Dante, the

Poem of Fernán González, Spanish Drama, the Chanson de Roland, and two more terms of Old Provençal. Pound did not take Rennert's classes in Portuguese, but they may have been included in his Special Work of the previous year. Finally, of course, Rennert ran out of courses, and Pound had to encounter less pleasant personalities. Even in the fall of 1906, he was forced to take French Phonetics with Rennert's new assistant, J. P. W. Crawford, and this resulted in a blank space in his record. Students were not assigned grades in courses in the Penn Graduate School. They had little tesseras in which the courses they took were listed, and the professors merely signed their names at the end of the year to signify that they had done a sufficient amount of work.

Pound's academic woes are apparent in his tessera's record for the spring. The following courses were entered under his name, and yet not a single one has a signature next to it:

COURSE	INSTRUCTOR	HOURS
Chaucer	Child	2
Drama	Schelling	2
Literary Criticism	Penniman	2
Current Criticism	Dept.	1
Contemporary Poetry	Weygandt	2

A student needed twenty-four course hours in order to graduate, and since Pound had amassed eleven hours in his first year and six in the fall term, he needed to pick up only seven hours to meet the requirement for a doctoral degree. However, two disasters occurred: he flunked Prof. Penniman's Literary Criticism, and he abandoned Dr. Schelling's Drama course (probably after telling him, as Hilda reported, that Shaw was equal to or better than Shakespeare). The other classes were also never finished.

The primary nemesis seems to have been Josiah Penniman, who not only taught Literary Criticism but was also the dean of the College faculty. To alienate this man, who later became the Provost of the University, was lethal. Yet Pound, who proudly saw his first literary essay appear that October in the *Book News Monthly*, was not about to take any nonsense from an academician who was not even publishing. Pound expressed his judgment of this type of teacher in "How To Read," written in 1929: "Those professors who regarded their 'subject' as a drill manual rose most rapidly to positions of executive responsibility (one case is now a provost). Those professors who had some natural aptitude for comprehending their authors and for communicating a general sense of comfort in the presence of literary masterwork remained obscurely in their less exalted positions" (*Literary Essays*, pp. 15–16). This entire essay can be seen as a diatribe against the Penn Graduate School. For example, Rennert is doubtlessly referred to in the following passage: "A professor of Romanics admitted that the *Chanson de Roland* was inferior to the *Odyssey*, but then the Middle Ages were expected to present themselves with apologies, and this was, if I remember rightly, an isolated exception. English novelists were not compared with the French." In short, Pound wanted to create a department of Comparative Literature, and was frustrated, just as today many schools tend to divide literary studies almost entirely along national lines. In an unpublished autobiographical essay of the 1930s, Pound said: "In 1907 I achieved the distinction of being the only student flunked in J.P.'s course in the history of literary criticism. So far as I know I was the only student who was making any attempt to understand the subject of literary criticism and the only student with any interest in the subject."

It is all too easy to make Penniman a whipping boy here. Dull as the man obviously was, he was doubtlessly pushed to his limit by his ambitious, aggressive charge. Even the mild-mannered Felix Schelling, who corresponded with Pound on and off into the 1930s, seems to have felt more comfortable when Ezra was addressing him from a distance. The same feeling obviously pertained to the rest of the professoriat. Cornelius Weygandt was a smooth, polished, wealthy man of the type that many Ivy League schools of the period liked to have around for decoration. Weygandt came into a lot of money, and yet, Pound complains twice in letters to Felix Schelling, he was too cheap to buy a copy of the poet's work and asked for a free one (*Selected Letters*, Nos. 113, 129). Still, Weygandt did offer a Contemporary Poetry course that touched on people like Lionel Johnson, a friend of Yeats and first cousin to Pound's future mother-in-law, Olivia

Shakespear. It was Weygandt who had arranged for Yeats to talk at Penn in 1903 when Pound was off at Hamilton. Weygandt spoke freely and often about the Irish poet in class, since Yeats had entertained him in Ireland in 1902, when the professor was putting together a book on contemporary poetry. Pound remembered Weygandt's course as one of those curiosities in which the reading material was far more beneficial than the teacher guiding it.

By far the person with the most ambiguous attitudes toward Pound was Schelling. When Pound wrote to the professor in 1916, suggesting that Penn establish a fellowship for gifted creative talents (not including himself), Schelling retorted, in effect, that the university did not exist for the exceptional man—which is quoted, among other places, in *Impact* (p. 264). Then in 1920 Homer Pound went to Dr. Schelling in an attempt to procure a doctoral degree for his son. Pound says about this, in the same passage:

> As a test I offered a few years ago my Cavalcanti *Rime* (not the essays reprinted in *Make It New*, but the paleographic edition) to an American university in lieu of thesis for doctorate: it was rejected. This caused me no surprise, but anyone interested in assessing the value of university degrees is invited to compare that volume with any batch of theses for Ph.D. that he fancies.

The meeting between Homer Pound and Dr. Schelling was cordial, and the professor promised to look into the situation. He even seems to have taken the trouble to speak about it with colleagues and to write to some outsiders for their opinions. Of course, the basic reason given for the refusal was bureaucratic: Pound had not collected enough class hours. Ezra was very skeptical in his letter of February 1, 1920, to his father: "Rennert (a poor thing without backbone) said in 1911 that he wd. accept Spirit of Romance . . . as substitute for Doctors Thesis" and "Rennert proposed me for Fellowship in 1911 or 12 but being a natural worm he backed down when someone objected that I wasn't going to be a professor." That "someone" was either Penniman or Schelling. The latter ended the matter once and for all by saying that, since the formal requirements had not been met, a degree could only be offered for Pound's "very clever verse," but Schelling (who was supposedly a critic of English verse] felt incompetent to judge that. And so ignoring Pound's criticism entirely—which already had a world-wide influence—they decided not to grant the degree—or even later to consider an honorary one.

It was no surprise, Hilda says, when the University told Pound in the spring of 1907 that his fellowship would not be renewed. Then came a second insult: he was not asked to stay on as an instructor. The university had firmly and unequivocally closed its door in his face. Of course they were all prepared to write glowing recommendations for him for jobs out in the hinterlands, but in their own bailiwick, affairs were different.

Pound's anger against Penn seethed for years, until he wrote a much-quoted letter to the Alumni Secretary from Rapallo on April 20, 1929:

> Any news that the grad. school or any other "arts" segment
> of the U. of P. had started to take an interest in civilization or
> " the advancement of knowledge" or any other matter of interest
> wd. be of interest. . . .
>
> In other words, what the HELL is the grad. school doing and
> what the HELL does it think it is there for and when the hell did
> it do anything but try to perpetuate the routine and stupidity
> that it was already perpetuating in 1873?
>
> P.S. All the U. of P. or your god damn college or any other god
> damn American college does or will do for a man of letters is to
> ask him to go away without breaking the silence.
>
> *(Selected Letters,* p. 225)

Meanwhile the winter of 1907 was also a bad one for Aunt Frank. We last mentioned that redoubtable lady in connection with the Euripides play of 1903 that drew both her and her beau, Dr. James Louis Beyea, down to Philadelphia. Pound mentions her often in letters from Hamilton, since he dropped down to New York occasionally on weekends and tended to use her boarding-house as a stopover place en route to Philadelphia. By 1904, "Uncle James," as Ezra called the man, moved into the end-house of "The Weston" at 28 East 47th Street, where Aunt Frank had been quietly but efficiently enlarging her operation. The Scottish gentleman, who hailed from Goshen, New York, ran his practice out of a handsome building called "The U.S. Senate'" just south of

Stuyvesant Square at 235 Second Avenue. Together, Aunt Frank and the doctor were rather affluent figures. Pound refers to this segment of her life as "her later and encrusted period" (*Indiscretions*, p. 28).

At some point in 1906 she decided to make Dr. Beyea husband number three. They were probably married by Dr. Parkhurst in his church (where the transplanted records are defective) rather than in Dr. Beyea's church, the University Place Presbyterian, where he was an elder. Shortly before this time, Robert Goelet, who owned the land under Aunt Frank's operation, gave her the jolt of her life by telling her that he was planning to tear down all of the houses on the eastern end of the block in order to erect an enormous luxury hotel that would be called the Ritz-Carlton—named for the famous hostelries of London and Cannes. The hotel started rising and in 1909, it was ready to open for business. In its heyday, it would become a mecca for café society until its sentimental closure in the early 1950s.

The news of the demolition must have had a devastating effect on Frances Weston, since twenty years of her life or more were bound up with that block. Her boardinghouse had a strong reputation in the South and was even known to people in Europe. Of course, she could simply settle back and take her financial gains over the years (which were by no means negligible) and play the role of a society wife of a famous doctor, but that was never Aunt Frank's style. She was too dynamic, too much a part of the center of things to allow herself to be shunted aside into a sedentary role in life.

And so, about 1905 she made a decision that would have an enormous effect on her own life and that of Ezra, who was still one of her potential heirs. Columbia University had been stalled in its "temporary campus" at 49th and Madison for about forty years after moving uptown from the Wall Street area. They owned the rose gardens across from St. Patrick's Cathedral that would some day become Rockefeller Center, but they still felt that they needed more room for the future. And so in 1897 they sold their land on 49th Street and then moved up to their present location on Morningside Heights, on the grounds of an old asylum. The buyer of the downtown property was the Berkeley School, a prep

POUND   RICHARDSON   DRISCOLL   TOLL

Ezra playing chess with other team members; taken from
The Hamiltonian of 1906, after Pound's graduation.
(*Courtesy of the Burke Library, Hamilton College*)

The old wing of the New Weston Hotel on the right, with the new wing on the left. (*Photo by Percy L. Sperr; courtesy of the U.S. History, Local History and Genealogy Division of the New York Public Library*)

school that could see the enormous profits to be reaped when a non-profit institution wheels and deals in big-city real estate, and very soon they sold out too, moving to the upper West Side to cheaper quarters off Central Park. Then a "société anonyme" known as the 49th Street and Madison Avenue Company purchased the site. They razed most of the hideous buildings (which had, for the most part, belonged to the New York Deaf and Dumb Institution before Columbia), parceled up the land, and threw up a rather handsome hotel that was described in this way in a brochure issued during the summer of 1906:

THE NEW WESTON

Madison Ave. and 49th St.

New York

THE NEW WESTON, a new modern fireproof apartment hotel, has just been completed and will open for the reception of guests on October 1st, 1906.

The Hotel is of twelve and one-half stories, and built on the site lately vacated by Columbia University.

It is centrally located, seven blocks from Grand Central Depot and 42nd Street Subway Express Station, two blocks from 50th Street Elevated Road, and the Madison Avenue Surface Cars pass the Hotel.

All the apartments have outside exposure and are flooded with sunlight. The single rooms are all outside and handsomely furnished. . . .

FRANCES A. BEYEA
Proprietor

Aunt Frank had really moved up in the world. As Pound entered his second disastrous year of graduate school, she entered her equally disastrous role as manager of a huge new hotel that was run by The New Weston Company, in which she was a major shareholder, along with the Doctor. From the first, things seem to have gone badly. Numerous mortgages were taken out on the property, indicating that Mrs. Beyea did not have the capital necessary to run such an ambitious outfit. In a world of boarding-houses, she could compete, but the world of luxury hotels is far more competitive, and numerous others had a jump on her. The brochure from which the information given above was taken has two lines crossing out words: one, the "American" of American plan, indicating that the idea of running a major hotel on a boardinghouse plan simply did not work; and then Aunt Frank's name itself. By 1908, in a letter to Isabel from Europe, Pound expresses the hope that Aunt Frank will come out of her problems "sunny side up"; another, written on February 11, 1909, says that he is glad that the poor lady is not selling matches in the street, and has enough money to go south and escape her problems for a time.

The sad outcome of the dream is recounted completely in *The New York Evening Mail* of June 10, 1909:

TO SELL HOTEL

The New Weston, a twelve-story hotel at the northeast corner of Madison avenue and Forty-ninth street . . . is to be sold in foreclosure early next month by Joseph P. Day. The action is brought by the Knickerbocker Trust Company against the Forty-ninth Street and Madison Avenue Company and others, to secure a just mortgage which with interest amounts to about $170,000. There are back taxes, etc., aggregating $21,000 on the property.

The hotel was leased in 1906 to The New Weston Company, which a couple of months ago went into the hands of a receiver.

The receiver was the Hotel Securities Corporation, which finally on February 24, 1911, sold "all furniture, fixtures and equipment now in the hotel" to one George L. Sanborn, according to the indenture records at the Register's Office of New York City. Sanborn ran it successfully until the 1960s, when the old hotel, with a new northern wing, was razed to create another undistinguished business tower. Aunt Frank and Dr. Beyea actually lived in the hotel by 1907, and for a time he even ran his practice out of there. But by late 1909, when the game was up, he was back at his old address on Second Avenue, and in Pound's visit of 1910, Ezra had trouble finding his aunt because she seemed to be living in semi-reclusion.

The effect of Aunt Frank's financial debacle on Pound's personal life cannot be underestimated. If the New Weston had worked out well, Pound could have inherited considerable money, since Frances was childless and had always adored him. Pound's bitterness toward the whole catastrophe comes through in a letter written to Louis Zukofsky on September 8, 1931, where he says that the New Weston was "the drain wot swallered all the fambly forchoons and left me bareassed on the pavement." In other words, Aunt Frank merely repeated the terrible errors made by dear old Uncle Ezra Weston with his artistic colony in Nyack, and it is doubtlessly Ezra Weston's voice which we hear in Pound's rhetoric, almost as if he were lamenting his wife's little tragedy. Had Pound become an heir to the New Weston holding, he would have been a very rich man, and his entire attitude toward society—the unequal distribution of wealth—might have softened. But this was not to be.

As for Aunt Frank herself, Ezra had no choice but to forgive her. She had done too much for him in other ways, and would, even in her worst period, sneak him a little money to help him get away on his cheap steamer after the Crawfordsville Incident. In Canto 84, written when she was long since dead, he still remembered that vivacious woman, and compared her to "Carson the Desert Rat," who lost a lot of money in mining:

> and my old great aunt did likewise
> with that too large hotel
> but at least she saw damn all Europe
>   and rode on that mule in Tangiers
>   and in general had a run for her money
>
> (p. 539)

It was at this nadir in the summer of 1907 that Ezra Pound met a girl whom he thought would be his true beloved. Her name was Mary Moore, and she happened to come from Trenton. If Hilda Doolittle was a Greek nymph out of some long-lost past, Mary was the girl from the next suburb whom one remembers from last summer. Photographs of her reveal a lively, vivacious young woman with a frank, pretty, open face, and with her hair piled up high on her head. She often wore bright, loose-fitting dresses that never seem to be quite as long as most girls' dresses were in this period. She clearly had a carefree, happy-go-lucky manner that contrasted with the moody introspectiveness of the Dryad.

Mary came from a "very good" family. Her father, Henry C. Moore, was vice-president of the company that ran the Trenton streetcars. Mary was no great intellect, but that did not seem to matter to the youthful Pound, although it might have mattered a great deal if they had gotten married. He met her at the little town of Scudders Falls, New Jersey, which is now on the northernmost city limit of Trenton, on the banks of the Delaware River. Pound was staying there at the country place of John Scudder, a not-too-bright young man whom he was tutoring in French, to help him gain his entrance into Williams College. (After several academic misadventures, Scudder would graduate from the Wharton School of Business and become a banker himself.) John broke up the tutorial session one afternoon and drove his buggy downtown into Trenton to pick Mary up at her lovely house at 136 West State Street, across the street from the New Jersey State House. Charles Norman, who became well acquainted with Mary, relates their encounter in his biography *Ezra Pound* (pages 21–23). When the buggy returned to the house, Ezra was lying out on the front porch on a hammock. As Mary bounced up the stairs, she caught sight of what she later called "a head of Lancaster County *stroobly*" (Pennsylvania Dutch for "uncombed, matted material"), and she said something like: "What have you got over there in the hammock—a mop?"

Instead of feeling insulted, Pound was challenged. He liked her brash, outspoken manner, which matched his own. The next time that John Scudder visited Mary's house, he took his tutor along. In no time, the tutor had beaten out his student in the competition over the girl. Mary and Ezra would go for long walks along the Delaware Canal, and sometimes they would go canoeing on the river. On at least one occasion, she tipped the boat over, but since the Delaware is relatively shallow, they had no trouble clambering back into the canoe, and Ezra used his hands to paddle them home.

They got to know the river very well during that idyllic summer of 1907. There was a big rock up by Washington Crossing

where they liked to picnic, and they explored the little islands
and coves down by Roebling. They sailed by "periplum"—a favorite Poundian word—by heart and mind, the way the Phoenician
sailors did, instead of by fixed charts or Father Doolittle's stars. It
was a paradisal world that lingered on for decades in Pound's
mind. Especially in the claustrophobic quarters at Pisa, in sight of
the mountains where the clouds hung low and heavy, he thought
back to those far happier days of his youth:

> The Pisan clouds are undoubtedly various
>   and splendid as any I have seen since
> at Scudder's Falls on the Schuylkill
>   by which stream I seem to recall a feller
> settin' in a rudimentary shack doin' nawthin'
>   not fishin', just watchin' the water,
>   a man of about forty-five
>   nothing counts save the quality of the affection
>   (Canto 87, p. 466)

Despite the confusion of the Delaware with the Schuylkill, which
runs past Penn, the image of the meditator in his natural setting is
calm and clear. It has the easy, relaxed quality of the Confucian
scenes painted in Canto 13:

> Kung walked
>   by the dynastic temple
>   and into the cedar grove,
>   and then out by the lower river . . .

Jobless and very uncertain about his future, Ezra Pound was
absolutely certain that he wanted to marry Miss Moore. When he
took the West Trenton train on its direct run to Wyncote, he
wrote her letters and sent her books, along with a photograph of
himself. He invited her to have lunch with him at Wanamaker's
Tea Rooms while she was en route to Richmond. She told Charles
Norman that she did get a chance to meet Mrs. Pound, and she
found that lady every bit as "pixyish" as her son.

Two years later, from the totally different world of London, he
would dedicate a small book of poems to her, the *Personae* of
1909:

THIS BOOK IS FOR
MARY MOORE
OF TRENTON, IF SHE
WANTS IT

The dedication would become almost as famous as the book itself. It was used again in the much-expanded *Personae* of 1926, which is Pound's most widely read book. There is something catching about the simple-sounding alliteration of "Mary Moore" brushing against the semi-aristocratic tag "of Trenton." When Mrs. Mary Moore Cross died in the 1970s, many of the headlines on the United Press releases that covered her death still used her maiden name, as if she had never acquired another identity. There was also something memorable about the terse and casual: "if she wants it." Decades of readers have pondered that question, and for a long time Mary pondered it too.

ELEVEN

THE CRAWFORDSVILLE INCIDENT

In the late spring of 1907, the new president of a struggling Presbyterian college in western Indiana wrote to the Fisk Employment Agency in Chicago to advertise a position at his school. He was Dr. George Lewes Mackintosh, a dour Scottish doctor of divinity who had just buried his first wife and was praying for a second. The position advertised was one of three that had just been created as Wabash College was trying to enlarge its curriculum in order to compete with nearby giants like Notre Dame, Purdue, and Indiana. Mackintosh and his trustees had decided to divide the Modern Language Department into two sections. One would continue German under the instruction of Dr. Robert King. The new unit would add Spanish to existing French courses, and required a new man. The position was that of a lowly instructor, but it was grandly billed as Chairman of the Department of Romance Languages—a department that would consist, in fact, of this single individual.

Ezra Pound heard about the job through the Penn Graduate School, and since other offers from places like Franklin and Marshall or Temple were not forthcoming, he wrote to Crawfordsville, the home of the school, assembled recommendations, and prepared himself for an interview in Philadelphia. The interview was a great success. Mackintosh hired Pound on the spot, and went back to Indiana thinking that he was collecting a great new faculty for the future. After all, Wabash's star seemed to be on the rise. Under its Indian football coach, the "Little Titans" were defeating powerhouses twice their size. As a result, the school was now being called in athletic quarters "The Yale of the West," while the town of Crawfordsville was proudly referring to itself as "The Athens of the West."

Pound was also enthusiastic at first. He wrote in August to his mother, who was away from Wyncote, that he had nailed down the job without even having his shoes shined (Paige Carbon 72). He bragged about being the head of a brand-new department, with great opportunities for the future, since he was eligible for a professorial appointment the following year. Of course the pay, to begin with, would be poor, but "Mac" had promised him that the future would indeed be bright.

In reviewing the brief but stormy confrontation between Wabash College and Ezra Pound—a confrontation that has become a *cause célèbre* in the annals of American poetics and education—it is hard to be objective. Most Wabash alumni are sensitive about the affair, seeing Pound's behavior as a gross exercise in bohemian exhibitionism that has made the college appear prudish and provincial. Pound's followers, on the other hand, have looked upon the college and the town as the sixth circle of desolation or hell, as Pound variously described it, without considering the fact that the college may well have had its own side in the case.

Concerning Pound, one has to admit that the rebellious young poet from Wyncote was not in any position to condescend to his new job, since no one else—especially his alma mater—wanted him. Then, too, Pound was no innocent; he knew precisely what he was getting into. Having spent two years in upstate New York, which he had already described as a cultural wasteland to many people, did he honestly think that the Athens of the West would live up to its noble name?

There was also clearly an error of judgment on Mackintosh's side. Since he interviewed Pound personally, he must have had some inkling about what he was getting into. Mackintosh had a local reputation for being humorlessly pragmatic. How could he possibly have believed that this long-legged, dramatic *poète* would be comfortable in a town that idolized the recently deceased author of *Ben Hur*, General Lew Wallace, as its most illustrious citizen? Did Mackintosh really believe that a young man who had already seen gay Paree on several occasions would be content to

President Mackintosh, who hired and fired Ezra Pound at Wabash College. (*Courtesy of the Lilly Library, Wabash College*)

The campus of Wabash College, viewed from South Grant Avenue, where Pound lived across the street. Ezra had his office in Center Hall, where the well-worn pathway leads. (*Courtesy of the Lilly Library, Wabash College*)

spend weekends in Indianapolis or Chicago? From the start, the error was twofold—and complete.

There is no doubt from the few letters that survive for that summer that Pound was already feeling qualms before he left. Not only did he hate to leave the cutural East, but he very much wanted to stay with Mary Moore, whom he was beginning more and more to see as the future Mrs. Pound. Mary Moore plays a vital role in all that happened. She kept writing him teasy, flirtatious letters that always seemed to be promising something— from a long visit to marriage. Finally she exploded a bombshell: she told the poet that she was in love with another man, who had the improbable but poetically justifiable name of Oscar Macpherson. This wounded Ezra to the core, and made his isolation in Indiana even more unbearable than it might otherwise have been.

Everyone around Pound tried to pretend that the new job was a godsend. His neighbors in Wyncote, the Whitesides, threw a little farewell party on September 11, and both Mary and Hilda Doolittle (who was still waiting in the wings) were invited. Hilda also exchanged letters with Pound, but unfortunately her choleric father destroyed them after the debacle. As a result, to reconstruct the affair, we have only local information, Pound's letters to Mary (housed at Penn), and a few letters to Lewis Burtron Hessler, who had gone from Penn to teach rhetoric at the University of Michigan, and to Viola Baxter. It is doubtful that any of these four people might have received "the whole truth" from Pound concerning the Crawfordsville Incident, since the three young women were all potential brides and the young man was a rival. Fortunately, a Wabash student of the 1950s named James Rader set about the task of compiling a cache of testimony about the Pound affair from every conceivable source, and his interviews with alumni and townspeople provide much of the information that follows.

Pound went to Crawfordsville in a way that suggests that he was trying to avoid it. Instead of taking the direct overland route via the Pennsylvania Railroad to Indianapolis, he was drawn to the New York Central Line (thinking back to his Hamilton days) and so found himself passing through Buffalo, Cleveland, Galion,

Anderson, and finally the desired destination. He wrote letters to Mary Moore en route, complaining about the cornfields and gossiping about the fellow travelers. Letter No. 9 contains a self-drawn caricature, with the young scholar weighted down by a heavy coat and two heavily laden suitcases. His trunk with his numerous books would follow.

Upon arriving in the town, Pound bedded down in the prime hostelry, The Crawford House. He wrote Mary a letter (No. 10) on its stationery, saying that he was looking for a room, since he could not afford the lavish hotel quarters; but he would return to the hotel often, since its Dining Room offered the best culinary fare in town. Curiously enough, Crawfordsville in 1907 was much more lively than it is today. Aside from its splendid rail connections with Chicago and Indianapolis, there were several hotels in the downtown area, as well as numerous theaters, saloons, and restaurants.

When he arrived, Pound told his parents that the town struck him as rather "southish" in atmosphere (Paige Carbon 78), and it is easy to see why. Crawfordsville has numerous long, tree-lined streets flanked by many stately homes. The rhythm of the town is as slow moving as the Sugar "Crick" that wends its way on the northern edge of the city, meandering toward its inevitable union with the Wabash. The college at the end of the century looked like a bit of New England dropped into the midst of the American heartland. It has changed greatly over the years, casting off its earlier rugged, stone appearance for a rather slick Edwardian brick cast. The Lilly Company of chemistry fame has built the school a shiny new library to replace the inadequate one of Pound's day. The poet complained bitterly about the lack of books for his fledgling department, and spent most of his time studying in the Carnegie Reading Room—a charming Greco-Roman structure that still serves as the local library.

Pound's office was located in Center Hall, in the South Wing near the President. This proximity very soon proved to be dangerous, since Pound liked to smoke his Bonhommes Rouges, and smoking was expressly forbidden both by the college and the State of Indiana (the "Red Gentlemen" were sent to him from the East by Mary, Hilda, and his parents). Mackintosh is known to have

Crawfordsville's main street in 1907, with the Old Post Office on the near right and The Crawford House with its porch extending over the sidewalk. The Music Hall Theater was around the corner on the first transverse street to the left. The streetcar tracks are those of a local traction company that ran hourly cars to Indianapolis during most of the day.

(Courtesy of the Lilly Library, Wabash College)

PROF. EZRA POUNDS
Romance Languages

Ezra Pounds, professor of romance languages, graduated from Hamilton College in 1905 and took his Master's degree at Pennsylvania University the following year. He took a fellowship in romance languages which enabled him to study abroad. He spent most of his time in Paris and Madrid, studying French and Spanish literature. While abroad he wrote his thesis on the "Graciso" and the plays of "Lope de Vega" which is soon to be published. He then had a second year of graduate work at Pennsylvania University, after which he spent some time in individual research work and tutoring. Professor Pounds is the author of several articles dealing with different phases of his work, and is a contributor to the Book Lovers Magazine.

What is the matter with the press club?

Watch the faculty end men for stunts!

Ezra Pounds—Ezra should have been a blacksmith.

Prof. Alva H. Ford, assistant professor in mathematics, is a son of Old Wabash, graduating in 1906. He is also a graduate of State Normal School. He has had seven years' experience teaching and was principal of the New Market schools for the last two years. He intends to make a specialty of mathematics and will enter an eastern university.

PROF. ALVA FORD
Assistant Mathematics

The vita of the new chairman of the Romance Languages Department as it appeared in the October 1907 issue of *The Wabash,* with some elusive comments about "end men" and "blacksmiths." (*Courtesy of the Lilly Library, Wabash College*)

caught the young instructor at least one time in the act of puffing, and to have threatened dire action if the crime was ever repeated. And so, from the start, there were frictions and warnings.

The school year started almost as soon as Pound arrived. Wabash was on a trimester system, with registration for the fall term on Monday, September 16. The next day classes began. *The Crawfordsville Journal*, which kept an eagle's eye on the school, ran a regular column entitled "College News," and there they said for that day: "The three new professors, William B. Duff, Joseph Rolleheaven [Rodeheaver], and Ezra Pounds [*sic*], were on hand in chapel this morning . . . the latter will teach the romance languages." This misspelling of Pound's name would establish a precedent. It was picked up in the college publication called *The Wabash* in its opening issue that year in October. There one sees a photograph of Professor Pounds in profile, looking stiff and determined, and below this there is a brief history. One is not sure at this point if the misspelling is intentional or not; after Pound had left, however, one is sure of intended malice. That same issue of *The Wabash* contains some puzzling statements, which Pound himself interpreted as digs:

> Watch the faculty end men for stunts!
> Ezra Pounds—Ezra should have been a blacksmith.

"End men" were the comedians in blackface shows who sat on the side chairs. The reference here seems to have been to the compulsory chapel services, where newer members of the faculty sat on the ends. Was Pound clowning around in his first appearances? The blacksmith remark seems to have been aimed at making fun of Pound's wiry frame, which was clearly not the mesomorphic type that one finds in a smith.

Pound taught three different classes at Wabash: an elementary Spanish class (with thirty boys) and two beginning French sections (one with fifty-seven, and one with fifteen). All of his courses were conducted in the morning, so he had his afternoons free, as well as his weekends. He told Mary in Letter 13 that the schedule was delightful; he was able to read and write poetry, and when she made her pilgrimage out to the Midwest, he would have plenty of time to play with her. In this letter, he addressed her as

"Grey Eyes," but elsewhere he employed the rabbit image, and often he dreamed up names like "Maridhu," just as he had done with H.D. Frequently he signed his letters with a light, filmy design that was meant to suggest a dragonfly. More secret troubadour signs.

On September 24, *The Crawfordsville Journal* reported an event that had ominous overtones: "Dr. Mackintosh gave the students a heart to heart talk this morning at the close of the chapel exercises. He emphasized the absolute necessity of all the students living up to the college rule in regard to drinking and other forms of immorality." It was well known that many of the fraternities permitted drinking in their houses, and some of the students imbibed in the back rooms of the downtown saloons. Property owners along Grant Avenue on one edge of the campus complained about the noise at night as various "Greeks" came back from the Goose Nibble section down by the river, where the less privileged girls of the community were known to entertain the more privileged college boys. This is the proper time for stressing the importance of chapel attendance. Students who cut frequently could be expelled from the school. If faculty members missed chapel, it was assumed that they were sick, and frequently the newspaper, which monitored every type of event, would comment on this. When President Mackintosh left town on business, his replacement as chapel leader was dutifully noted. Pound's absences in the future would not escape notice.

The national news that fall was largely about the Rockefellers, and the football team dominated local news. On September 18, *The Journal* said: JOHN D. ROCKEFELLER / SLIPS OUT OF CLEVELAND / TO NEW YORK CITY. On the 20th: FOR FIRST TIME ROCKEFELLER'S / INTEREST IN THE STANDARD / MADE KNOWN / Owns One-Fourth of Stock. Pound would later stress the inequity of a society in which people close their eyes toward shady financial dealings but keep them fixed on others' personal lives. Meanwhile, the Little Titans opened their season with a smashing victory over Rose Polytechnic Institute 27–0, and followed with a resounding win over Earlham, 25–0. On October 12, they defeated Purdue up at Lafayette by a safety, 2–0, and everyone was waiting for the big game with the mighty

Henry Zwingli McLain, the beloved bachelor professor of Greek
who lived in the Halls' room later occupied by Pound.
(Courtesy of the Lilly Library, Wabash College)

The house of the Hall sisters, with the arrow pointing to the second-floor quarters occupied by Professor Pound. (*Courtesy of the Lilly Library, Wabash College*)

University of Michigan at Washington Park in Indianapolis on October 19.

On that day, most of Crawfordsville went to Indianapolis for the game—including the President and Pound. The *Wabash College Record* described the outcome as follows: "Although outweighed thirty-one pounds to the man, we held the score down to 22 to 0, and it took Michigan more than thirty minutes to score the first point." The loss was accepted with good humor: "Cheers for the visitors are given with a spirit." Pound described his visit to Indianapolis in a letter to his mother (Paige Carbon 81), saying how pleasant it was to taste a bit of culture in the larger city. If one wonders why Pound did not go there more often (or to Chicago), the answer has to be his measly salary, and the fact that teachers were paid only three times a year, at the beginnings of the trimesters.

Soon after arriving, Pound moved into his first private residence, a peculiar structure that was located off Milligan Terrace at 500 Meadow Avenue. He described this new place to Mary Moore (Letter 11) as having Gothic windows and being set in the most wooded part of the town. The house was originally built in the middle of the nineteenth century by the Abbott family from a design executed by a man who was languishing in prison. Its sloping A-frame roofs and elaborate Gothic windows mark it as the product of a man who was allowing his fantasy to run wild, since he himself could not do so. The property was then bought by a wealthy gentleman named Joseph Milligan, who had married a girl named Harriet Fullenwider. She was the sister of Chalmers E. Fullenwider, a real estate man who had an office opposite the Crawford House. Chalmers advertised rooms for rent, and Pound obviously went to him when he wanted to find private quarters. Chalmers, who was living in the place himself, spoke with his sister, who at first was reluctant to let the young instructor in. Eventually, however, she was persuaded to allow Pound to have the north wing with its private entrance on Meadow Avenue. In Paige Carbon 79, Pound told his mother how thrilled he was to have his own entrance, which was located just three minutes from his office, and free access to all the milk and cream and fruit that he wanted, as well as the use of the large parlor room for entertaining when the Fullenwiders were not using it. But complications soon set it.

Trouble started when Chalmers' wife, the former Fannie Shipman from Kentucky, was visited by her sister, Mary Moore Shipman Young. This second Mary Moore (and Pound played up the coincidence in his letters back to Trenton) had been widowed when still young, and had come to Crawfordsville to be near her sister while she worked as a nurse. She was a lovely southern girl who quickly befriended young Pound, who proceeded to fall in love with her. Then a further complication arose. Old President Mackintosh met the young "widder," as Pound later called her, and fell in love with her himself. This was scarcely a safe triangle for the young instructor to become involved in. When Pound left, he of course dissolved the triangle; but as he crowed in a 1959 letter to James Rader, Old Mac never got the pretty widder after all.

Mary's presence in the house led Pound to ask for more frequent use of the parlor and music room to entertain her—and this caused the wood-burning furnace to have to be heated for much longer periods; and so the troubles compounded. Pound did not have access to the kitchen, and the bathroom setup was also not ideal. The young instructor really began to make himself unwelcome when he started to entertain students in his room until the wee hours of the morning. Very soon, the Fullenwiders requested his departure. And although he maintained his friendship with Mary Moore Young, Pound bade the little gingerbread house adieu forever. Already on October 14 (one of the few dated letters), he wrote his parents that he had to find a new place with a bath, gas, and furnace heat, and on October 20, just after the Michigan game, he said that he had found it.

This second place was almost assuredly one located on South Washington Street near the Big Four Railroad Depot. It was recalled by a number of Wabash alumni, some of whom remembered the Spartan furnishings with affection. But like the previous place, there was a problem with heating and a private bathroom. It seems highly likely that this is the place where Pound met a certain stranded vaudeville girl who was living across the hall

Close-up of Professor Pound(s).

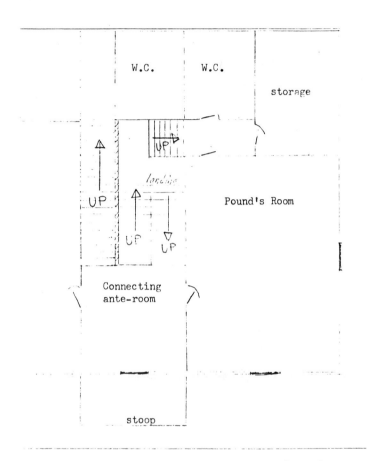

The interior design of 412 South Grant Avenue, as drawn by a
student who lived there in the 1950s when the house was
demolished. (*Courtesy of Thomas Dewey*)

from him and to whom he very kindly dispensed food and coffee. This story—which we might call the "Food-Sharing With a Roomer" tale—accompanies, and is sometimes confused with, the more famous "Orphan in a Snowstorm" tale that led to Pound's dismissal.

Tale A, as we shall call it, was described carefully by Pound in a letter to Hessler that has been quoted extensively:

> Two stewdents found me sharing my meagre repast with the lady-gent impersonator in my privut apartments.
>
> keep it dark and find me a soft immoral place to light in when the she-faculty-wives git hold of that jewcy morsel. Don't write home to me folks. I can prove an alibi from 8 to 12 p.m. and am at present looking for rooms with a minister or some well established member of the facultate. For to this house come all the traveling show folk and I must hie me to a nunnery ere I disrupt the college. Already one delegation of about-to-flunks have awaited on the president to complain erbout me orful langwidge and the number of cigarillos I consume.

This letter has an accompanying envelope with a postmark of November 11, and so the chronology forms very clearly. It is only at this address that the actress could have been living in the same house with Pound. In Tale B, the girl is encountered suddenly in the street—and it is conceivable that the same girl could have been involved. It is perhaps worth mentioning that, in reviewing the whole situation with Rader in the 1950s, Pound clung to his innocence and the details cited in Tale A, even though he also disseminated the alternate version. He indicated to Dr. Kavka that he had had "an affair with a former actress."

In Letter 17 to Mary Moore, he also speaks of a lady male impersonator who is stalled in Crawfordsville because she has no money. Pound says that she is British, and cannot make her subtle act with monocle and tuxedo appeal to the Hoosier masses. Then in Letter 37 (the order being totally suspect), he says that Mary Young has admonished him about giving coffee and salads to the variety performer who is living across the hall. Again, two students are the villains, catching the good Samaritan during one of the feedings in his room (sometimes this event is put rather early in the morning). Mary Young suggests that he get married as soon as possible to re-establish his respectability (a strong hint to the Trenton Mary), and in any case an immediate move was called for.

And so Pound moved again—this time to a place that would put him away from traveling acts and into an atmosphere of warmth and comfort. The winter was now coming on, and it would be a bitter one. In Paige Carbon 84, the poet writes home that he is thinking about taking a bungalow with the young instructor Carey Stevens, and in Carbon 86 he writes that he is going to move again on Monday. He suddenly abandons his plan of sharing a place with Stevens and moves instead into the fateful house at 412 South Grant Avenue, across from the campus.

The house on Grant Avenue belonged to a pair of spinster sisters, the Misses Ida and Belle Hall, who let out rooms to bachelor professors. When Pound moved in on the upper floor of the south side of the duplex, Instructor Rodeheaver was already living there below him. The Hall girls lived in the north part of the house. They were tall, prim, talkative ladies who liked to sit on their front stoop and watch the world go by. They wore cameos attached to black silk ribbons, and maintained strong ties with Dear Old Wabash and its preacher-president. In some ways, it seems as if the Hall sisters were members of the Board of Trustees. Certainly they affected college policy in a way that would seem scandalous today. They were also active in the town's social life. On September 20, 1907, *The Journal* reported one sister's movement as follows: "Miss Ida Hall returns this afternoon from Jacksonville, Ill., where she has been the guest of friends for a week."

The Hall sisters were also staunch members of the Center Presbyterian Church, where the previous occupant of Pound's quarters, Professor Henry Zwingli McLain, had been stricken with a fatal hemorrhage in his pew in January of that year. For several months, his room had lain empty, almost as a memorial. Professor McLain had been a cherished member of the Wabash faculty. As a teacher of Greek, he had lived the life of a confirmed bachelor, devoted to some lost ideal of Hellenic beauty. With Kantian precision, McLain almost wore a path out between his room with the Halls and his office in Center Hall across the street. He was a perfect third in that house where the lives were lived utterly without reproach—or love. When Pound moved in, the Hall Sisters undoubtedly imagined that the young boarder would be rather like "dear Zwingli." They had obviously not heard the gossip that was already accruing around this "peculiar" young teacher from back East.

Facing a year that was a far cry from Uncle Ezra's Manhattan or the suburbs of Philadelphia or the Venice of his dreams, Pound did three things: he wrote poetry (which has mercifully endured), made what friends he could among the faculty, and sought out acquaintances in the town. Let us consider the poetry first, since Pound's departure from Crawfordsville would occur in February of 1908 and his first book of poems would appear only four months later. Therefore, whatever cannot be dated earlier was most probably written during this four-month span.

Pound mentions several poems in his letters to Mary Moore, and some of them are spoken of as earlier creations, such as two Villonauds or poems written in honor of the Old French poet François Villon:

> Drink ye a skoal for the gallows tree!
> François and Margot and thee and me,
> Drink we the comrades merrily
> That said us, "Till then" for the gallows tree!
>
> (*A Lume Spento*, p. 26)

Letter 20 mentions "A Rouse," which is a highly pagan invitation to join a fertility rite in southern France, with the April Queen of Provençal popular song:

> Follow! Follow!
> Breath of mirth,
> My bed, my bower green of earth,
> Naught else hath any worth.
> Save ye, "jolif bachillier"!
> Hell take the hin'most!
>
> (p. 77)

Letter 27 mentions a poem called "Baltasare" that is not in *A Lume Spento*, as well as the poem, already cited, for Kitty Heyman: "Scriptor Ignotus." It is believed that he wrote "Cino" at this time, which expresses a desire to break loose from puritanical con-

173

formity and to live the free and creative wandering life of an Italian troubadour:

> Bah! I have sung women in three cities,
> But it is all the same;
> And I will sing of the sun.

(p. 17)

The Collected Early Poems of Ezra Pound contains two poems with notations that they were written in Crawfordsville. One, "Ballad of the Sun's Hunting," is a vigorous pagan piece with strong pantheistic overtones:

> My soul hath caught the sun out-riding
>   By creations' t'other side.
> The sun hath kissed her lips out-right
>   And hath my soul to bride.

(p. 264)

The other is a very long poem titled "Quia Amore Langueo" (Because I Languish With Love; from the Song of Songs):

> Tho I steal sweet words from long ago,
> Tho I sing in the sun and the rain,
> I bid thee come where the west winds blow
>   Quia Amore langueo
> And forget the world and the old world pain
>   Quia Amore langueo.

(p. 265)

The poem's mention of pain is doubtlessly pointed. The important thing to note is that during these difficult months, Pound affirmed his faith in what he loved by continuing to write . . . "the quality of the affection that has carved the trace in the mind." That is all that would ultimately matter.

As for the faculty, they at first seemed quite affable and pleasant. Professor King, the German instructor, drove Pound around to help him find a room and also had him to dinner. "Danny" Hains, the Greek instructor, held a tea for the faculty at the beginning of the year and impressed Pound as being not only quite decent but even a kindred soul (Paige 76, 77; Moore 13). According to the Rader correspondents, Hains was one of the few who defended Pound during his crisis, and when the young instructor was asked to leave, Hains took over those courses which were not canceled.

There was also a mild-mannered math professor from Tennessee named Cragwall who was likable, as well as Prof. Milford of the English Department and his young assistant Carey Stevens, who has already been mentioned. Stevens had just received his B.A. the year before and had worked in advertising in New York during that summer, but was called back to help Milford grade the composition papers for the entire school. According to a letter written by Pound on March 27, 1959, to Rader, when Stevens heard that Pound had been fired, he exclaimed, in effect: "Jesus! I wish I'd been fired too!" Stevens left Wabash shortly after that, going on to a very successful career in advertising in Chicago, and seldom if ever returning to his alma mater.

Three others would leave Wabash shortly after Pound did. Instructor Rodeheaver would take his psychology knowledge elsewhere, and Rollo Walter Brown, Professor of Rhetoric, would move upstairs to Harvard. Perhaps the strangest refugee was the successful football coach, Francis M. Cayou, who went off to try his luck in a bigger school out west, failed, and spent the last years of his life largely in Indian garb, speaking his native Omaha dialect and refusing to talk about his Wabash years. It was this man—not Ezra Pound—who later haunted the college. Looking over the roster years later, there would not be the material for a happy reunion.

If some of the faculty members were passable, their wives tended to be unmitigated disasters. As Pound wrote to Hessler, he yearned for the effete east, with its decadent culture and kissable girls. Yet there is reason to believe that Pound was not without female companionship. For one thing, he saw a lot of Mary Young, who introduced him to a friend of hers named Cassandra Rowland, a lovely, golden-haired woman from the South. Cassandra was married to Sam Rowland, an official of the local Water & Gas Co. Sam had been born in Philadelphia and had attended college in Pennsylvania; he and Cassandra had married in Germantown, and so enjoyed a Philadelphia connection with Pound. Ezra was a frequent visitor to the Rowland house, according to the testimony

175

of Cassandra's sister, Viola Baylis (later Wildman). Viola herself dated Pound often, and when the "Snowstorm" episode occurred, she staunchly defended her suitor. As she told James Rader years later:

> Finally the tragedy of giving his decency to an "Orphan in the Storm" (his expression). This was his Swan Song at Wabash. Ezra Pound was stunned, bewildered, when he came to tell me his side of the story. Out of a snowstorm he brought a stranded chorus girl to his room, heated water for tea over his gas-light flame, "to bring warmth to her frozen body," gave her his bed, where she slept "safe as in her mother's arms," while he lay, fully clothed on the floor, wrapped in his topcoat. Thus his landlady found them. He was amazed at the narrow-mindedness of the Wabash College officials and their action against him. Again he had given too much, not wisely nor well! He lost his professorship and was branded a Libertine. He was lost to Crawfordsville—the world swallowed him—for me, a few letters and then silence. My saga is almost ended—today, 50 years later, he will have completely forgotten me.

Despite the melodrama, her loyalty is the same that could be found in Hilda Doolittle, Mary Young, and Mary Moore. In short, the people who knew Pound best tended to believe him.

An important friend in the town was a young painter named Fred Vance, who lived at 309 South Plum St. with his parents. Fred had studied art in Chicago, and had then gone off to paint in Paris and Rome. In one of his letters to Rader from Rapallo, Pound recalled that Fred had been a student of the painter Puvis de Chavannes. He told Rader that he wrote some lines about Fred and his father, George, in his Ur-Cantos, but could not work them into the finished product. The lines dealing with the Vances occur in the rejected Canto 2:

> I knew a man, but where 'twas no matter;
> Born on a farm, he hankered after painting;
> His father kept him at work;
> No luck—he married and got four sons;
> Three died, the fourth he sent to Paris—
> Ten years of Julian's and the ateliers,

Ten years of life, his pictures in the salons,
Name coming in the press.
                              And when I knew him,
Back once again, in middle Indiana,
Acting as usher in the theatre,
Painting the local drug-shop and soda bars,
The local doctor's fancy for the mantel-piece;
Sheep—jabbing the wool upon their flea-bit backs—
The local doctor's ewe-ish pastoral;
Adoring Puvis, giving his family back
What they had spent for him, talking Italian cities,
Local excellence at Perugia,
                              dreaming his renaissance . . .

The local paper had indeed announced in September that Fred Vance was back home in Indiana. It seemed that he might have a big job pending in New York, but it did not materialize. Fred was working as a painter with his father, George, who also doubled as an employee at Lacey's Book Store. The two eventually got jobs to decorate the local Elks Club, across the street from the library, and later won major contracts to do murals for a theater in New Orleans and the U.S. Grant Hotel in San Diego. Although Pound thought that Vance had made an Icarus-like escape to California, he died in his cottage near Crawfordsville in 1926, from acute indigestion.

Pound was very close to the two Vances, and included them in the many soirees he held in his various rooms during the fall term. These were sardonically described by an alumnus named Fred H. Rhodes (with the elder Vance probably mistaken for an undertaker):

> Almost immediately upon his arrival, Ezra gathered around himself a small group of advanced thinkers in the arts. The nucleus of this group was, of course, Pound himself, but associated with him were a local artist and a local undertaker. . . .
>
> Professor Pound was wont to hold, in his rooms, soirees to which a very few privileged disciples were invited . . . I attended one of these soirees. After the preliminary formalities, Pound seated himself on a chair, while his disciples and satellites dis-

posed themselves gracefully, but somewhat uncomfortably, cross-legged on the floor, at the feet of the master. The leader then began a spirited but disconnected discourse on many topics, leaping from subject to subject with the agility of a mountain goat. His dissertation was, at appropriate intervals, broken (but not interrupted) by sage interjections of agreement from the artist and by the hearty applause of the undertaker. The subordinate satellites listened with rapt attention and numbing legs. I do not now remember the message of the master, although I seem to recall that he was disdainfully critical of the current trends in social and political life, in economics, in art, in education, and in other fields in which he was equally an authority. . . . Enlightened and inspired, we went home.

Despite this acid account, it is known that Pound devoted a great deal of his time to his students—and that may have irritated the faculty as much as anything else. He himself confessed to Mary Moore that he was sometimes indiscreet in the remarks he made in class. He told his charges that one of the major purposes of religion was to popularize art (Letter 37), and he asked the athletes to please shower before attending class. Some alumni reported that he lectured occasionally with his back turned to the students, while he gazed contemplatively out the window. And there were all sorts of varying comments about his outrageous dress, which allegedly included large, floppy hats and capes and canes; although, conversely, there were several former students who said that his dress was not in any way unusual.

Lest we think that Pound was a total failure, there were numerous comments to the contrary. Possibly the most eloquent came from a man named Robert Winter, who went on to teach Romance languages for several years at Northwestern, and then moved to Beijing University in China, where he was still living in 1984 in his nineties. Following is an excerpt from a letter that he wrote to a young Oriental student named Rujie Wang, who later studied himself at Wabash:

Ezra Pound . . . had been given a room in a little boardinghouse where they usually put teachers who had no family. Crawfordsville was then a little uncivilized village. Some wild puritan from the college went to see Pound and found one of the local women teachers in his room asking him some questions about phonetics. He immediately rushed back to Wabash headquarters and ordered them to write an official letter to Pound demanding that he leave town by the next train!!! A few hours later I happened to go to see Pound and he showed me the letter and then picked up a volume of Browning's poems and read to me the poem with the title (I think) *Seen by a Contemporary*, which begins "I only knew one poet in my life" and goes on to say how a man had watched "a man in the streets of Voladolid" who walked up and down observing and taking notes about everything and who was, of course, a poet, but who was thought to be a spy! Then Pound said goodbye, left Crawfordsville and went to Italy. We wrote to each other for about a year. In one of his letters he said that I was the most civilised person in Crawfordsville. Then he met T.S. Eliot and stimulated him to be a good poet. I fled from the USA. I kept Pound's letters as my most precious possession. By that last evening with Pound I had suddenly been *awakened*!!! Without Pound, I probably would now be an idiot crawling about in Crawfordsville. As it is, I am a belligerent atheist in China!

It is now time to reconstruct the last chapter of the "incident," whatever it was. No explanation is, or probably ever will be, absolutely accepted by everyone. A great deal depends on what one thinks about Pound. If it has any value at all, one must remember that Pound, to the very end, proclaimed his innocence, even when the matter was long a dead issue. He said in a letter to Ingrid Davies on April 4, 1955, that it was not until he got to England, when men were scarce in the war, that he passed beyond the innocent caresses of the early 1900s.

The fall term came to a close on December 20, and, with twenty-six hours of railroad track lying between him and home (so he calculated), Pound decided not to make the holiday trip. He had already spent Thanksgiving more or less alone, frying oysters on a chafing dish that he used to entertain guests with—a utensil that was earning some notoriety, as we shall see. Two days before Christmas he wrote a lonesome-sounding letter to Mary Moore, and Viola Baylis said that he paid her a Christmas visit, bringing her chocolate-covered cherries, one of his favorite sweets. He also spent some time with the Vances.

The New Year of 1908 dawned with the State of Alabama going dry and the sensational Stanford White murder trial opening in New York City. The weather of the New Year was first relatively mild, but soon turned very bitter. From the tenth of January on into mid-February, there were numerous snowstorms and blizzards. But for those who could make it out at night, the local theaters were offering a wide variety of bills, and many lovely ladies graced the boards, despite the brutal chill:

Monday, Jan. 6: MAJESTIC THEATER: Alice B. Hamilton, Character Singing Comedienne

Thursday, Jan. 9: MAJESTIC THEATER: Annette Link, Soubrette

Monday, Jan. 13: MAJESTIC THEATER: Maudie Minerva, Novelty Act

Tuesday, Jan. 14: GRAND THEATER: Burk & Erline, Automobile Girls

Thursday, Jan. 16: MAJESTIC THEATER: Emmett & McNeill, Singing and Dancing Sisters

Saturday, Jan. 18: MUSIC HALL (the main theater) Latimore-Leigh Stock Co. High Class Vaudeville / No Smoking

The second trimester began on January 7, and Pound was there to greet his charges. But very soon something strange seems to have happened. *The Wabash,* in its monthly edition of February, mischievously hinted at some mysterious event by inserting a series of one-line tags among its chronicle of events:

Ezra was not at chapel on Jan. 13.
Ezra was not at chapel on Jan. 14.
Ezra was not at chapel on Jan. 15.
Ezra was not at chapel on Jan. 16.
Ezra was not at chapel on Jan. 17.

Any reader would automatically assume that the great misadventure happened here, but *The Crawfordsville Journal* informs us that the actual denouement occurred a good month later. The

Ezra was not at chapel on Jan. 13.

After "Three Weeks" we promise to get back to studying.

Eller has promised to get a new shot when he hears from Michigan.

One senior says, "The moon has it on us. He can get full on a quarter."

One senior was heard to lament that he didn't have pink cheeks like Cochran's.

"Blondie" Patton has a new dog and now both the master and the dog are called "Pat."

Prof. Gibson sometimes when excited talks rather emphatically, all unconsciously however.

Muncie translates in German A, "unter den wilden Buben" as "among the wild bubbies."

Have you noticed Jerome Schultz's new vest? A little gray, some white, enough silk edging to be very neat.

Ulrich asked Dr. Mackintosh about changing from ethics to logic, and the answer was, "Yes, Mr. Ulrich, I'll be glad to get rid of you."

We don't remember seeing any account of the junior-senior foot ball game in the last number of THE WABASH.

Advice for Mills, '10, (if you don't know him, he is the large, fat freshman.) "Unbutton your coat and wipe your chin."

"Bud" Herron is glad that the Glee Club is going to Muncie. When there with the militia he met some old friends as well as one new one.

As yet, owing to the sensational scaricty of certain volumes, only a few of us are in a position to feel beholden to Mrs. Glyn for her sublime and bestial conceits.

Prof. Milford in English III— "Anglo-Saxon poetry has a swing similar to the rocking of a cradle." Very true. But what do the juniors in Eng. III know about cradles?

Ezra was not at chapel on Jan. 14.

Let freshmen take the advice of always saying necktie when they mean necktie. One man was aiming at calling it cravat, but he said cravanet, and no one knows sure that he knew the difference.

Emanuel, '10, has been adjudged the possessor of more than the usual apportionment of college spirit. He yells for the college song on all occasions as a man howling for the life-line.

This page and the following are taken from the February issue of *The Wabash*, with Pound's attendance record in chapel duly noted.
(Courtesy of the Lilly Library, Wabash College)

Ezra was not at chapel on Jan. 15.

The youngster outside the chapel door on Jan. 16, and sticking closely by Prof. Thomas, was "Bobbie" McCain. It was one of his first visits to the college and he didn't seem at all disturbed by the general hub-bub.

Prof. Rhodeheaver has, you might say, "fooled 'em." Some of

School at Indianapolis. His work is with the evening classes. Although pleased, he means to get back in college to finish before many terms.

Ezra was not at chapel on Jan. 16.

The college men who put in about a week of service in the militia to quell the car strike riots at Muncie have returned very thor-

JUNIOR CLASS OFFICERS
Brown. Pres.
Glasscock, Vice-Pres.   Linn, Sec.-Treas.

the most studious men in college this term registered for Bible study. They wanted the two credits and didn't see the need of getting them by work in all cases. Report has it that they are beginning to be awakened.

Herbert Henry, a former '09 man, left college at Christmas time to take a position as chemistry assistant in the Winona Technical

oughly tired out. They slept in skating rinks, the court house, etc. Perhaps those things account for their weariness, though we Athenians might say that it was the contrast between Crawfordsville and Muncie. We know whereof we speak. Crawfordsville is unequaled.

Of all poor specimens of freshman ignorance this instance is the most flagrant. Republican pri-

issue of Saturday, February 15, after mentioning a recent blizzard, says:

Prof. Ezra Pound Leaves

Prof. Ezra Pound, instructor of Romance Languages in Wabash College, has resigned his position and left yesterday for his home inu [*sic*] Philadelphia. Prof. Hains will take his classes in French and John Wilson, a student with five years knowledge of Spanish, will take the classes int hat [*sic*] language temporarily. Robert Winter will relieve Prof. Hains of one of his beginning classes in Greek.

Clearly, Pound left on Friday, February 14. This departure date is confirmed by an entry made in the Treasurer's Report of the college. It contains a sudden, extraneous doling out of money that followed the two regular payments issued at the starts of the two trimesters:

Ezra Pound
Feb. 12: Amt. paid him, balance salary to February 29, 1908 (order
     G.L.M.) $200.

This made Pound's total salary through February 29 $447.50, which is as much as some of the other young instructors received for the entire year. And so, far from being issued cursory walking papers, Prof. Pound was paid rather handsomely to depart the premises. A week later, the Country Editor of *The Crawfordsville Weekly Review* wrote in his column: "We presume that when Ezra left he took his chafing dish with him." Strange how a simple cooking tool could assume such gigantic importance to a whole community!

As for the culminating event itself, James Osborne and Theodore Gronert, who wrote *Wabash College: The First Hundred Years*, have told the story this way:

The end came on a bitterly cold night in his first winter at Crawfordsville. He had taken the rooms vacated the year before after long occupancy by Professor McLain. After reading late into the night he walked downtown through a blizzard to mail a letter. On the street he met a girl from a stranded burlesque show, penniless and suffering from the cold. He took her to his warm rooms. She spent the night in his bed, he on the floor of his study. He went off to his eight o'clock recitation in the morning. The ladies from whom he rented the rooms, the Misses Hall, went upstairs to make the bed and found in it the girl from burlesque. Their only experience with roomers was with Professor McLain. This confrontation bewildered them. They telephoned the President, and a trustee or two. Shortly after there was a discussion between these gentlemen and Mr. Pound, a discussion at distinctly cross purposes. The elder statesmen really did not have the kind of minds they were at once suspected of having, but on the contrary recognized an impulsive action that was not only innocent but excellently charitable. But they were aware too, from the accumulated evidence of several months, of a gulf too wide to be bridged between two different philosophies. And they were content to use the occasion to make an arrangement about their contract that encouraged Mr. Pound to shake the dust of a small middle-western Presbyterian college forever from his feet, and content to rejoice in his subsequent triumphs in poetry.

(pp. 291-92)

This is the classic version of the tale, although the alumni supply a wealth of variants of every conceivable kind. Alumnus Roy G. Pearce said that two girls were involved with Pound (and he confessed that he himself had bedded two down from the ill-fated show), while others said that Pound slept in the hallway outside his room that night or in his cold classroom. Pound insisted that the girl involved was a male impersonator, telling Rader in a letter of June 20, 1959, that she "could never have gotten to first base" in a burlesque show, and also that she was extremely grateful to him five or ten years later when he saw her back in her native England. Still, both Mary Moore (in an interview in the Carl Gatter Scrapbook No. 3) and Hilda Doolittle (in *End of Torment*, p. 24) indicate that they too received the "orphan in the storm" version of the tale.

The important thing from Pound's point of view is that he did not give in. He stood his ground, and that was why he was paid rather handsomely to depart. If he had quietly capitulated, Mackintosh would have simply booted him summarily out of the school. Pound was not without his defenders—like Mary Young, who tried to intercede personally with the President—but to no avail. The poet decided to leave at once. He packed up his trunk with his valuable books, which would trail far behind him, and he instructed the two "buzzards" to sell his furniture, but he never received a cent.

Alumnus David Glascock has the final word:

> I believe that I am the last man to have seen Mr. Pound before he left Crawfordsville. I saw him at the Big 4 Station, South Washington Street, and talked with him until he boarded the train leaving the city. In the course of our conversation I asked him why he was leaving. He replied that he was fired. (Later on he gave me another account.) I asked him why? He replied that the college board fired him because they said he had had a girl in his room. I asked if he had had one. He said, "Yes I did." And when he denied it and asked the board to prove it they could not and because they could not they reinstated him. It was then that he told me he told the board "To go to Hell" and resigned.

Unlike the doomed souls in the London Cantos, he left "with pride, with dignity."

But that was not the end of the "high comedy," as Pound later called it to Rader. In its March issue, *The Wabash* concocted this little riddle:

> Math problem: Solve for the unknowns (if any): "Lbs. + drams —scruples = 23."

Translated, the riddle meant: "Pounds (Ezra's acquired name) added to dramatic stars without any scruples leads to a 23"—and even in 1907, "23" meant "skiddoo." As if this wasn't enough, there was a poem with the title of "23":

> There are many cantankerous tumors,
> But none so noisome as rumors.
> The Powers, they said, "Zounds;
> We'll have to can Pounds,
> He's going too far with the roomers."

The mention of "roomers" here throws us back once again to Version A, the starving actress across the hall. To Dr. Kavka, Pound spoke of an "affair with an actress," implying a long time. Ah, well . . .

The *Annual Catalogue* issued on May 11, 1908, said: "there have been several changes in the personnel of the faculty. Herman B. Dorner, instructor in Botany, Francis M. Cayou, instructor in Physical Culture, and James I. Osborne, assistant in German, have resigned, as have William A. Ellis, professor of Education, and Ezra Pounds [misspelled to the end], instructor in Romance Languages." They noted that the course in Spanish, which had been very successful that year, would be continued. In 1910, when they named a regular man to the job, there was no mention of his ill-starred predecessor. It appeared that Wabash College had completely forgotten the illustrious founder of its Romance Language Department.

Yet neither Pound nor Wabash could ever forget each other. For both, the encounter had been too traumatic. Pound had failed in his first real attempt to break totally free of his family's economic control, and this failure would cause him to be partially dependent on them for some time. Furthermore, it colored even darker his attitude toward jobs in general, and especially those in Academe. As he indicated in letters from Venice, it took weeks if not months for him to put his nerves back in order.

Wabash, meanwhile, was saddled with a very embarrassing event. To some people, the very name "Wabash College" has become synonymous with provincial prudery. Whether one regards the Crawfordsville Incident as high comedy or low camp or borderline tragedy, it was not just a silly event that frittered away. It remains, in spite of the circumjacent humor, a rather serious study in cross-purposes between the creative and the academic minds, the liberal and the conservative, the urban and the provincial. Even today, many a young academician trudging off to the hinterlands toward a school with no name and a fortune yet to come thinks about the event with a certain sigh.

Yet fortunately for both Pound and the school, neither was permanently damaged. Pound went on to become one of the greatest poets of the twentieth century, while Wabash College—like the river for which it was named—just keeps rolling along.

Fate (or something) had spoken.

♦ TWELVE
EASTWARD HO!

It was a long trip back through the cornfields, with plenty of time to think.

Pound had failed in his first attempt to escape parental control. And he had also flunked out of Academe, since his dismissal would not be an easy thing to live down. Yet that didn't bother him, since he was simply using the Grove of Academe as a way of climbing toward Parnassus. Now if ever, he was determined that his calling was that of a poet. He might still teach in the future, but not in any official capacity.

More serious, though, was his attitude toward his native country. Up until this time, he had been extremely patriotic, viewing America, and especially the West, as if he were a pioneer like Thaddeus Coleman Pound. Suddenly, that optimism was fading. The West was no longer a frontier; it seemed simply a wasteland where the culture of the East had not yet penetrated, and indeed never might, because it was so firmly in the hands of neo-Puritans.

If culture was lacking, so was love. He was now twenty-two years old and still had no clear idea whom he was going to marry. Of course Mary Moore was always in the picture, but was she serious? If he was a dragonfly, she was a butterfly, always darting from one socially well-placed beau to another.

But behind Mary, there was Hilda. . . .

Still, his first task was to explain the Incident to his parents. As he rode through the Midwestern countryside on his way to the Main Line, he decided to tell the story—improbable as it might seem to many—this way: he had met a girl in a storm, had put her up for the night in his bed while he slept elsewhere, and had been reported by the Hall sisters to the authorities. Farfetched as the "good Samaritan" story was, it would be more acceptable to his female friends than a story involving a long-standing relationship with an actress (however innocent).

And so, when he arrived at home on Fernbrook Avenue, he told his distressed parents the story of the orphan in the storm. Isabel behaved as expected: she was shocked by the firing and the presence of an actress in her son's life, but she was also fiercely loyal, steadfastly refusing to acknowledge the slightest hint of wrongdoing. Yet her concern for her social position really left her no choice. Homer was his usual, good-natured, forgiving self. Of course he was also upset by the whole affair, and he could well imagine what all the neighbors would say, but he also stuck by his son.

However, the rest of the world—with the exceptions of Mary Moore, Hilda Doolittle, and William Brooke Smith—were not in any way as sympathetic at all. News of the incident permeated the suburbs from Wyncote to Upper Darby. When it reached the Penn Graduate School, there were howls of laughter privately and cries of moral indignation publicly. This was all that anyone needed to finally bar the difficult Mr. Pound now and forever. If doors had earlier been closed, now they were locked and barred.

Mary Moore forgave Ezra his indiscretions, but when he proposed to her, she quite firmly said no. She was as usual involved with one of her many "Princeton beaux" and other suitors. Eventually she would settle down with a businessman named Frederick Cross—that Cross she bore, Pound would say—and become a respectable Montclair matron. *Sic transit gloria mundi.*

Ezra began dating Hilda almost immediately upon arrival, hoping somehow to persuade Mr. Doolittle to permit their marriage. Hilda wrote to Bill Williams, before Ezra even arrived home, that she was engaged to him in a letter of February 12. She told Bill that she was prepared to live the rest of her life with this poor, mistreated victim of a philistine society. She would gather the dismembered limbs of Atthis or Osiris and restore him to his primal state of glory.

Ezra waited for a few weeks, and then decided to face Papa Doolittle in a head-on encounter. He took the cross-county trolley to the observatory and there, in an atmosphere of telescopes and astral charts, he asked for the Dryad's hand. At first, Charles Leander was speechless. He had heard all of the gossip through his society-conscious wife, and he knew that this moment was coming. Yet when it actually came, he scarcely knew how to vent his indignation. Finally, in short, impassioned spurts, he exclaimed, focusing his far-ranging eyes upon this impetuous intruder: "*What*! Why . . . you're . . . nothing but a *nomad*!"

That was the end of that.

Hilda returned the ring (presumably the same ring that Kitty Heyman had given Ezra and that Ezra had given to Mary Moore before it was returned to him). Still another door had slammed shut.

Hilda was very dejected by her father's action. Ezra told her that, since their marriage was impossible so long as they lived in Philadelphia, they would have to accomplish it abroad. He had decided that his only recourse was a flight to Europe. He knew that Kitty would be touring the European continent for most of the rest of the year, and he had already discussed the possibility of being her agent. Once abroad, he would publish a book of his poems at his own expense and dedicate it to Hilda. But then Ezra went to see poor William Smith, and observed that his young friend was dying. After that death, he would dedicate his first book to Smith instead. . . .

The sudden, unpremeditated changes in plans drove Hilda to distraction. She now felt entirely manipulated by her parents and her lover. She wrote a letter to Bill Williams on March 7, saying that her engagement to Ezra had suddenly been called off (with no details mentioned), and that Ezra was about to depart for Gibraltar.

In Ezra's mind, Europe was now the only answer. But he still had to get there. True, the money from Wabash arrived, but he would need more than that if he was planning to subsidize his own publication. Of course he could depend on the Kitty-mama once he was there, but he could not locate her in time to get the fare.

Once more he appealed to the mercy of his father. Homer was again sympathetic, but he assured his son that he was not going to support him for the rest of his life. He would only contribute some money if Ezra could bring him in writing the testimony from some authority that his poetry showed promise for the future.

Ezra racked his brain. After much, much thought, he finally came up with the name of Witter Bynner, who was the poetry editor of the fashionable *McClure's Magazine*. Bynner had introduced A. E. Housman's poetry to America and might appreciate Pound's pagan tendencies. Ezra wrote him a letter, and Bynner asked to see the poems, inviting the young poet to New York.

Years later Bynner recounted the interview with Pound to the biographer Charles Norman. He vividly remembered how the young poet looked: "I should say that his jacket, trousers and vest had each a brave color, with a main effect of purple and yellow, that one shoe was tan, the other blue, and that on a shiny straw hat the ribbon was white with red polka dots" (*Ezra Pound*, p. 26). In other words, Mr. Pound was already dressing in the extravagant way that he would affect in London during the following year.

Bynner recalled that Ezra read his poetry enthusiastically and insistently, and compared him to Vachel Lindsay (a comparison that Pound would find unappealing). When the reading was over, Bynner was more than happy to write a supporting letter to Homer. He even suggested that Pound should send him things in the future that he might pass on to his own publisher, Small, Maynard Company of Boston. They would bring out Pound's *Provença* in 1910.

Ezra dropped in on Aunt Frank in New York and got the little bit of money that she could contribute to his flight. He then returned to Philadelphia, where Homer was impressed enough by Bynner's letter to come up with the money for a cheap ticket to Europe. Pound went downtown to see "a fellow named Smith," according to the post-postscript of *The Spirit of Romance*, and the travel agent sold him passage on a glorified cattleboat to Gibraltar. Then Smith did a surprising thing. He wrote a letter of introduction for Ezra to a certain Sullivan of London who had a connection with Covent Garden Market. It was Sullivan who told Pound about an opening as a lecturer at the London Polytechnic Institute, where the poet delivered the lectures that were eventually published as *The Spirit of Romance*. These lectures enabled Pound to stay in London and to meet Dorothy Shakespear, who, with her mother Olivia, came to hear the exciting young American discourse on the troubadours and Dante.

Having failed with Hilda, he then wrote a letter to Mary, informing her that sunny Italy was calling, and that he would "saila da boat on the Santo Patriks day." He invited her to come and see him off.

Then, as time was running out, he wrote to Bill Williams, saying that he wanted very much to visit him in Rutherford. This visit took place just a few days before March 17. Pound stayed at the Williams home, where the two spoke endlessly about poetry. Pound showed Bill some of the poems that would appear shortly in *A Lume Spento*, while Williams showed Pound his long Keatsian poem called *Endymion*, which Pound praised.

Mary Moore showed up on St. Patrick's Day on the Hudson River to see him off on the R.M.S. *Slavonia*. In a letter written aboard the ship, he apologized for having mussed her hair when he embraced her in a passionate farewell. She promised him that she would come and visit him in Venice, and then she went back to her happy, comfortable life in Trenton.

The whistles sounded, the smoke rose, and the *Slavonia* sailed slowly but surely out of the Hudson River and into the Atlantic Ocean. Ezra Pound was leaving America, the land of his birth—not permanently, but decisively. He had decided that he had to return to Europe, the land of his people long before they had come to America in the seventeenth century. Despite his deep love of his native land, he had found it progressively harder to bear. In this respect, he was by no means unusual, for before and after him went Henry James, T.S. Eliot, Gertrude Stein, and scores of others. Expatriation was becoming a good old American custom.

As the New York skyscrapers faded in the west, and the *Slavonia* faced the Atlantic, Pound had to feel both invigorated and yet afraid. After all, he had a relatively small amount of money in his pocket:

> so that leaving America I brought with me $80
> and England a letter of Thomas Hardy's
> and Italy one eucalyptus pip

(Canto 80, p. 500)

Still, he had both genius and courage. He had failed in Indiana, but he would not fail where it mattered. Of this he was sure. He was now moving out to face for the first time the reality of his true existence. The adventure of his life was actually just beginning, and he was ready to accept it:

> And then went down to the ship,
> Set keel to breakers, forth on the godly sea . . .

(Canto 1, p. 3)

◆THIRTEEN

Venice and *A Lume Spento*

We know from an envelope accompanying Letter 45 to Mary Moore that he was already ensconced in Gibraltar by early April and had even visited Madrid. Letter 44, which is undated, was written aboard the Royal Mail Steamship *Slavonia* on the ship's stationery to the "most delectable of rabbits all," describing a rather stormy crossing. The following letter mentioned again the hellish weather and his desperately played poker games, in which he cleared just enough money to pay the steward's tips, but not enough for cigarettes. He speaks of having to write "arrangement notes" for Kitty to the four corners of Spain, and of his plan to remain at the Bristol Hotel in Gibraltar for about a month.

Then suddenly in the next letter Pound has been to Tangiers, where Aunt Frank had ridden the mule, looking up a remote cousin of John Scudder and talking to the bandit Raisuli; he was trying to write interviews and stories for *Harpers* and other magazines, and he spoke of being on the fringe of some kind of money racket in order to survive. This was made clear in the autobiographical sketch done for Louis Untermeyer:

> 1908 landed in Gibralter [*sic*] with 80 dollar and lived on the
> interest for some time. Life saved by Yusuf Benamore (tourists
> please note and use the Benamore family if couriers are required).
>
> (p. 19)

Yusuf, the Jewish guide, has already been described in Chapter 9. In Letter 46 to Mary, Pound clearly speaks of his transactions as "graft," and later he referred to them as "the gombeen business" or exchange racket, which was perilously close to the commerce of the evil goddess Usura. Gibraltar was overrun with British soldiers and sailors, and hence did not offer the tranquility that was necessary for putting his nerves in order.

In Letter 46, Pound speaks about getting seasick on his return from Morocco, and then of moving on to Cadiz and Seville. With a romantic flourish that suggests the carefree life of a troubadour moving from castle to castle, singing his songs of love for woman after woman, Pound adds: "Here today & on the wind tomorrow." This is precisely the voice that can be heard in the poem "Cino" in his first book of poems. In a world that was either too rigid like Crawfordsville or too corrupt like Gibraltar, he sought a mean that would offer him sun, laughter, beautiful women, and fluidity, and soon he was on his way there: Venice.

Mary Moore received a card from Pound from the North Italian city of Vicenza, postmarked April 25, as well as Letter 47, which announced his arrival in Venice and even his forthcoming publication, with the address of 861 Ponte San Vio. His father got a more laconic communication dated April 26: "I still eat." And so Pound arrived once again in the city of his dreams, for Venice was the place where he felt most at home—even more so than in Rapallo. It is the place where he would spend many of his later years in his "Hidden Nest" with Olga Rudge. But from the time of its founding, when the people of the Veneto region fled to the sandbars of the Adriatic to escape the marauding Teutons and their own decadent Greek and Roman rulers, Venice has always symbolized liberation—even, as to Thomas Mann, in death.

In 1908, Venice looked very much the way it looks today. It was also quite expensive, because Italy was then experiencing one of its most prosperous decades, often referred to as "the beautiful epoch." The perpetual king Victor Emmanuel III sat woodenly on the sidelines while Prime Minister Giovanni Giolitti was master-fully orchestrating the many dissonant elements of Italy's mixed society. Socialism was running rampant in all the classes, but because of its general acceptance, it was fairly well under control, while communism was still largely an idea that was causing trouble in Russia and up in the North.

The pre-war decade was an epoch of Puccini's rich, lush music (Pound sometimes called him Spewcini); of Marinetti's sometimes crazy futuristic art, with hymns to automobiles (Pound would encounter him later in London); of that flickering spectacle that was known by the Greek name of *kinema* (*Ben Hur* was one of the first Italian productions); and of that dashing figure, Gabriele d'Annunzio, whose flagrantly adulterous affair with the aging actress Eleonora Duse had all of Italy atwitter (there being no Misses Hall to report them to the authorities). D'Annunzio's play *La Nave* (The Ship) was a great tribute to the Venetian past; the way that the work advocated brutality on the part of aristocrats to control the masses seemed, however, to look to the future. In nearby Forlí, a young man named Benito Mussolini was writing angry editorials for the socialist newspaper *Avanti*, while socialists were marching in Milan, farmers were striking around Parma, and the South, as usual, was experiencing earthquakes or one natural disaster after another. But up in Venice, perennially lapped by the warm, all-encompassing Adriatic, with its swarms of dolphins in sight of the Belltower, all of that chaos and confusion seemed remote. Venice had scarcely acknowledged the fact that it was a part of the relatively new Italian state, for after it had fallen to Napoleon, Venice was finding it difficult to acknowledge anything that was "real."

Enchanted by the detached beauty around him, the penniless American refugee could sit on the steps of the Customs House (Dogana) and gaze across the canal at the pink and white marble splendors of St. Mark's Square and dream of a timeless past:

> I sat on the Dogana's steps
> For the gondolas cost too much, that year,
> And there were not "those girls," there was one face,
> And the Buccentoro twenty yards off, howling "Stretti,"
> And the lit cross-beams, that year, in the Morosini . . .
> > Gods float in the azure air,
> Bright gods and Tuscan, back before dew was shed.
>
> (Canto 3, p. 11)

The "Stretti" comes from a popular Neapolitan song that was howled that year by the gondoliers from the Bucintoro Club nearby (where the Golden Bark of the Doge was housed, in which he used to ride out and marry the Adriatic Sea by throwing a ring into it). The word means "close, tightly embraced," and occurs in "The Spanish Girl" in this way:

> So close, so close
> In the ecstasy of love
> The Spanish girl knows how to make love
> Mouth to mouth
> All the night and day.

This sensual refrain could be heard all over town that summer, and it lingered in Pound's mind with the tenacious hold that popular songs tend to exert on us all.

Despite his poverty, Pound was soon on his way back to mental health. In Paige Carbon 88 to Isabel, he says that he is "almost" himself again; then he quickly mentions his Italian publisher (the letter is dated simply June, 1908) and speaks about having to move on to London and wanting very much to meet "Bill" Yeats, whom he already treats as a familiar. He wrote Letter 50 to Mary on stationery that was quietly removed from the Royal Danieli Hotel, and proudly announced that he was staying in an even better place that looked out on the All Saints canals. Having left the San Vio Quarter, where he lived between the Academy Bridge and the church of Santa Maria della Salute, he was now at Calle dei Frati 942. He would later describe his quarters this way in Canto 76:

> well, my window
>> looked out on the Squero where Ogni Santi
> meets San Trovaso
>> things have ends and beginnings

(p. 462)

He told Mary that his new quarters were in the ruins of what was once a palatial setting. It had a sweeping view of the Grand Canal on one side and the Giudecca Quarter on the other. Next door was a garden with the San Trovaso Church, and across the little canal behind the house was a "squero" or yard for parking and refurbishing gondolas. The cover of the 1965 edition of *A Lume Spento* contains a lovely photograph of the setting. He tells Mary that he would like to linger on indefinitely in Venice, but fears that it will soon be necessary to start drifting northward.

Certainly Venice was doing wonders to drive out the trauma of Crawfordsville. He noted whimsically at the start of *Indiscretions* that the "Queen of the Adriatic" was a good antidote for the "Athens of the West." His renewed sense of power comes through in a little poem called "San Vio," which was a part of his *San Trovaso Notebook*, that was included in the 1965 edition of his first work:

> Old powers rise and do return to me
> Grace to thy bounty, O Venetian sun.
> Weary I came to thee, my romery
> A cloth of day-strands raveled and ill-spun,
> My soul a swimmer weary of the sea,
> The shore a desert place with flowers none.

(p. 115)

He expressed the same idea in Canto 26:

> And
>   I came here in my young youth
>   and lay there under the crocodile
> By the column, looking East on the Friday,
> And I said: Tomorrow I will lie on the South side
> And the day after, south west.
> And at night they sang in the gondolas
> And in the barche with lanthorns;
> The prows rose silver on silver
>   taking light in the darkness. "Relaxetur!"

(p. 121)

He did indeed relax, shifting his positions as he lay under the famous statue of St. Theodore striding the crocodile that stands in St. Mark's square.

During this visit and others, Pound came close to knowing "the stones of Venice" as had that other earlier visitor, John Ruskin. He knew by heart the palaces and the churches, as well as the paintings inside them. In one section of the *Pisan Cantos*, he begins by mentioning the Academy Bridge, the houses along the Grand Canal that belonged to families like the Vendramini and the Contrarini, and beautiful churches, such as St. Mary of the Miracles, with its stone carvings of mermaids by Tullio Lombardo

[Pound mistakenly calls him Romano]; St. George of the Greeks; and St. George of the Slavs [Schiavoni], which contains the painting by Victor Carpaccio that shows Christ "in the place of skulls":

> with the new bridge of the Era where was the old eyesore
>   Vendramin, Contrarini, Fonda, Fondecho
>   and Tullio Romano carved the sirenes
>   as the old custode says: so that since
> then no one has been able to carve them
>   for the jewel box, Santa Maria Dei Miracoli,
> Dei Greci, San Giorgio, the place of skulls
>   in the Carpaccio
> and in the font to the right as you enter
>   are all the gold domes of San Marco

                                        (Canto 76, p. 460–61)

When Allen Ginsberg met Pound in the 1960s and wanted to know the locations of the places mentioned here, Pound could tell him—down to the last chip in the stone.

Soon he was determined to bring his poems out in print. He had built up a large repertoire, and he knew that unless he had a book, he could not attract enough attention to his work. He therefore went to the establishment of one A. Antonini, who agreed to do the book for a reasonable fee. But the printing soon ran into trouble when Signor Antonini ran out of the letter "w," which is not regularly used in Italian. Fortunately the printer was able to find some more, and the work appeared late in June.

Like all fledgling authors, Pound was racked by feelings of inadequacy and doubt. He even considered throwing the proofs [*bozze*] into the canal:

> by the soap-smooth stone posts where San Vio
> meets with il Canal Grande
> between Salviati and the house that was of Don Carlos
> shd/I chuck the lot into the tide-water?
>   le bozze "A Lume Spento"/
>   and by the column of Todero
>   shd/I shift to the other side
>   or wait 24 hours

                                       (Canto 76, p. 460)

Mary de Rachewiltz tells us in the 1965 edition of *A Lume Spento* (p. 113) that by "shifting" he meant going into something commercial, as well as changing physical position. For a time his wallet was quite bare. He made a lunch of sweet potatoes and had a supper of barley soup (*minestra d'orzo*). He recalled this simple but hardy fare much later in Canto 102:

> Barley is the marrow of men,
> 40 centess' in my time
> an orzo.

(p. 729)

Forty centesimi were not very much money.

But soon his life picked up again: the Kitty-mama arrived on her tour of Europe. She first admonished her ward for failing so miserably at Wabash, and then saw that he was properly fed. She asked him to come north with her at the end of the summer to Paris and London, and he wrote to the Paris headquarters of the *New York Herald* announcing the possibility of future concerts there for Miss Heyman on her way back to America. He had always been entranced by her playing, and he now began to envision himself as her manager in a serious manner. In a letter of June 14, he wrote to Hessler at the University of Michigan to ask him to try to line up some engagements in the Detroit area. He confessed that he had gone to an employment agency to look for work, but when the clerk realized that he was rejecting some perfectly good jobs because he wanted to work only parttime in order to write poetry, the man told him sarcastically in French: "You are young, and have your illusions." The fact that they were speaking in French might also indicate a reason for leaving Italy at that time. For a time, Pound even entertained the idea of being a gondolier, but when he was given a test at the squero, he found that it was harder to manipulate those long, thin boats in the narrow canals than it looked. And so, the job as Kitty's manager did not look bad. It would offer him a chance to travel to all sorts of exotic places: San Francisco, Rio, Buenos Aires—places that the poet never visited later.

Pound's genuine admiration for Kitty's performances is revealed in a poem called "Nel Biancheggiar" (In the Whitening), which appeared in his second book that year, *A Quinzaine For This Yule*, in December:

> Blue-grey, and white, and white-of-rose,
> The flowers of the west's fore-dawn unclose.
> I feel the dusky softness whirr
> Of color, as upon a dulcimer
> "Her" dreaming fingers lay between the tunes . . .

(A Lume Spento, 1965, p. 109)

The second line of the poem supplies the dedication for this book, to "The Aube of the West Dawn." There is also a poem called "Aube of the West Dawn: Venetian June," which tells how a certain Malrin fell in love with the Dawn; the subtitle clearly indicates Kitty as the inspiration, since she was at the center of his world that June.

Miss Heyman was not alone. She had a young piano student from Richmond named "Babs" Derby in her entourage, as well as others whom Pound would refer to in letters later as "the gang in Venice last summer." They enjoyed themselves with all the delights that the city has to offer: coffee at Florian's in the square, opera at the Fenice Theater, swimming at the Lido, and D'Annunzio's latest play. Memories of that carefree summer flooded back over the poet when he sat in his strict confines in Pisa years later:

> and the Canal Grande has lasted at least until our time
> even if Florian's has been refurbished
> and shops in the Piazza kept up by
> artificial respiration
> and for La Figlia di Jorio they got out a
> special edition
> (entitled the Oedipus of the Lagunes)
> of caricatures of D'Annunzio

(Canto 76, p. 456)

In that same canto, he remembered a funny event that happened as he and Kitty Heyman were trying to track down the extravagant writer:

> Does D'Annunzio live here?
> said the american lady, K. H.

"I do not know" said the aged Veneziana,
　　"this lamp is for the virgin."

(p. 461)

The old Venetian woman's devotion to the Virgin Mary stands
in marked contrast with the dashing lover, whom many people
today see as a kind of prototype for the whole Fascist movement.
D'Annunzio was vigorous and bombastic, given to broad gestures,
like bombarding the Italian-populated parts of Yugoslavia with
propaganda leaflets. Pound was drawn to the man's sense of drama,
despite his reservations about the dramatist's use of words:

there is no doubt that D'Annunzio
　　　　could move the crowd in a theatre

(Canto 93, p. 630)

Suddenly toward the end of June, *A Lume Spento* appeared, in
a press run of only 100 copies selling for five lire ($1.00) apiece.
The book was supposed to have untrimmed edges, but the first
twenty copies were trimmed, and so they were sent to Homer
Pound to distribute as review copies. Ezra himself wrote a letter to
Homer Pound's old friend from Wisconsin, Ella Wheeler Wilcox,
asking her if she would be so kind as to review his book. In the
December 14 issue of something called the *New York American-
Journal-Examiner* she effused some rather mindless words of
praise. The *Book News Monthly*, which had already published the
poet's essays, was fairly critical, noting the poet's talent, but
commenting on his immaturity in its issue of May, 1909. The
reviewer there detected the excessive influence of Walt Whitman
(precisely the person who was not in the poems) and suggested
that the young artist simplify his style. This suggestion had some
merit, since the excesses of Dante Gabriel Rossetti and Swinburne and Ernest Dowson, who *were* there, were all too apparent.
Still, when he later saw this book up in London, "the greatest
poet of the English-speaking world" would find it promising and
"charming."

Up to this point, there has been cause to mention most of the
remarkable pieces in *A Lume Spento*. The most important one

199

that has gone uncommented upon is "Na Audiart," a Provençalish ballad written to a lovely but uncooperative lady (of whom there were many in Provence, as well as in Pound's life):

> Though thou well dost wish me ill,
> > Audiart, Audiart,
> Where thy bodice laces start
> As ivy fingers clutching through
> Its crevices,
> > Audiart, Audiart,
> Stately, tall, and lovely tender
> Who shall render
> > Audiart, Audiart,
> Praises meet unto thy fashion?
> Here a word kiss!

(p. 21)

The handling of the meter is subtle and ingeniously recalls the troubadours at their finest, especially Bertran de Born, who sang to this woman in a poem in which he assembled the features from a host of beautiful women because no single one could give him solace. Yeats would sense that Pound had a genuine feeling for Provence that he was able to transmit both in his essays and his adaptive verse, just as Eliot would see that Pound's grasp of the sensibility of François Villon in his Villonauds marked the re-entry of a vigorous, masculine element in English verse that had become muted with the Victorians.

It was stated earlier that in 1965, when the poems were being reissued with *A Quinzaine For This Yule*, Pound called them "stale creampuffs." This judgment was too severe. Granted that many of the pieces are sentimental and archaic-sounding, twelve of them were salvaged for the definitive collection of *Personae* in 1926. Like his predecessor Rossetti, Pound was imbued with the spirit of Dante. He had devoured the Italian's treatise on poetry, *De vulgari eloquio* (On Common Speech), but he had not mastered its meaning. He was wavering between an artificially precious diction like that in "Donzella Beata" (close to Rossetti's "Blessed Damozel") and an embarrassingly modern piece like "Nicotine: A Hymn to the Dope" or "Mesmerism" (with an epigraph from Browning), where the language is "vulgar" in the wrong sense:

Heart that was big as the bowels of Vesuvius,
Words that were wing'd as her sparks in eruption,
Eagled and thundered as Jupiter Pluvius,
Sound in your wind past all signs o'corruption.

(p. 28)

The twelve poems that moved on into *Personae* tended to show two lasting influences: the Roman Ovid, who was with Pound from the Cheltenham Academy, and the Englishman Robert Browning, who had died just around the corner in Venice at the Palazzo Rezzonico. Pound had read Browning carefully—especially with Hilda—and had admired that poet's handling of persona or poetic voice. He expressed this same assumption of the personalities of others in his own work in a poem called "Histrion," which appeared in his second book in London:

Thus am I Dante for a space and am
One François Villon, ballad-lord and thief,
Or am such holy ones I may not write
Lest blasphemy be writ against my name;
This for an instant and the flame is gone.

(1965 *A Lume Spento*, p. 108)

Pound's finest handling of what Browning called "interior monologue" occurs in "Cino," which has already been discussed. The technique of writing poems through the minds and voices of others is, of course, the basic organizing principle for *The Cantos.* There a whole symphony of voices speaks under the direction of the mastermind running the show. This concept of a major poem mediated through a series of smaller lyrics (or miracle plays) is still another idea that the young Ezra Pound had learned from Dante, as he reveals in *Spirit of Romance* (p. 153).

The weakest poems in *A Lume Spento* tend to be those that touch on Celtic myth or Arthurian romance. Both the long, introductory "La Fraisne" (The Ash Tree) and "Praise of Ysolt," written for Is-hilda, sound like pallid imitations of Yeats and his friends. Pound's forthcoming encounter with the Irish master would soon convince him that he should not try to imitate the work of a man who has already perfected his style and staked out a certain "turf" for himself.

201

The strongest poems are those written with Ovid in mind. It is easy to trace the uninterrupted influence of the Roman poet on Pound's work, from the early poem "The Tree" to sections of the Later Cantos, where the Ovidian world-view is integrated into the poet's whole concept of the universe:

> "From the colour the nature
> > & by the nature the sign!"
> Beatific spirits welding together
> > as in one ash-tree in Ygdrasail.
> > > Baucis, Philemon.
> Castalia is the name of that fount in the hill's fold,
> > the sea below,
> > > narrow beach.
> Templum aedificans, not yet marble
> > "Amphion!"
>
> (Canto 90, p. 605)

One sees here the tentative outreachings of 1908 coming to a fruitful end.

All too soon the summer of 1908 was ending.

Pound wrote to Mary Moore that he would be leaving Venice in August, drifting northward to Paris and London, and he told his parents the same thing, emphasizing the importance of meeting Yeats. Later, he mentioned the cold, economic facts: he was going to London largely because Kitty's tour was going there—before heading off for Germany—and he was quite firmly under her wing. And so, if our Parsifal had no money, he nevertheless did have a very clear notion as to where the Grail Castle lay, and for the time being at least, he had Katherine Ruth Heyman as his Kundrie.

On leaving the city, Pound wrote a poem called "Partenza di Venezia" in which Venice first appears as a sensual woman:

> Ne'er felt I parting from a woman loved
> As feel I now my going forth from thee,
> Yea, all thy waters cry out "Stay with me!"
> And laugh reflected flames up luringly.

However, in the last stanza, the city becomes a spiritual object that can perform miracles—a Grail indeed:

As once the twelve storm-tossed on Galilee
Put off their fear yet came not nigh
Unto the holier mystery,
So we, bewildered, yet have trust in thee,
And thus thou, Venice,
              Show'st thy mastery.

                    (1965 *A Lume Spento*, p. 99)

He had to have trust in something, since he was approaching his twenty-third birthday and was still not sure quite where he was going in the world. But he did have faith—in himself, in his craft, and in the survival of poetry written with the highest possible standards. Having basked in the southern City of Water, he would now face the Metropolis of the North. Since he could not go back home, and he could not support himself in the city of his dreams, he had no choice. He would have to face London—and conquer it.

The building described in *Patria Mia* with the unsightly water tank on the roof (still there 70 years later). This view from across Gramercy Park is close to the one that Pound had in 1910 from his quarters at the corner of 21st Street and Fourth (now Park) Avenue.

◆CODA

HAILS AND FAREWELLS:
1911...1939...1958

This book should properly end here, but we shall fill out Pound's love-hate relationship with his native land, which was a thing that would last to his death.

We are all familiar with how, on entering London with little more than a handful of pounds, promises from Kitty, and a boxful of poetry books printed at a vanity press in Venice, he took the world of English poetry by storm. The details of that conquest, fascinating as they are, are too complex to go into here. Suffice it to say that in the space of two years, the name of Ezra Pound, which had been reviled in Philadelphia and unknown in most of New York City, was soon beginning to be heard everywhere in the English-speaking world.

The credit for Pound's Conquest of London has to be attributed in a large part to the kindly publisher and bookseller Elkin Mathews, who brought out Pound's second book, *Quinzaine*, toward the end of 1908. At Mathews' clubby place of business Pound met the learned and hospitable Ernest Rhys, who introduced him to May Sinclair, who introduced him to Ford Madox Ford, who introduced him to Violet Hunt, who introduced him to Brigit Patmore, who introduced him to Richard Aldington—to whom Pound introduced Hilda Doolittle when she finally turned up in

London. These three (despite what Aldington said later) founded Imagism, a frontal attack on nineteenth-century pomposity and artificiality, whose repercussions continue to be felt.

Elkin Mathews also arranged for Pound to meet a promising young poet from Oxford named James Griffyth Fairfax, who presented Pound to a society woman named Mrs. Alfred (Aunt Eva) Fowler, who, in turn, presented him to Olivia Shakespear, who soon began to attend Pound's lectures at the London Polytechnic Institute, which were later published (through Rhys' promotion) as *The Spirit of Romance* in 1910. Pound found Olivia the most charming woman in London, and he was also captivated by her daughter, the lovely and talented Dorothy, who eventually became his wife. Olivia was the lover of William Butler Yeats, and so the avenue to "the greatest living poet of the English-speaking world" was assured. Yeats and he became fast friends, and Ezra served as the older man's secretary during World War I. Even Yeats, great as he was, found that he could learn something from this brilliant, rather disturbing, but always compelling young man from America.

There is no doubt that the Ezra Pound who shocked, titillated, and then instructed the Edwardian London of 1908 to 1910 was not a naive poetaster like the rude Joaquin Miller of California who had preceded him. Pound did not create his impact by his garish clothes or his compulsive acts, such as eating the floral piece during a dinner (frankly, would the son of Isabel and Homer Pound ever do a crude thing like that?). His impact was intellectual, and it was deep and penetrating. I am not suggesting that he taught James Joyce (whom he met through Yeats) everything that Joyce knew, any more than he fully instructed T.S. Eliot (whom he met through a letter from Conrad Aiken) or even Yeats himself. That would be excessive. Yet he did have an effect on most of them (Joyce possibly the least)—even if it was only to help them get published (but where would Joyce be today if Ezra had not been there behind him?). The one major English-speaking poet of the twentieth century whom Pound did not seem to teach much to (besides Wallace Stevens) was William Carlos Williams. But that was because "Bill" had removed himself from Pound's influence by staying home and delivering babies. If we follow what

Hugh Kenner has established as "the Pound tradition," we have to acknowledge the powerful effect that the Philadelphia triad of 1905—Bill, Ezra, and Hilda—had on everything that followed.

But if Ezra was a social and intellectual success in London, he confessed to his mother in Paige Carbon 104 that he still had not solved the problem of how to win his daily sustenance. Sheer economic survival would dog him until he left London in 1921. This difficulty explains why economics bulked so large in Pound's view of an ideal society.

Finally, the nagging inability to "make it big" financially forced Pound's possessive mother and a capitulating Homer to call for their son's return from abroad. Homer had been advancing Ezra small sums during the two years after his flight, but now the family felt that, since Ezra had won an international reputation, he should return to his homeland and bask in his freshly acquired glory. Pound, of course, resisted tenaciously. London was far more exciting then than anything New York had to offer, and New York was the only city he could envision living in. But by January 31st of 1910 he had applied for a fellowship at Penn (which, of course, would not be granted), and he vaguely talked about being home for the summer. On February 23, he applied for a teaching job at Hobart College in upstate New York—showing that the Wabash trauma seemed to be receding. In March "Bill" Williams arrived from Germany, and he and Ezra enjoyed the cultural events together. Then Ezra fled to Italy, especially Verona, on a brief visit. In a letter of April 2, he was back in London, telling his father that Witter Bynner's company in Boston was going to issue *Spirit of Romance* in America, and—suddenly he was back in the United States.

Pound went first of all to Philadelphia, where his family was still deeply involved in its Christian Endeavor work. During this visit, they lived in the city near the Mint or out in the western suburb of Swarthmore, subletting their house; it was not until 1911 that they were back in Wyncote. This dislocation was obviously unsettling to Ezra, but he had already decided that if he was going to live in America, it would have to be New York.

He moved first to Waverly Place in Greenwich Village and then to an apartment on Park Avenue South off Gramercy Park.

At first the clamor and the hubbub of the metropolis managed to keep his mind away from Europe, but he soon missed the companionship of Ford Madox Ford and Violet Hunt (at whose Lodge he played tennis almost every day) and Yeats's famous soirees, and dinner with the Shakespears. Of course, he got caught up in the rhythm of the Big City. He went to the Metropolitan Museum of Art to look at pictures and to the Metropolitan Opera to hear music. After much searching, he finally found Aunt Frank, who was lying low after her debacle. She was usually staying with Cousin Sadie Wessells out in New Jersey, and would die in Sadie's house in Belmar in 1914, along the Atlantic Coast. Poor Aunt Frank was just a vestige of her usual self. Since she no longer had a job to occupy her time, she did not know quite what to do with her life. She also seems to have had a strained relationship with her husband. Dr. Beyea had taken a house up on the Upper West Side near Alexander Hamilton's Grange. Although the two of them would maintain their marriage to the end, when Aunt Frank died on July 29, 1913, she was laid to rest with her first and only true beloved, Ezra Brown Weston in Cypress Hills.

Even Pound's old love interests had changed. Father Doolittle kept forbidding Hilda from seeing Ezra—international reputation or not—and so the poet asked her to come secretly to New York, where they once again pledged their love for one another. Hilda promised faithfully that she would cross the Atlantic soon—and she did. But by then it would be too late. Pound also had dinner with Viola Baxter, who was now living in New York City, but, like Mary Moore, she had other romantic attachments too. He would stay friendly with both these young women, but the flame no longer burned very fiercely for either.

While walking on the streets one day, he bumped into John Yeats, the father of the poet, who in turn introduced him to a lawyer named John Quinn, who later proved to be very valuable to Pound and many others as a patron of great generosity. The three of them went off to Coney Island one night in August, and had a delightful time riding elephants and shooting at targets in a gallery.

Pound also went out to Plainfield to have dinner with William Baldwin Wadsworth, Ma Weston's friendly relative. There he listened to the family talk about their sporting cars and stocks. Pound not only touched the kindly old William for a small loan, but also asked for some advice. At this time he seems to have been planning some kind of business deal—possibly beginning a magazine—in concert with a questionable entrepreneur named Francis S. "Baldy" Bacon. Baldy had run a variety of businesses which are catalogued in Canto 11, where his equally questionable buddy Mons Quade is also mentioned. To Pound, this duet seemed to represent the essence of all that was dubious in the world of business. Yet he kept in touch with both over the years, recommending to Wyndham Lewis on September 11, 1939, when Lewis was contemplating a move to America, that he look Baldy up at 80 Maiden Lane on Wall Street as well as "that ass Quade" in Washington.

As for the more fashionable world of finance, Pound visited Charles David Wadsworth and his sons on Central Park South in their elegant townhouse. But they too seemed somehow removed, with their adulation of Longfellow and apparent ignorance about anything that he seemed to be doing. No, kind and cultivated as they were, they were still not kindred spirits. And so he plunged more deeply into his work. He was studying Guido Cavalcanti that fall, and on November 22, Small and Maynard brought out his first book of poems in America: *Provença*. This cheered him up, and he was even more happy when he spent Thanksgiving Day with the Williams family in Rutherford. There was always plenty to talk about with Bill. They both had great plans for the future—and strangely, many of those plans would come true.

Yet from the start, this visit was doomed to failure. The lovable Westons were gone, and the city that he had known and loved in his childhood was changing. Pound admired the mammoth splendor of the old Pennsylvania Railroad Station, with its gigantic columns. He also loved the glistening spire of the Metropolitan Life Insurance Company, which was next door to Dr. Parkhurst's gem of a church. But a beautiful building that he could see nearby on Gramercy Park was spoiled by an unsightly watertower, and the brand-new New York Public Library was "another example of botch, of false construction," with its hideous roof and partially concealed third floor. Even the beautiful tower of the

Metropolitan had its imperfection, since the clock "projects in a very ugly manner" (*Patria Mia*, p. 17).

Mainly, however, it was the people who put him off. He could not stand the crowds on Seventh Avenue, with their endless pushing and shoving. The new immigrants from central and southern Europe seemed to be trying to brush him aside in the same way oldtimers like the Westons had disappeared, along with the boardinghouse and roominghouse. And so, in February of 1911, Pound boarded a ship and returned once again to the Europe of his family's past.

Back in Europe, he watched the First World War descend, and was deeply moved by the deaths of friends like the sculptor Henri Gaudier-Brzeska. Then, after the war, when he expected things to improve, nothing significant happened. He moved over to Paris, which was experiencing the wonderful but highly artificial life of the 1920s. There he encountered a host of writers like the friendly Hemingway and the hostile Gertrude Stein. Finally, however, he could not stand the perennial busy-ness of the place, and so he moved to the Italian Riviera, to the quiet port of Rapallo, where he and Dorothy lived above a hotel on the promenade downtown, and Olga Rudge, whom he had met in London at musical events, lived up in the hills.

But with Italy came Benito Mussolini; the two were inextricably intertwined. And, however bad Mussolini may look with hindsight, he seemed in the 1920s to be putting Italy back on its feet after its post-war slide. Pound, trying to understand the financial inequities that exist in societies, was now deeply immersed in his studies of economics and Chinese, especially Confucianism. To him, Mussolini seemed cut in the mould of a benevolent Chinese emperor, a true patriot who was trying to free his country from the control of evil international money men. Always an impassioned zealot when he saw what he considered a proper cause, Pound now devoted all his energy to free the world from the vices of Usura or Monetary Crime.

It was for this reason—with an honorary degree from Hamilton thrown in—that he made the desperate trip to America in 1939, ending a twenty-eight-year separation with his homeland. Pound had been corresponding with a number of Congressmen, and was hoping in vain to have a private meeting with Franklin Delano Roosevelt about various economic reforms that he felt were drawing the United States into a European war that was being waged purely for financial reasons. But of course he failed in his mission. Roosevelt did not see him, and the few Congressmen with whom he spoke seemed incapable of doing anything to prevent the fated course of events.

And so Pound went back to Italy.

World War II broke out in Europe, and gradually America was drawn into it. At this point, seeing his direst fears proving true, Pound was unable to maintain his silence. In 1941 he began his broadcasts for Radio Rome, despite the fact that everything sane should have urged against them; yet his sense of caring for America—rather than his desire to overthrow it—has to be seen as the important motive. The tragic ending has already been mentioned several times in this book. Italy lost the war, and Pound was turned over to the American authorities, who put him first in the detention camp at Pisa for about six months, and then hauled him across the ocean in November of 1945 on a purely involuntary return. Declared unfit to stand trial for treason, Pound was remanded to St. Elizabeths under the care of psychiatrists in early 1946, where he languished until his release in 1958.

Compared with the other seven "golden-tongued traitors" who were indicted with him, Pound had a hard time indeed. The fates of the others, who were all spokesmen for Nazi Germany, were:

MAX "OKAY" KOISCHWITZ: died in 1944, apparently of a heart attack, in Berlin; case dropped.

EDWARD L. DELANEY: quondam film salesman and vaudeville hoofer; captured in Czechoslovakia in 1945, but released; rearrested in 1947, flown to America, but charges dropped for lack of sufficient evidence.

JANE ANDERSON: the stylish, beautiful wife of Deems Taylor and then of the Spanish Count of Cienfuegos; never arrested; charges dismissed for lack of evidence.

FREDERICK WILHELM KALTENBACH: the so-called American Lord Haw-Haw; fled eastward; died in mysterious circumstances in a Russian prisoner camp; case dismissed.

ROBERT HENRY BEST: tried in Boston in 1948; sentenced to life
imprisonment with a fine of $10,000; died in federal custody
in Missouri on December 21, 1952—six years before Pound
was released.

CONSTANCE DREXEL: the self-styled member of the Philadelphia
Drexel clan who was no such thing, having been born in
Darmstadt, Germany; never arrested; charges dismissed in
1948; died peaceably in Waterbury, Connecticut, on August 28, 1956, the same day as George H. Tinkham, Pound's
friend from Massachusetts who served in the House of Representatives.

DOUGLAS CHANDLER: the "Paul Revere" of Radio Munich; sentenced
in Boston in 1947 to life imprisonment with a fine of $10,000;
sentence commuted by President John F. Kennedy on August 5, 1963, on the condition that Chandler leave the United
States. He did so immediately, fleeing to Germany and disap-
pearing forever.

With the exception of Chandler, it is clear that Pound got a much
harsher treatment than did the others.

Once again, it is not the purpose of this book to promote
propaganda or to preach. If Pound suffered imprisonment in St.
Elizabeths for twelve long years, he still got better treatment than
William Joyce (the British Lord Haw-Haw), who was executed by
the people of Britain for treason even though he was not a citizen
of that country, or Mildred Gillars (Axis Sally), who was tried and
imprisoned by the United States Government in 1949 and not
freed until twelve years later on July 11, 1961. Conversely, if
certain people feel that Ezra Pound cheated the American government by feigning insanity and then led a life of sybaritic pleasure
in St. Elizabeths, those who visited the poet tell a quite different
story. There are easier places than a madhouse in which to create
a literary salon. It is to Pound's credit that, despite the hysteria
and madness around him, he never stopped thinking and writing—and loving his native land. The Later Cantos, which were
written here, never surrender the thread of American history that
begins to unravel from Canto 30 onward. From his room on the
hill in the southwestern part of the city, Pound could see the

dome of the Capitol, which shines like a beacon at night out over the Potomac Plain. With that light came thoughts of T. C. P., who orated beneath that dome, and Uncle Ezry, who lived for a time just around the corner on Capitol Street. And all of the Presidents whom he wrote about: Jefferson . . . Adams . . . Jackson . . . Van Buren.

After his release in 1958, Pound fled for the third time to Italy. He came back to America only one more time—on a surprise visit in 1969 to see J. Laughlin of New Directions, his longtime publisher, receive an honorary degree from Hamilton.

In 1972 he made the last journey he would ever make, from the Church of San Giorgio Maggiore to the Island of San Michele, where he was buried in a cemetery reserved for non-Catholics. This final resting place reinforces what William Carlos Williams always insisted: try as Pound might to adopt Italy as his second home, he would always remain something of an outsider there. For Pound's true home was not Italia. It was the EU-nited States: from the Wayside Inn and the Captain's House at Duxbury to the lumber booms at Chippewa Falls and the roaring falls at Shoshone; from the old quad mellow in the October light on The Hill at Hamilton to the green, arching groves of Wyncote; from the chattering microcosm of the boarding house, with the laughter of Uncle Ez and Monsieur Fouquet and the impassioned readings of Ma Weston to the silken rustle of Aunt Frank and the invisible ghost of Harding Weston. These were the memories that haunted. These were the memories that clung.

Whether in the hellhole outside of Pisa or the asylum on the hill or the last sanctity of the Hidden Nest, they were also the things that redeemed:

What thou lovest well remains,
                          the rest is dross
What thou lov'st well shall not be reft from thee

WORKS CITED IN THE TEXT

I. BY EZRA POUND

ABC of Reading. New York: New Directions, 1971.

A Lume Spento. New York: New Directions, 1965 (1st ed., 1908).

"Autobiographical Outline (for Louis Untermeyer)." *Partisan Review*, 28 (1962), 18–21.

Cantos. New York: New Directions, 1972.

Collected Early Poems. Ed. M. J. King with intro. by Louis Martz. New York: New Directions, 1976.

Guide to Kulchur. New York: New Directions, 1970.

Impact. Chicago: Regnery, 1960.

Indiscretions: Pavannes and Divagations, pp. 3 ff.

Jefferson and/or Mussolini. New York: Liveright, 1970.

Letters to Ibbotson, 1935–1952. Ed. V. I. Mondolfo and M. Hurley. Orono: Maine, 1979.

Literary Essays. Ed. T. S. Eliot. New York: New Directions, 1972.

Patria Mia and the Treatise on Harmony. London: Owen, 1950.

Pavannes and Divagations. New York: New Directions, 1958.

Personae: Collected Poems. Rev. ed. New York: New Directions, 1971.

Selected Letters, 1907–1941. Ed. D. D. Paige. New York: New Directions, 1971 (1st ed., 1950).

Selected Prose, 1909–1965. New York: New Directions, 1973.

Spirit of Romance. New York: New Directions Paper, 1968 (1st ed., 1910).

II. BY OTHER AUTHORS

Doolittle, Hilda (H. D.) *End to Torment.* Ed. N. H. Pearson and M. King. New York: New Directions, 1979.

—— *Hedylus.* Redding Ridge, Ct.: Black Swan, 1980.

—— *HERmione.* New York: New Directions, 1981.

—— *Selected Poems.* New York: Grove, 1957.

Fries, Robert F. *Empire in Pine.* Madison: Wisconsin State Historical Society, 1951.

Guest, Barbara. *Herself Defined: The Poet H. D. and Her World.* New York: Doubleday, 1984.

Hall, Donald. "E. P.: An Interview." *Partisan Review,* 28 (1962), 22–51.

Hidy, R. W., F. E. Hill, and A. Nevins. *Timber and Men: The Weyerhauser Story.* New York: Macmillan, 1963.

Kenner, Hugh. *The Pound Era.* Berkeley: University of Press, California, 1971.

Mariani, Paul. *William Carlos Williams: A New World Naked.* New York: McGraw-Hill, 1981.

Norman, Charles. *Ezra Pound.* Rev. ed. New York: Funk & Wagnalls, 1969; Minerva Paperback, 1969.

Osborne, James, and Theodore Gronert. *Wabash College: The First Hundred Years.* Crawfordsville: Banta, 1932.

Reck, Michael. "A Conversation Between E. P. and Allen Ginsberg." *Evergreen Review,* 55 (1968), 27 ff.

Robinson, Janice S. *H. D.: Life and Work of an American Poet.* Boston: Houghton Mifflin, 1982.

Rosholt, Malcolm. *Lumbermen on the Chippewa.* Rosholt House 1982.

Stock, Noel. *Life of E. P.* Expanded ed. San Francisco: North Point, 1982 (1st ed., 1970).

Torrey, E. Fuller. *Roots of Treason.* New York: McGraw Hill, 1983.

Twining, C. E. *Downriver: Orrin H. Ingram and the Empire Lumber Co.* Madison: Wisconsin State Historical Society, 1975.

Williams, William Carlos. *Autobiography.* New York: Random House, 1951.

——*In the American Grain*. New York: New Directions Paper, 1956.

——*Paterson*. New York: New Directions, 1963.

——*Selected Essays*. New York: New Directions, 1969.

——*Selected Letters*, New York: Random House, 1954, 1968.

DOCUMENTATION

Since the sources of most items such as newspaper articles, letters, census records, and city directories are obvious from their contexts in the text, this section is meant merely as a supplement. The major work of Pound for the writing of this book is *Indiscretions*, which has been published in *Pavannes and Divagations* in the most recent edition (see Works Cited In The Text). Also important are the letters of Pound to his parents, known as the Paige Carbons, currently housed in the Beinecke Library at Yale. Occasional references are also made to the analysis of Pound by Dr. Jerome Kavka (File No. 58, 102), which is readily available in stencil form from the Public Affairs Office of St. Elizabeths Hospital in Washington.

INTRODUCTION

Citations of the radio speeches are from *"Ezra Pound Speaking"*: *Radio Speeches of World War II*, ed. Leonard W. Doob (Westport: Greenwood, 1978), arranged by date. See *Charles Olson and Ezra Pound*, ed. C. Seelye (New York: Viking, 1975), pp. 3–5, for a poem about Pound's Americanism, with the epithet "Montana."

1. IDAHO AND T. C. POUND

The major source is *Indiscretions*, along with the Centennial Issue of the *Wood River Journal* for Hailey. The archives of the *Milwaukee Sentinel* has a complete file on the activities of T. C. P., available through interlibrary loan. Literary portraits occur in John Gregory's *Industrial Resources of Wisconsin* (Milwaukee, 1870); *The United States Biographical Dictionary* (Chicago, 1877), pp. 402–05; *Dictionary of Wisconsin Biography* (Madison, 1960), p. 291; *Biographical Directory of the American Congress, 1774–1971* (Washington, 1971); *Wisconsin Senate Journal* (April 23, 1915). The Wisconsin Legislative Reference Bureau supplies extensive clippings and articles upon request; the Historical Society of Wisconsin provides obituaries and speeches, including the letter against Blaine's candidacy for the President (Milwaukee, 1884).

Papers for the Union Lumbering Co. are obtainable from the Minnesota Historical Society, but since they are a part of the Weyerhauser archives, they are subject to censored use. Thaddeus' political acts are recorded in the U.S. Congressional Record for appropriate dates and the *Wisconsin Assembly Journal.* His eulogy is in the *Wisconsin Session Laws: Acts, Resolutions and Memorials* (Madison, 1915), pp. 991–92.

The early history of the Pound family is traceable in the *Quaker Records: Rahway and Plainfield Monthly Meetings,* supplemented by reports from upstate New York; available through Society of Friends Genealogical Service, New York City. Extremely important is Ora Eugene Monnette, *First Settlers of Ye Plantations of Piscataway and Woodbridge . . . 1664–1714* (Los Angeles, 1935), Vols. 1 and 5.

For general books on lumbering and railroads, see Hidy, Twining, Rosholt, and Fries in Works Cited In The Text.

For Pound's poem on the Chippewa Spring and the reminiscences of Thaddeus, see *Chippewa County: Wisconsin Past and Present,* Vol. 1 (Chicago, 1913; actually 1914); see entry B6 in the Gallup bibliography.

2. UNCLE EZRA WESTON

The primary sources for this chapter are contained, often with photographs of documents, in the author's article "Ezra Pound's New York, 1887–1908: A Recreation" in *Paideuma, 12* (1983), 55–87. The Municipal Archives of the City of New York contain death records and census reports. The New York Public Library has an extensive photographic collection, and its Genealogical Room also has valuable directories and records. The major genealogical article is "The Descendants of Edmund Weston of Duxbury, Mass., For Five Generations" in the *New England Historical and Genealogical Register, 41* (1887), 285–96; also valuable is D. W. Howe's *Howe Genealogies,* rev. G. B. Howe, 2 vols. (Boston, 1929).

The veterans' files of the National Archives have the complete pension story of Harding Weston, with his history in veterans' homes until his death. The Nyack Public Library has a file on Ezra Weston, with maps of his property. The Hopkinton Public Library has information on Mt. Auburn Cemetery, where Mary Weston is buried.

3. THE WADSWORTHS

Primary documentation contained in the author's article "The Wadsworths, the Westons, and the Farewell of 1911" in *Paideuma, 12* (1983), 305–47. Ma Weston's primary sources were *Two Hundred and Fifty Years of the Wadsworth Family in America* (Lawrence, 1883) and *The Poetical Works of Henry Wadsworth Longfellow,* 6 vols. (Boston, 1886). Also consulted were the archives of the *Plainfield Courier* and the *Harvard Class Reports.*

4. PHILADELPHIA

All material here is heavily indebted to the preliminary researches of Carl Gatter, which are contained in twenty-one scrapbooks in the Rare Book Room of the University of Pennsylvania Van Pelt Library. These consist of information about individuals (Books 1 to 3), newspaper clippings and transcriptions (Books 9 and 10; I have used these liberally for the Hatboro and Jenkintown publications), information about the Cheltenham Academy (Book 16), and so on. Gatter's account of Pound's visit in 1958 is contained in Book 8.

Also useful is the Homer Pound scrapbook from Rapallo at the Beinecke for local photos. For Pound's interview with Ginsberg, see Reck in Works Cited In The Text.

5. AUNT FRANK AND EUROPE

The main details of the trip come from the passages cited in *Indiscretions.* For Parkhurst, see the *New York Times* obituary of Sept. 9, 1933; for Train, the same on Jan. 20, 1904. Train's autobiographies are: *An American Merchant in Europe, Asia, and Australia* (New York: Putnam, 1857); *The Downfall of England* (Philadelphia: Peterson, 1862), and *My Life in Many States and in Foreign Lands* (New York: Appleton, 1902). Parkhurst's major works include *My Forty Years in New York* (New York: Macmillan, 1923) and *Our Fight with Tammany* (New York: Scribner's, 1895).

6. PENN AND A DRYAD

The University of Pennsylvania Archives supply the main facts about Pound's academic record, supplemented by Emily Mitchell Wallace's "Penn's Poet Friends" in *The Pennsylvania Gazette* (Feb., 1973), 33–36. *Hilda's Book* is printed at the end of *End To Torment.* William Brooke Smith's vital statistics can be found on Death Certificate 9577 in the Philadelphia City Archives, and his academic record in the Archives of the Philadelphia College of Art. Bryn Mawr supplies the record for Hilda. See Robinson and Guest in Works Cited In The Text.

7. "BILL" WILLIAMS

The Penn Archives and the Wallace article mentioned above are important, along with Williams' own works. See Mariani in Works Cited In The Text. For Olson's report on Pound's comments on Williams' background, see *Charles Olson and Ezra Pound*, ed. C. Seelye (New York: Viking, 1975), xxii and elsewhere.

8. HAMILTON AND A DREAM

The Burke Library of Hamilton College has a special Pound collection with letters, documents, pictures, etc., from which all of the facts for this chapter were gleaned. Also useful is Frank Lorenz' brochure *Ezra Pound at Hamilton College: A Summing Up, 1905–1969*, issued by the college in 1980.

The New Yorker article appeared on August 14, 1943, pages 16–17. The Yale Broadcasting Co.'s tribute to Pound resides in script form at the Beinecke.

Fred C. Robinson's "'The Might of the North': Pound's Anglo-Saxon Studies and 'The Seafarer'" appeared in *The Yale Review* (1982), 199–224.

The Humanities Research Center at the University of Texas, Austin, holds many of Pound's textbooks: Henry Sweet's *Anglo-Saxon Reader in Prose and Verse*, 7th ed. (Oxford, 1898); E. Moore's *Tutte le Opere di Dante Alighieri*, 2nd ed. (Oxford, 1897); Propertius, *Elegiae*, ed. L. Mueller (Leipzig: Teubner); A. C. Swinburne, *Laus Veneris* (New York: Carleton, 1866); and the three vols. of the Temple Classics edition of Dante's *Divine Comedy* (London, 1903), inscribed 1904.

9. PENN AGAIN AND EUROPE

The Penn Archives and the Wallace article are the primary sources. Williams' two letters to his brother Ed are at the Lockwood Library at the State University of New York in Buffalo. The Viola Baxter (Jordan) letters are at the Beinecke; the Mary Moore letters are at the Van Pelt, Penn.

10. AUNT FRANK AND MARY MOORE

The correspondence of Pound to Mary Moore is in the Van Pelt Library at Penn. Pound's grades are in the Penn Archives. For Aunt Frank's debacle, see my article in *Paideuma*, 12 (1983), 55–87. Details about the New Weston Hotel may be found in the hotel collection at the New York Historical Society. The Zukofsky letter is at the Humanities Research Center in Austin.

11. THE CRAWFORDSVILLE INCIDENT

Most of the details are supplied from the James Rader collection of documents at Wabash College, supplemented by local sources in the Lilly Library of Wabash and the Crawfordsville Public Library, for newspapers. My article in *Paideuma*, 13 (1984) contains a full summary of the facts, followed by extensive excerpts from witnesses, assembled by Rader, as well as Pound's letters to Rader. The Hessler letter quoted about the students discovering him with the woman is taken from Noel Stock's *Life of Ezra Pound*, rev. ed. (San Francisco: North Point, 1982), p. 41. The letters to Moore are at Penn; to Hessler and Ingrid Davies, at Texas; to Viola Baxter (Jordan), at Yale. Harry R. Fullenwider supplied me personally with details about the Gothic house, now owned by the Lakeside Press. Rujie Wang graciously granted me permission to print the letter from Robert Winter, which is in his possession.

12. EASTWARD HO!

The letters from Hilda to Williams are at the Lockwood Library, Buffalo. Pound recounted the story of his proposal to Michael Reck, among others: *E. P.: A Close-Up* (New York: McGraw-Hill, 1973), p. 9.

CODA

The fates of the other seven accused of treason are culled from the files of *The New York Times*. The letter to Wyndham Lewis about Bacon and Quade is housed in the Rare Book Room at Cornell.

INDEX

226